Reassessing the Impact of Teaching Assistants

'This is the most up-to-date, comprehensive and ~~detailed~~ account of the work of teaching assistants in this country ... essential reading for all teachers and senior managers in schools, local authority support services and teaching assistants themselves.'

Peter Farrell, Professor of Special Needs and Educational Psychology, School of Education, University of Manchester, UK

'*Reassessing the Impact of Teaching Assistants* is an essential read for school leaders seeking to develop conceptually sound models of inclusive service delivery that account for the full range of student diversity, including students with disabilities and other special educational needs.'

Professor Michael F. Giangreco, Department of Education and the Center on Disability and Community Inclusion, University of Vermont, USA

'This book will inspire you to take a fresh look at the role of your TAs, and maximise their impact in the classroom. I commend it to all school leaders and teachers.'

Roz Sendorek, Headteacher, Oakfield First School, Windsor, UK

Over the last decade, teaching assistants (TAs) have become an established part of everyday classroom life. TAs are often used by schools to help low attaining pupils and those with special educational needs. Yet despite the huge rise in the number of TAs working in UK classrooms, very little is known about their impact on pupils.

This key and timely text examines the impact of TAs on pupils' learning and behaviour, and on teachers and teaching. The authors present the provocative findings from the ground-breaking and seminal Deployment and Impact of Support Staff (DISS) project. This was the largest, most in-depth study ever to be carried out in this field. It critically examined the effect of TA support on the academic progress of 8,200 pupils, made extensive observations of nearly 700 pupils and over 100 TAs, and collected data from over 17,800 questionnaire responses and interviews with over 470 school staff and pupils.

This book reveals the extent to which the pupils in most need are let down by current classroom practice. The authors present a robust challenge to the current widespread practices concerning TA preparation, deployment and practice, structured around a conceptually and empirically strong explanatory framework. The authors go on to show how schools need to change if they are to realise the potential of TAs.

With serious implications not just for classroom practice, but also whole-school, local authority and government policy, this is an indispensable text for primary, secondary and special schools, senior management teams, those involved in teacher training and professional development, policy-makers and academics.

Peter Blatchford is Professor in Psychology and Education at the Institute of Education, University of London, UK and was the DISS Project Director.

Anthony Russell is a researcher at the Institute of Education, University of London, UK, and was a school teacher and science advisor.

Rob Webster is a researcher at the Institute of Education, University of London, UK, and worked for many years as a TA.

Reassessing the Impact of Teaching Assistants

How research challenges practice and policy

Peter Blatchford, Anthony Russell and Rob Webster

Routledge
Taylor & Francis Group

LONDON AND NEW YORK

First published 2012
by Routledge
2 Park Square, Milton Park, Abingdon, Oxon OX14 4RN

Simultaneously published in the USA and Canada
by Routledge
711 Third Avenue, New York, NY 10017

Routledge is an imprint of the Taylor & Francis Group, an informa business

British Library Cataloguing in Publication Data
A catalogue record for this book is available from the British Library

Library of Congress Cataloging in Publication Data
Blatchford, Peter.
Challenging the role of the teaching assistant : reassessing practice
and questioning policy / by Peter Blatchford, Anthony Russell and Rob
Webster. -- 1st ed.
p. cm.
Includes bibliographical references and index.
1. Teachers' assistants. I. Russell, Anthony, 1942- II. Webster, Rob,
1976- III. Title.
LB2844.1.A8B53 2012
371.14'124--dc23
2011024011

ISBN: 978-0-415-68763-8 (hbk)
ISBN: 978-0-415-68764-5 (pbk)
ISBN: 978-0-203-15196-9 (ebk)

Typeset in Bembo
by GreenGate Publishing Services, Tonbridge, Kent

MIX
Paper from
responsible sources
FSC
www.fsc.org   FSC® C004839

Printed and bound in Great Britain by
TJ International Ltd, Padstow, Cornwall

Contents

Endorsements

The substantial and counter-intuitive research findings that underpin this (book) set it apart.
Seamus Hegarty, Editor of the European Journal of Special Needs Education

This is a most welcome book ... high quality and (will have) a substantial impact.
Professor Geoff Lindsay, Director of Centre for Educational Development, Appraisal and Research, University of Warwick, UK

This is the most up-to-date, comprehensive and detailed account of the work of teaching assistants in this country. It provides a readable description and analysis of the findings from a large scale research project that began over eight years ago. There are important implications in the findings for the recruitment and deployment of teaching assistants in mainstream schools and for ensuring that they make an effective contribution to raising the achievements of all children. It should be essential reading for all teachers and senior managers in schools, local authority support services and teaching assistants themselves.
Peter Farrell, Professor of Special Needs and Educational Psychology, School of Education, University of Manchester, UK

Blatchford, Russell and Webster have taken the research on teaching assistants to the next level by correlating their use with student outcomes and providing compelling explanations for their unexpected findings. Their DISS project data represent arguably the most comprehensive, large-scale, longitudinal study pertaining to teacher assistants conducted to date. The evidence holds important implications for schools internationally. *Reassessing the Impact of Teaching Assistants* is an essential read for school leaders seeking to develop conceptually sound models of inclusive service delivery that account for the full range of student diversity, including students with disabilities and other special educational needs.
Professor Michael F. Giangreco, Department of Education and the Center on Disability and Community Inclusion, University of Vermont, USA

'Pupils supported by Teaching Assistants do no better than those who are left alone' (*Times Educational Supplement* 05.09.2009). Did this headline misrepresent the most detailed study yet undertaken of TAs' work in schools? *Reassessing the Impact of Teaching Assistants*, the eagerly awaited book of the DISS project, argues that whilst TAs improve classroom discipline, and reduce teachers' stress levels, they can stand in the way of children's learning. But there are solutions. This book will inspire you to take a fresh look at the role of your TAs, and maximise their impact in the classroom. I commend it to all school leaders and teachers.
Roz Sendorek, Headteacher, Oakfield First School, Windsor, UK

List of illustrations

Figures

Tables

Boxes

Acknowledgements

The authors would like to thank the following people for their help with this book.

First of all we acknowledge the valuable input of our colleagues on the DISS project. Paul Bassett conducted all the statistical analyses, including the pioneering multilevel regression analysis of pupils' progress in relation to the amount of support from TAs. His analyses of the systematic observation data has broken new ground in educational research. Penelope Brown had main responsibility for the systematic observation component of the research and had a main role to play in the general day-to-day management of the project. Clare Martin had a key role to play in the management of quantitative data.

Julie Radford is a colleague in the Department of Psychology and Human Development at the Institute of Education (IoE) who specialises in interactions in classrooms and the learning of language skills, and the verbal and non-verbal resources of children with language difficulties. Julie conducted the Conversation Analysis reported in Chapter 6 and co-wrote the chapter with us.

Christine Rubie-Davies is from the University of Auckland in New Zealand and during a sabbatical stay at the IoE she drew on her valuable experience as a teacher educator and researcher and took a lead role in the Instructional Talk Analysis reported in Chapter 6. She was also a co-author of this chapter.

We also thank the following colleagues who contributed to the research in other ways: Naomi Haywood and Maria Koutsoubou were researchers who worked on the case studies in Strand 2 Wave 1 and Strand 2 Wave 2 respectively. Selma Babayigit conducted the Strand 2 Wave 1 systematic observations with Penelope Brown.

We thank Margaret Lankester and Ann Brown for their help with transcribing data, and the small team of data-enterers.

Many thanks to Sue Briggs, Peter Farrell, Olga Miller and Alan Radford who under severe time pressures kindly read through an earlier draft of the manuscript. We also thank three anonymous reviewers of the book proposal for their support and helpful suggestions.

We would like to thank the headteachers, SENCos, teachers and local authority staff who contributed to our DISS project working groups, and to the numerous school staff we have had the pleasure of working with on rethinking the role of TAs.

We particularly want to thank Roz Sendorek for being such a wonderful critical friend, who supported the project and also provided invaluable feedback on a draft of the book. Roz was ever helpful in letting us try out observation systems in her school and has worked with us in public sessions on the DISS project. She gave a valuable headteacher's perspective on the reality of life in schools, and always stood up for the TAs!

We thank Michael Giangreco for his pioneering work in this field, for his advice and for being so responsive to our work. We also thank our colleagues who contributed in various ways to the project, from the administrators to academics, and in particular to Dylan Wiliam, Geoff Whitty and Andy Tolmie for their support. We also thank Alison Foyle of Routledge for her support, and her efficient and speedy responses.

The DISS research was funded by the then Department of Children, Schools and Families (DCSF), now the Department for Education (DfE), and the Welsh Assembly Government, and the authors thank them for the professional way the research was managed.

We also thank our research managers at the DCSF and the members of the DISS project Steering Group who worked very hard to support the research.

We would especially like to thank the many school staff (teachers, headteachers and support staff) who contributed to this research by completing questionnaires (all 17,800 of them!) and other forms, allowing us to observe and interview them, and being so helpful and professional during our visits to schools.

All of these people have contributed in numerous ways to our developing understanding of the role and impact of TAs, but none should be held responsible for the views expressed in this book. In a similar way, the opinions expressed in this book are those of the authors and do not necessarily reflect those of the funders, members of the Steering Group during the period of the research funding (2003–2008), or the views of the present government in the UK.

Chapter 1

Introduction

There has been a huge and unparalleled increase in the numbers of paraprofessionals working in schools, particularly classroom- or pupil-based support staff, referred to throughout this book as 'teaching assistants' (TAs). This book provides the most comprehensive picture of the consequences of this change for schools, teachers, pupils and the TAs themselves.

We start with a vignette that provides most of the essential results from the Deployment and Impact of Support Staff (DISS) project and reveals the key themes we will be addressing in this book. It provides a description of one small extract of classroom interaction between a teaching assistant and a pupil. We then put this into context by drawing on further information on the classroom interactions and behaviours at this moment in time, the TA's activities over the school day, and then information from the TA, the class teacher, the headteacher and the general context provided by government. In this way the small piece of classroom interaction between a TA and a pupil is nested in progressively wider sources of information and influence. Finally, we provide information on the relationship between the amount of support the child receives from a TA and the pupils' attitudes to learning (e.g. independence and motivation), and their academic progress.

All the information provided is real and comes from – and is representative of – data collected as part of the DISS project, though the names and some minor details have been adapted. The vignette describes the situation in a primary school but most of the details, with some differences concerning the deployment of TAs, which we will describe in this book, also apply to the situation in secondary schools.

1.1 A vignette

Meet Reece. He joined Year Six at Dalebrook Primary School in September. In his previous school, Reece had been placed on School Action because he had difficulty with reading and numeracy. School Action is the first of the three commonly understood levels of special educational need (SEN) used in England and Wales. Pupils on School Action require interventions that are additional to or different from those provided as part of the school's usual differentiated curriculum. When Reece arrived at Dalebrook, he was assessed by Jackie, the school's special educational needs coordinator (SENCo), who felt that his speech and language skills were delayed and so she raised her concerns with the local authority's education department.

A speech and language therapist then assessed Reece and agreed with Jackie. The therapist recommended that the Reece be placed on School Action Plus. School Action Plus is the second level of SEN. Teachers of pupils on School Action Plus receive advice or support from outside specialists, so that alternative interventions to those provided through School Action can be put in place. To help develop his communication skills, Reece, together with a small group of his Year Six (10–11-year-old) classmates who have similar problems, are taken out of the class twice a week to take part in an intervention programme. The intervention is delivered by someone that Reece has got to know well: Mandy. Mandy is the teaching assistant (TA) in Reece's class. She often sits with Reece in class and supports his learning throughout the day.

Deploying Mandy in this way is Mark's idea. Mark is Reece's teacher. As he feels he does not know enough about how to teach children like Reece, Mark thinks it's useful for Reece to have additional support from Mandy, because she has more experience of helping children who have difficulties with learning. Mandy, like the other experienced TAs at Dalebrook, has been at the school longer than most of the teachers. She started as a volunteer parent-helper twelve years ago when her children attended the school.

There has been a steady increase in the number of TAs at Dalebrook driven to a large extent by the availability in this local authority of funding to support the inclusion of children with SEN. Dalebrook's headteacher, Liz, decided that increasing the number of TAs she employed was a cost-effective way of meeting the needs of her pupils with SEN. It wasn't just the new cadre of TAs that swelled the school's workforce. In the early 2000s, Liz also began recruiting a number of other new support staff and widening the roles of existing support staff: Alan – the part-time caretaker – became a full-time site manager; and Crystal arrived as the school's first finance officer.

One reason for the expansion in support staff was as a result of the New Labour Government's response to a crisis in teacher recruitment and retention, a key cause of which had been excessive teacher workload. The then education secretary likened this ambitious programme of 'remodelling' to changes made in the health service: 'In our hospitals and GP [general practitioner] practices, we have seen how nurses have grown into roles which were once the strict preserve of doctors. And we are clear that this development has helped doctors, just as it could teachers, to concentrate their energies on more difficult matters, to the benefit of those in their care'. Such reform, claimed the minister, 'can only help to raise standards'.

It looks, therefore, as if the TA's role in the education of a child with SEN is a good thing. Despite Reece's learning needs, Mandy's support seems to enable him to be included in a mainstream classroom, to access the same curriculum as his peers, and make progress academically.

It's a morning numeracy lesson in Mark's classroom. He is teaching his Year Sixes how to round off numbers. Mark begins by asking the class to discuss in groups what they think a whole number is. He then explains how to round whole and decimal numbers up and down to the nearest whole number, with reference to place value, and demonstrates this on the whiteboard. Afterwards, the pupils are given a worksheet of progressively challenging rounding problems to complete. As he hands her copies of the worksheet, Mark tells Mandy that Reece need only complete the first 15 problems.

Mandy begins to work through the problems with Reece, which entail rounding whole numbers to the nearest ten. As she does so, it's clear that Mandy has misunderstood the difference between a whole number and a round number: 'Seven would be closer to ten, wouldn't it? Because ten is a whole number. So whole numbers are like tens and things like that'. As the lesson continues, Reece begins to disengage from the task. This often happens with Reece, and Mandy's strategy for getting him back on task is to remind him of the teacher's expectations: 'Come on now, Reece. Mr Simmons wants this work finished by the end of the lesson. We've got to get this done.'

When Mandy sits next to Reece, Reece finds himself the focus of her attention far more often than he finds himself the focus of Mark's attention. The instances when Mandy interacts with Reece last longer than any conversation Reece has with his teacher. Reece is also more active in his interactions with Mandy compared to his interactions with Mark. When Mark talks to Reece, it's as part of his whole class delivery, so Reece's role is as a passive member of the class audience; he's one of the crowd.

In today's numeracy lesson, Mark and Mandy take up their usual positions. Mark spends the first half of the lesson (about 30 minutes) teaching from the front of the class, then, as the pupils complete the worksheet, he roves around the room. On occasions, he stops for a few minutes to work with a group at one table. Mandy's default position is to sit beside Reece on red table. Joining them are Nathan and Shaun (who, like Reece, are on School Action Plus) and Carla (who has a statement of SEN for moderate learning difficulties). Mandy is on-hand to explain concepts and instructions and to prompt the pupils in ways that Mark is unable to do from the front of the class. Mandy hardly ever sits with the pupils on the other tables who are the middle ability pupils and higher attaining pupils. These children receive much more of Mark's time overall than the pupils on red table. What is more, the four red table pupils are often separated from Mark and the mainstream curriculum in other contexts. For example, they often work with Mandy away from the classroom.

Working with pupils and supporting their learning therefore seems to be Mandy's primary role, and the extent to which this is the case is brought home to her later that day. Mandy has been asked to complete a work pattern diary as part of a large national survey. Today, Mandy had been ticking, from a long list of tasks, the activities she did at 20-minute intervals throughout her six-hour working day. Before she posts it off, she works out that she spent almost two-thirds of her day (four hours) doing what the survey calls 'direct learning support for pupils' – or as Mandy thinks – 'teaching'. Her responses to the survey – which in her experience are common for a TA – show that she spends much more time teaching than helping the teacher or helping pupils in other ways.

The survey went on to ask questions about the hours Mandy worked and the hours that she was paid for. The time she spent coming in to school early, staying beyond her contracted finish time – all time for which she was not paid – added up to nearly three hours a week. She also knew that her TA colleagues and some of the other support staff also worked extra hours for which they were not paid. The school relied a lot – albeit, it seemed, unintentionally – on the goodwill of its support staff. In order to do her job effectively, Mandy needed to do certain things in her own time. She felt a strong sense of duty to Reece and the other children she supported, and if it meant using her own time in order to ensure she could do right by them, then so be it. Take today for instance: getting in a little early to talk to Mark about the day's lessons; preparing some resources for art in her lunch hour; staying behind after 3pm to feedback to Mark about, among other things, Reece's struggle with the rounding off task in numeracy; and assessing pupils' work from the latest speech and language intervention session.

In fact, if Mandy didn't meet with Mark in her own unpaid time, there would be almost no opportunity for them to communicate at all. As it is, Mandy often feels under-prepared. For example, there had been no time to discuss the numeracy lesson that morning, so Mandy had to tune in to Mark's delivery in order to pick up the subject knowledge that she needed. This can be quite frustrating, particularly when Mark is introducing instructional techniques she has never seen before.

The national survey in which Mandy was participating also collected data from teachers and headteachers. Mark completed a questionnaire that sought his experiences as a teacher working with TAs and his views on the impact TAs had on him as a teacher, and on his pupils.

First the survey asked Mark about the training he had received in relation to how he manages and organises Mandy's work. He thought back to his PCGE pre-service training two years ago. He recalled a so-so half-day session on working with TAs, and had not received anything on his induction at Dalebrook on this topic. Overall, his training on working with TAs was quite scant.

Mark was also asked about the opportunities he had for planning and feedback with Mandy. His responses echoed the sentiments expressed by his TA: communication with Mandy was limited to break, lunchtimes, and before and after school.

The survey asked Mark to consider the impact Mandy has on his teaching and on pupil learning. For Mark, the support Mandy provided for Reece and the other pupils on red table was invaluable in terms of providing the individualised help that these pupils required and allowing him to get on with teaching the rest of class. She also helped him to keep pupils on task and limit instances of disruptive behaviour, so Mark could teach without interruption.

Another way in which Mandy allows Mark to concentrate on teaching is by taking on some of his routine administrative tasks, for instance: photocopying; collecting dinner money; and putting up classroom displays. Mark responded positively to the survey questions about the impact Mandy has on his job satisfaction, stress and workload.

As part of the survey, Liz had been sent a version of the survey for headteachers to complete, and it asked her to comment on the impact of all the support staff at Dalebrook. She believes that the introduction of new support roles and the expansion of the roles of existing support staff has had a positive effect on the performance of the school. But most of all, Liz feels that Mandy and the other TAs have helped to raise standards by making an important contribution to children's learning. Liz summed up her view like this: 'Without the TAs, this school would fall apart.'

Both Liz and Mark's responses to the survey questions about the impact of TAs, though impressionistic, are based on their professional expertise and careful judgments. They both concluded that TAs have a positive impact on pupils' learning, behaviour and their 'soft' skills, such as confidence, motivation, concentration and independent working.

However, the study's researchers were able to objectively and reliably measure the impact of TA support on pupils, because they had asked Mark and hundreds of other teachers to provide data on the amount of support pupils received over the school year from TAs. The researcher also collected data on the attainment of 8,200 pupils in English, mathematics and science at the beginning and end of the year. They even had ratings completed by teachers on whether pupils had improved in terms of their soft skills.

Surprisingly, the results were very different to the views expressed by Liz and Mark. There was no evidence that the support provided by TAs like Mandy improved pupils' soft skills over a school year. More worryingly, the results showed that relative to other pupils who received little or no TA support, the more support pupils like Reece received from TAs, the less progress they made in English, maths and science over a school year, and this was even after controlling for the factors likely to be related to academic attainment and the reasons why pupils were given TA support in the first place (i.e., prior attainment and SEN status). What, wondered Liz and Mark, could account for these surprising results?

The vignette shows the general way in which TAs can be seen to be of great assistance to teachers and schools, through help with routine activities, and, on the face of it, to pupils as well in terms of more individual attention, in particular, for those in most need. But it also shows serious inadvertent problems for pupil learning that have arisen out of this arrangement. In this book we describe these problems and what can be done to overcome them. First, though, we give more details on the increase in numbers of TAs.

1.2 The increase in TAs in schools

One of the most profound changes in UK schools over the past 15 years or so has been the huge and unprecedented increase in support staff. The number of full-time equivalent (FTE) TAs in mainstream schools in England has more than trebled since 1997 to about 170,000 (DfE 2010a). At the time of writing, in 2011, 43 per cent of the mainstream school workforce[1] in England are support staff, and over half of these people (54 per cent) are TAs (DfE 2010a). TAs therefore comprise almost a quarter (24 per cent) of the workforce in English mainstream schools: 32 per cent of the nursery and primary school workforce; and 12 per cent of the secondary school workforce. The most up-to-date and comparable figures for Wales show that TAs make up a third (33 per cent) of the school workforce[2] in the maintained sector, and account for 75 per cent of all support staff (Statistics for Wales 2010). TAs make up 44 per cent of the Welsh primary school workforce, and 17 per cent of the secondary school workforce. In a third UK territory, Scotland, TAs[3] constitute a smaller, but still significant proportion of the publicly funded mainstream school workforce[4] (17 per cent), and account for 58 per cent of all support staff (The Scottish Government 2010). TAs make up 24 per cent of the Scottish primary school workforce, and 9 per cent of the secondary school workforce.

Government statistics for England also show an increase in numbers of a new form of support staff introduced in the mid-2000s: higher level teaching assistants (HLTAs), more on whom below. In 2006, there were 5,500 HLTAs in mainstream schools[5] – just under 4 per cent of all TAs; but by 2010, the number of HLTAs had trebled, and around 9 per cent of all TAs had this status (DfE 2010a).

This rise in TAs can be seen as part of a general increase in education paraprofessionals with similar roles worldwide. We have found it surprisingly hard to obtain up-to-date and reliable information on numbers of TAs (and their equivalents) in other countries. Data from the US Department of Education (2010), for example, shows a 6.2 per cent increase in the FTE number of teacher aides between 2003 and 2005 – from 370,300 to 393,400. From 2006, data for teacher aides was aggregated with data on other paraprofessional personnel employed to provide special education and related services to pupils, so we cannot be exact about teacher aide numbers. However, the number of paraprofessionals overall continued to rise, and in 2007, there were 412,500 such people working in US schools.

Giangreco and Doyle (2007) describe increases in support staff in schools in Australia, Italy, Sweden, Canada, Finland, Germany, Hong Kong, Iceland, Ireland, Malta, South Africa, as well as the USA. TAs, therefore, appear to be a growing part of the school workforce in many countries, though this has been more pronounced in the UK.

Later in this chapter we will describe the developments that have driven the growth in school support staff in the UK and also the expansion of the roles and responsibilities many now have. We can say right at the outset of this book that the findings from the DISS study show that the general effect of these initiatives has been that TAs now often occupy a role in mainstream schools where they interact with pupils – principally those not making expected levels of progress and/or those with learning and behavioural difficulties. They often supplement the teacher's input in class by providing more opportunities for one-to-one and small group work both in and out of the classroom.

This is a profound change, though one which has to a large extent occurred with little debate or public discussion. The rise in the number of TAs has important consequences for teacher workloads, teacher roles, school management, school workforce 'remodelling' and ensuring value for public money spent on education (according to Whitehorn (2010), in 2008–2009 schools in England spent £4.1bn on TAs and other education support staff). The rise in the number of TAs has also caused important changes to the educational experiences of school pupils, including those with SEN. Giangreco and Doyle (2007) argue that, metaphorically, 'teacher assistant' issues are the tip of the iceberg; that is, they are the visible signs above the waterline, but that it is below the surface that there are potential dangers lurking in the form of fundamental unresolved issues and specific matters relating to practice and policy.

1.2.1 TAs in the classroom

Every reader of this book will have experienced a school classroom, and it is likely that those classrooms will all have had similar features. Typically there is a teacher, a class of pupils, and a physical space that is recognisably a classroom, in terms of the positioning of desks or tables, displays, whiteboard, and so on. Despite significant technological advances, this has been a stable environment within which generations of school children have been educated (albeit the whiteboard was once black!), and will probably remain the main environment for school-aged children for years to come. A long tradition of research and theory has attended to the nature of the classroom environment and its effects on learning and personal and social development (Shulman 1986; Doyle 1986). A number of studies have identified characteristics of schools that seem to be associated with the better performance of pupils (e.g. Rutter et al. 1979; Mortimore et al. 1988) and a separate strand has drawn on empirical classroom research to identify effective teaching (e.g. Brophy 1989; Creemers 1994; Creemers and Kyriakides 2008; Rosenshine and Stevens 1986).

These traditions of research together make up a large part of educational research, but all are largely predicated on a description of the classroom essentially involving a teacher, a class of students and a physical classroom. However, with the recent rise in numbers of TAs, there is now a different kind of educational input and a different kind of social and instructional dynamic within the school. It is our view, based on the findings from the research project on which this book is based, that many traditions of research and thought need to be fundamentally reworked to accommodate the recent increase in paraprofessionals in education.

This becomes clearer when we consider what is known about effective teaching. Though there are a range of new developments in education – for example, those involving ICT and distance learning – face-to-face interactions remain the defining feature of most classrooms and still lie at the heart of the learning process, and this is likely to be true across all types of schools, subject areas and age of child (Pellegrini and Blatchford 2000). Gage's (1985) conclusion in the mid-1980s still stands: 'Teaching is the central process of education'. In Chapter 6 we provide more detail on research and thought on effective teaching. Here, we just note the often taken for granted but high level of professionalism involved in good teaching, seen in terms of high levels of skill, responsiveness, reflectiveness, classroom management and subject and pedagogical understanding. It also means that such considerations about professionalism cannot be put to one side when large numbers of TAs now have, as we shall see in subsequent chapters, a main responsibility for teaching pupils. If TAs are involved in a direct instructional role, even for some of their time, then we need to be clear what they do, what activities and interactions they are involved in with pupils, and what effect these interactions have on pupils' learning.

The increase in the number of TAs has been accompanied by a growing, but still limited, body of research. Let us briefly summarise the main directions.

- First, there has been interest in the appropriate role of support staff in relation to teachers and teaching (in the UK – Bach *et al.* 2004; Beeson *et al.* 2003; Cremin *et al.* 2005; Farrell *et al.* 1999; Mistry *et al.* 2004; Moran and Abbott 2002; and Schlapp *et al.* 2003; and overseas – see Finn *et al.* 2000; Takala 2007; Logan 2006 and Angelides *et al.* 2009, for debates in the USA, Finland, Ireland and Cyprus respectively).
- Second, there has been interest in the role of support staff in relation to inclusion and supporting pupils with SEN (in the UK, Mistry *et al.* 2004; Moran and Abbott 2002; in Iceland, Egilson and Traustadottir 2009; and in the USA, Giangreco *et al.* 1997, 2005; Giangreco and Doyle 2007).
- A third area of research concerns the characteristics of support staff, in terms of gender, ethnicity, class and qualifications (Teeman *et al.* 2008).
- And, fourth, perhaps unique to the UK context, there has been descriptive and evaluative research on the role of support staff in relation to workforce remodelling and the impact of the National Agreement (Butt and Gunter 2005; Gunter and Rayner 2005; Hutchings *et al.* 2009; Thomas *et al.* 2004). Finally, other work has addressed the labour processes involved in the restructuring of teachers' roles and trade union responses (Stevenson 2007) and the erosion of teachers' professional jurisdiction (Wilkinson 2005). A useful overview of research and thought on support staff in the UK is provided by Burgess (2008).

Whilst this work provides valuable insights into the nature of TAs' work and their position in relation to teachers, it is widely recognised that it provides only limited information on the impact of TAs on teachers and pupils (see Alborz *et al.* 2009; Howes *et al.* 2003). This is a serious omission given the high stakes and high costs involved and the divided opinions about the value of support staff in schools. There have already been strong views expressed in the UK about the appropriateness of retaining 'cost-ineffective' TAs expressed in independent reviews of public sector spending, in the years following the 2008 global economic crisis (for example, Bassett *et al.* 2010).

The Deployment and Impact of Support Staff (DISS) project was a unique study in terms of length and scale and was set up to address the lack of research on support staff in schools. It sought to provide a rigorous description of the characteristics and deployment of support staff, including the nature of their activities and interactions with pupils, and to address their impact on teachers, teaching and pupils. This book describes results from the study on the impact of TAs. It can be said at this point that the main research findings on the impact of TAs on pupils' academic attainment, described in Chapter 2, were unexpected and troubling, and these results provide the key reference point for the book. It can also be said early on that we do not attach blame to TAs for these findings; far more likely at fault are factors governing TAs' work over which they have little or no control, much more on which will follow in Chapters 3 to 6.

The main point made in this book is that there has been an ad hoc drift toward a kind of deployment of TAs that, while conducted with the best of intentions, has resulted in unintended and unacceptable consequences. As is revealed in the vignette at the beginning of this chapter, for many in education, the use of TAs has become an essential way in which they can deal with problems connected to the integration of pupils with SEN, teacher workloads and job satisfaction, and challenges posed by curriculum initiatives and behaviour in school. We shall see that teachers are often well disposed toward the use of TAs in their classrooms, because TAs can give more individual attention to the small numbers of pupils who are struggling to keep up with the work, while the teacher can then devote herself more directly to helping the rest of the class.

We know from the work of Michael Giangreco and colleagues (Giangreco 2003, 2010; Giangreco and Broer 2005) that this situation is also occurring in US schools and informal communication with academics elsewhere suggests this is true of other countries as well (e.g. Australia, New Zealand and Hong Kong). The view seems to be that TA deployment, as we have just described it, seems a very sensible arrangement, and it is therefore no surprise if there is a reluctance to want to hear bad news about it, and sometimes a resistance to want to change things. But we will argue that unless we realise that current arrangements are themselves the cause of the problem, many lower attaining pupils and pupils with SEN will be let down. This book will describe the effects of TA deployment and then, in subsequent chapters, show how it has happened and, importantly, what we can do about it.

We believe that this book will be of interest to readers in many other countries. Although the increase in TAs and other support staff has been most marked in the UK, there has also been, as we have seen, similar growth in other countries as well, and the impression we have gained is that there are similar, though often unrecognised, issues connected to the use of TAs in these countries as well.

Before we describe the findings, we need first to provide the policy context for the increase of support staff in schools, and the DISS study. This inevitably has to be selective; our primary purpose is to show why there has been a vast increase in numbers of TAs in the UK, to indicate some of the resulting tensions, and to show the consequences of this for the educational experiences of pupils. The reader who wishes to move quickly to the key findings could turn straight to Section 1.5.

1.3 Reasons for increase in numbers of TAs

We argue that there are two main causes of the recent increase in TAs; first, concerns over teacher workloads and teacher retention which led to government policy (the National Agreement) within which TAs and other support staff were seen as central to addressing the concerns over excessive teacher workload and simultaneously raising overall pupil standards; and, second, the way in which TAs have become strongly connected to facilitating the inclusion of pupils with SEN in mainstream classrooms.

1.3.1 Teacher workloads

1.3.1.1 Curriculum initiatives

There have been a number of centrally-driven curriculum initiatives over the past 20 to 30 years. These have included: the introduction of the National Curriculum in 1988 and national end of key stage tests (the so-called 'SATs'); a new regime of school inspections carried out by the inspectorate, Ofsted (in 1992); the use of SATs results to construct and publish 'league tables' of school performance (in 1992); and the national literacy and numeracy strategies (in 1998 and 1999).

There have been many challenges for schools in implementing these policies, too numerous to cover here, but Hancock and Eyres (2004) have showed how TAs have been deployed in the implementation of the national literacy and numeracy strategies (NLS and NNS respectively) in England and report evidence from Ofsted to confirm that TAs have been substantially involved in their delivery; TAs, for example, played a key role in working with the one in four children Ofsted claimed found it difficult to meet government and school expectations.

On the whole, the use of TAs in the context of curriculum reform was seen as a positive development. Initially, for example, Ofsted supported the idea of TAs helping pupils with SEN. But by 2004 there was some recognition that the use of TAs needed to be looked at carefully. A review of reading standards carried out by Ofsted reported findings that it found 'unacceptable'. The report said that local authorities should 'ensure that teachers and TAs understand and use the [NLS] intervention programmes effectively', and that schools 'monitor the impact of support through assessing pupils' progress', in order to reduce 'the tail of underachievement' in terms of reading (Ofsted 2004a).

1.3.1.2 Teacher workloads and TAs

The 'performance culture' in education (Hancock and Eyres 2004), and the heavily bureaucratic processes that accompanied it, were major contributing factors to increased teacher workload and feelings of pressure in the mid-1990s. In its annual report on teachers' conditions of employment in 2001, the School Teachers' Review Body reflected the mounting concern within the teaching profession over excessive workload and its effect on morale, particularly in terms of recruitment and retention, and recommended that the Department for Education and Employment (as it was then) organise an independent review to investigate the matter further.

PricewaterhouseCooper (PwC) were subsequently commissioned to undertake the review, and in their final report, published in December 2001, recommended that the 'extension of the support staff role' was central to 'a programme of practical action to eliminate excessive workload and … raise standards of pupil achievement' (PricewaterhouseCooper 2001).

A month earlier (November 2001), the then Secretary of State for Education, Estelle Morris, made a speech to the Social Market Foundation that drew heavily on an early version of the PwC final report. The speech set out how the New Labour Government proposed to deal with the supply and demand problem facing the teaching profession and the shorter term issue of excessive workload. In her address, Morris echoed the PwC recommendation, proposing to greatly widen the role of TAs within a remodelled teaching profession. 'Delivering the wider standards agenda', it was claimed, 'hinges on securing this radical shift'. Boundaries between the role of the teachers and those of TAs and other school support staff were to be redrawn, with tasks traditionally seen as proper to teachers being shared partially or totally between them and support staff.

Despite there being little or no hard research evidence at the time that upheld the view that support staff in general, and TAs specifically, actually raised academic standards (Cook-Jones 2006), the government continued to build its case for enhancing the contribution of TAs in the White Paper 'Schools: achieving success' (DfES 2001), claiming that TAs had 'been central to what has been achieved so far in raising standards'. The government implemented a £350 million funding programme to improve and increase the support offered by TAs to both teachers and pupils, and recruit an additional 20,000 TAs by 2002.

1.3.1.3 The National Agreement: raising standards and tackling workloads

By 2003, the numbers of TAs and other support staff in English and Welsh schools were set to swell even further. In January 2003, the government, local government employers and the majority of school workforce unions signed the National Agreement: 'raising standards and tackling workload'. The National Agreement drew together policy aims concerning raising pupil standards, tackling teacher workload (including a concerted attack on unnecessary paperwork and bureaucracy), and creating new support staff roles.

In brief, the National Agreement set out three phases of reform through changes to the School Teachers Pay and Conditions Document. These took place in September 2003, September 2004 and September 2005. In September 2003, phase one set out measures to ensure that: teachers were no longer routinely required to carry out administrative and clerical tasks; all teachers and headteachers should enjoy a reasonable work–life balance; and those with leadership and management responsibilities must be given a reasonable allocation of time in which to carry out their duties. In September 2004, limits were put on the amount of cover teachers could be expected to do for absent colleagues. And with effect from September 2005, teachers were guaranteed at least 10 per cent of their timetabled week for planning, preparation and assessment (PPA), and were no longer required to invigilate external examinations and tests. The Training and Development Agency for Schools (TDA) and the Workforce Agreement Monitoring Group (WAMG) – the committee set up to oversee implementation of the Agreement, comprising all its signatories – also provided detailed guidance on implementation strategies. Alternative arrangements existed for Wales. Detailed guidance on what might be expected of two new support staff roles that were, in effect, created by the National Agreement – cover supervisors and HLTAs – was also provided by WAMG.

The National Agreement and remodelling of the workforce were connected but separable policies. Remodelling was seen as part of a much wider and ongoing process of modernisation in schools, and by the end of 2008 schools were expected to have reviewed and implemented new staffing structures.

The concern over recruitment and retention in the teaching profession was a main reason for the introduction of the National Agreement, and the proposal that TAs and other support staff should release teachers from routine and clerical tasks, in order to allow them to focus more on core teaching tasks (i.e. teaching pupils, preparing their lessons and carrying out assessments), was central to delivering early successes. In this sense, TAs (and some other support staff) are seen to have an *indirect* effect on pupil standards through helping teachers, not pupils, directly. In line with this expectation, we would expect to see – as the government at the time intended – a positive effect on teachers' workloads, decreased stress and increased job satisfaction.

But the government also proposed that TAs in particular should have a *direct* impact on pupil attainment through the 'kinds of teaching activity [that] could be delegated to trained, high-level teaching assistants and … those with further and higher education experience' (DfES 2002). The use of TAs in a direct instructional role has led to a good deal of controversy and, as we highlighted above, is a main theme of research on TAs. This is an important issue for this book, and in the next section, we look more closely at the direct versus indirect roles of TAs.

1.3.1.4 Direct versus indirect TA roles

One of the key issues in the use of TAs has been their appropriate role in the classroom and, in particular, the extent to which they should have a direct pedagogical role with pupils. A main problem is that there is a general lack of clarity with regards to this role, even though it lies at the heart of the successful use of TAs, and is at the centre of concerns about teachers' professional identities, which we look at later.

In line with what has just been said, one distinction we can draw is between a direct versus an indirect role in teaching and learning. As we noted above, the version of an indirect role encapsulated in the National Agreement is through the delegation of routine tasks, allowing teachers to focus more time and energy on the core functions of teaching. Connected to this would be better quality lessons, made possible by the provision of PPA time. So here the TA helps the teacher and the school, and this indirectly benefits pupils.

However, from an early stage in the policy process, there were views in favour of TAs having a more obviously direct role with regard to pupil learning. The following extract from a speech by Estelle Morris in 2001 echoes the PwC (2001) recommendation that TAs be integrated more fully into the delivery of teaching: 'Teaching assistants will be: supervising classes that are undertaking work set by a teacher, or working with small groups of pupils on reading practice … and covering for teacher absence' (Morris 2001).

Even before the developments that led to the National Agreement, there was an influential view that TAs could have a direct beneficial effect on pupil attainment, through an explicit, increased teaching role, albeit one constrained in terms of context or type of pupil.

> It is possible to imagine extensive use of para-professionals – for example in the management of small groups, in following up with individuals the themes of lessons taught to the whole class and in helping to manage pupils who are involved in seeking or analysing information through computers.
>
> (Barber 1997)

We can, therefore, map the origins of policy that positions TAs in a direct pedagogical role back more than a decade. Some authors, though, feel that this positive view about a direct role for TAs could actually be traced back to the 1970s (Ozga 2002; Ball 2003; Butt and Gunter 2005). The developments in the early 2000s, outlined above, culminated in the formulation of the National Agreement, though TAs' direct positive contribution to pupil attainment, behaviour and attitudes to schooling was never spelt out in the National Agreement (NA), only implied.

The most radical aspect of school workforce remodelling, therefore, was the expression of a direct role for TAs, which would extend the TA role into the heart of the teaching profession – as teachers of pupils. The NA suggested a number of ways in which schools could implement cover supervision and PPA arrangements, including doubling-up classes, using supply teachers and employing 'floating teachers'. However, the policy acknowledged the likelihood that most schools would use TAs (and/or support staff in similar positions) to lead classes when teachers were unexpectedly absent or taking their non-contact time. To this end, the government set about creating two new cadres of support staff: higher level teaching assistants (HLTAs) and cover supervisors. HLTAs – as the name implies – were experienced TAs whose competency could be defined against a new higher level professional standards framework. This new post was linked to 31 occupational standards, many of which, at one time, would only have been associated with the responsibilities of qualified teachers. With the introduction of the National Agreement, the gap between the work of TAs and the work of teachers narrowed even further.

It is not surprising that there were a number of concerns within the teaching profession about the proposed new roles for TAs. Ofsted (2002) stated that unless teachers have the necessary skills and adaptability to direct the work of TAs, then the whole agenda would be undermined. In an evaluation of the first phase of the National Agreement (which was concerned with transferring routine clerical tasks from teachers to support staff) Ofsted expressed concern that: 'Most of the schools visited by Ofsted … are not making the link between this aim and the overarching objective of improving education for children and raising attainment' (Ofsted 2004b).

One view, maintained for some time anecdotally, but given some formality by the National Agreement, and later in regulations introduced under section 133 of the Education Act 2002, was that TAs did not, nor were they intended to, 'teach' pupils. The NA made clear the intention that HLTAs were not interchangeable with, or a substitute for, a qualified teacher; but they could, it was claimed, 'make a substantial contribution to the teaching and learning process in schools and to raising standards of achievement by pupils' (DfES 2003a). The wording of this claim is noteworthy: teaching remained the job of teachers, but the role of TAs and HLTAs was less clear.

Underpinning these efforts to separate the roles of teachers and TAs was a rather muddled effort to downgrade the full expression of the pedagogical role of TAs into something helpful, pedagogically speaking, but not actually 'teaching' as such. This proved to be a hard line to draw. As we shall see in Chapter 5, these convenient distinctions between 'supporting' and 'teaching' (and other nebulous terms used liberally in the National Agreement documentation) do not stand conceptual scrutiny, nor – as we shall see – do they agree with observations of what actually takes place in classrooms. Another expression of a less than full version of a direct role was that, by only interacting with a few pupils in the class, TAs were playing a secondary, less directly instructional role. This may be the case in the context of the whole class, but it is again hard to sustain this view when applied to those pupils being supported by TAs.

Yet another attempt to define the separation of teaching and TA roles, which was written into the National Agreement, was through the notion that TAs in some undefined way 'work under the guidance of the teacher' or other education professional. This caveat appears to have legal significance, in terms of which adults have ultimate responsibility for pupils' learning and welfare. Once more, it is difficult to maintain this as a tenable distinction, not least, as we shall see, because in moment-by-moment interactions with pupils, TAs often have a lot of independence from teachers, and in many cases, there is very little pre-planning or ongoing supervision from the teacher.

As noted above, the National Agreement attempted to allay concerns that HLTAs, TAs and cover supervisors would take on a pedagogical role by offering the assurance that these support staff were not interchangeable with teachers.[6] Yet at the same time, the National Agreement defined overtly pedagogical tasks and functions of TAs as 'specified work': work that TAs could undertake 'in order to assist or support the work of a qualified teacher in the school' (DfES 2003b).

It is therefore clear that there was considerable confusion about the appropriate pedagogical role of TAs. This uncertainty about how the National Agreement would manifest itself in schools proved decisive in the National Union of Teachers' (NUT) (the largest of the teacher unions) decision not to sign the Agreement. It was the only teacher union not to put its name to the policy. In a statement to its members in January 2003, entitled *A Price too high*, the then General Secretary, Doug McAvoy, explained that the NUT 'refuses to accept an inadequate and educationally unsound package', in which 'the Government will have legitimised the employment of unqualified persons to teach whole classes'.

As the policy was implemented, it became clear that staff in schools were confused about, or chose to overlook, the intended distinction between teacher and TA roles. It seems that issues concerning who exactly was to teach and how this was to be managed were obviously not working out as smoothly as intended or envisaged. In July 2008, WAMG tried to clarify the position, highlighting: how TAs without appropriate training and skills were being required to supervise pupils; 'insufficient opportunities' for HTLAs to use their higher skills on a continuing basis; and confusion between how TAs should and should not be deployed in relation to cover for unforeseen teacher absence and PPA time (WAMG 2008).

This kind of discussion and dispute about defining the appropriate role of TAs is important and we will come back to it – with some possible solutions – in the final chapter of this book. But first, it is important to obtain a systematic picture of just how support staff are used in schools, and clear information on the nature and quantity of contact they have with pupils and teachers. This was a key aim of the DISS project and we shall see in the later chapters of this book how TAs are actually deployed in classrooms and how far in everyday reality TAs are engaged in direct versus indirect roles, and the extent to which the notion of 'specified work' is actually found in practice.

1.3.2 The education of pupils with SEN in mainstream schools

There is a very important additional development, predating the National Agreement, which has also played a major part in the deployment of TAs in schools, and which has further added to the urgent need to clarify their pedagogical role. This has been the significant rise in the numbers of pupils with SEN being educated in mainstream schools.

From 1991 to 2000, the balance of pupils with a statement of SEN between mainstream and special schools in England shifted dramatically. During this period, the number of statemented pupils in mainstream schools increased by over 95,000, representing more than 90 per cent of the total increase in statemented pupils. At the same time, the number of statemented pupils in special schools remained relatively constant. The consequence of this was that in 1991, around half of all pupils with a statement were being educated in special schools; but by 2000, this proportion had fallen to around one-third (House of Commons Education and Skills Committee 2006).

In addition to this group of pupils, there has been a steady increase in the number of pupils with SEN who do *not* have a statement. Since 2003, these pupils have been categorised as either School Action or School Action Plus; as we indicated in the vignette at the start of this chapter, the latter of these two gradings is given to children whose needs are seen to require a greater level of provision than those on School Action.

Whilst the proportion of pupils with a statement of SEN being educated in English mainstream primary and secondary schools has actually fallen slightly since 2003 – from 2 per cent to 1.65 per cent – there has been a steady increase in the proportion of pupils with SEN on School Action or School Action Plus – from 14.6 per cent in 2003, to 19.1 per cent in 2010 (DfE 2010b; DfES 2005). Taken together, in 2003, the proportion of pupils with SEN in mainstream schools (with and without a statement) was 16.6 per cent; the corresponding figure for 2010 was 20.7 per cent. The increase over this period is particularly noticeable in secondary schools: the proportion of pupils with SEN in 2003 was 15.4 per cent; for 2010, it was 21.6 per cent.

We need to point out that this book is not specifically about pupils with SEN, and the education of such pupils played a relatively minor role in the original conception of the DISS project. But it became more and more apparent, once the results emerged, that the education of pupils with SEN was closely connected to the deployment of TAs. Our purpose in this section is not to specifically address wider issues related to the education of pupils with SEN, but to show one main influence on the use of TAs, as well as provide further context for the educational experiences of pupils and factors affecting their progress.

The Warnock committee report (1978) and the subsequent Education Acts of 1981, 1993 and 1996 fundamentally changed policy and practice regarding the education of pupils with SEN in England and Wales. The Government's Green Paper *Excellence for all children* (DfEE 1997) introduced a new emphasis on inclusion for pupils with SEN. Nearly a decade before the National Agreement, and 27 years after the recommendations of the Plowden Report (1967) – which included the proposal to greatly increase the number of 'teachers' aides' – the 1994 Code of Practice (DfEE 1994) supported the idea of employing TAs to help pupils who had an individual education plan or a statement (Cook-Jones 2006).

There were immense challenges for teachers in adapting to the inclusion of pupils with SEN in their classrooms (Carrington 1999; Kellett 2004). As classrooms became more inclusive, teachers felt anxious and ill-prepared to meet this challenge, and did not feel they had the specialist skills or training to work with such pupils. Concerns over the adequacy of teacher preparation were still evident when the revised Code of Practice was introduced in 2001 (Callias 2001).

As numbers of TAs and pupils with SEN in mainstream increased in tandem, it was somewhat inevitable that TAs would take on a greater role in facilitating inclusion. Early studies and commentaries on this topic found that schools with high proportions of pupils with SEN 'frequently employed considerable numbers of TAs' (Ofsted 2004b), and that TAs 'can play a pivotal role in promoting inclusion of children with additional needs in mainstream schools' (Moran and Abbott 2002).

The 2004 Ofsted report also noted that it was an established practice in special schools for TAs to take part in 'planning and teaching lessons', and that with the introduction of the National Agreement, this was 'becoming more common in other schools'. One 'increasing' trend was the use of TAs to withdraw groups from the classroom, often using so-called 'intervention programmes' in literacy' (Ofsted 2004b). Similar developments were also occurring in the USA, where the 1975 'Education for all Handicapped' Act had led to increased number of TAs providing 'individualized instruction for students with learning disabilities' (Gerber *et al.* 2001).

As the numbers of pupils with SEN in mainstream schools increased, a number of broad tensions emerged. One tension was the seeming incompatibility between the aims of the 'raising standards' agenda with policies of inclusion. The increasing competition and the marketisation of education (Gibson 2004) had revealed 'apparent conflicts' in government policy between standards and league table discourse and the inclusive schools discourse, '[making] it more difficult for schools to become more inclusive' (Evans and Lunt 2002).

Another tension concerned the emergence of TAs as the preferred means for facilitating the inclusion of pupils with SEN. Ofsted voiced their concerns in reports in 2002 and 2006, with the latter report concluding that: 'Pupils in mainstream schools where support from TAs was the main type of provision were less likely to make good academic progress than those who had access to specialist teaching in those schools' (Ofsted 2006).

On the same issue, Giangreco and Broer (2005) were strong in their conclusions about the situation in schools in the USA: 'paraprofessionals have served as an analgesic for the perceived pressures of including more diverse populations of students with disabilities. Unfortunately, to date we have no compelling evidence that this model is an effective educational support for students with disabilities.'

Once again, what is apparent when reviewing the evidence from the UK and other countries is how limited the research evidence is on the deployment and impact of TAs on pupils and, in particular, pupils with SEN. It is vital that such information is collected in a systematic way and this was a main aim of the DISS project.

1.4 Paraprofessionals and public services

The increase of TAs and other support staff in education can also been seen in the wider context of an increase in 'paraprofessionals' across the public services. Professional roles in a number of sectors (e.g. medicine, social work, law, police and education) have been redefined, so that some activities previously performed by established professionals are now undertaken by others. Sherr (2007) describes the changes that have taken place in the legal profession:

> The results of specialisation in the legal profession, competition and changes in legal aid have led to a form of industrialisation within the legal sector. Legal work is often organised in a more standardised and repetitive fashion. Work is de-skilled and broken up into different activities which can be handled by lower level operatives.
>
> (Sherr 2007)

In the UK there has been for some time now a redrawing of the boundaries between the roles of established professionals and others who work in their respective fields. Thornley (1997), for example, reported on the use of health care assistants doing important clinical duties, a notion that – as we saw in the vignette at the beginning of the chapter – the then Education Secretary Estelle Morris evoked in her outline of the expansion of support staff roles. Education, as shown by the introduction of the National Agreement in 2003, was no different. In the UK, these developments were to a large degree driven by the modernisation agenda of the New Labour government, picking up on the work of the Conservative government in the 1990s, which was designed to improve the efficiency, economy and effectiveness of public services (see Hammersley-Fletcher 2006).

As we noted earlier, similar changes have been occurring in the USA, with the emergence of paraeducators, and outside of education, with paralegals and paramedics (although pre-service preparation and ongoing development may differ between professions (Wallace 2003)). Given what we have said in this chapter about the reasons for the growth of support staff in education in the UK, it is interesting to see the factors thought to have contributed to the changes in numbers and roles of paraprofessionals in American education. Wallace (2003) argues that as well as the inclusion agenda, these factors include shortages of teachers and related services personnel, and changing and expanding roles of school professionals as classroom and programme managers.

As we described above, workforce issues were a key factor in similar developments in the UK: in 2001, the then Education Secretary, Estelle Morris, used the broader action of workforce remodelling as a means to address anticipated recruitment and retention problems, which were due in part to an ageing teacher workforce, and the likelihood that fewer and fewer graduates would be drawn to teaching.

The growth of paraprofessionals has also been driven by costs. Professionals are expensive to train and tend to be more highly rewarded financially for their years of study and acquisition of professional knowledge and skills. Cheaper workers, taken on to reduce the workloads of the more expensive professionals, seem attractive because they can prevent a rise in the overall costs of running the service. Moreover, in the case of education, the hope was that because they were cheaper than teachers, increased use of paraprofessionals could make possible major inroads into the pupil:adult ratios in schools, and as a result, greater flexibility would arise (Barber 1997). Hancock and Eyres (2004) put it simply: 'their presence within schools is very convenient to government, LEAs and teachers at a time when the education system is under great pressure to improve. In short, they are a cheap and readily available source of potentially valuable labour.'

A number of authors have provided detailed analyses of factors and issues connected to this rise of a 'new professionalism' and disputes over the traditional divide between professional and paraprofessional (e.g. Bach et al. 2004; Butt and Gunter 2005; Nixon et al. 1997; Stevenson 2007; Thompson 2006; Wilkinson 2005) and it is not intended to cover this here. Our focus is more on the use of paraprofessionals in education and the educational consequences of their involvement. A theme to emerge across professions is the function of paraprofessionals in easing the working conditions of the professional groups they served, but also the general lack of studies addressing the paraprofessionals' position in this process of change and their impact. As we shall see, this is particularly the case in education.

There are several other themes and issues that have emerged from the broader study of paraprofessionals that we feel are relevant to the development of TAs in education and therefore worthy of mention. One is a concern over loss of professional status. In the past, a number of factors like closely guarded professional knowledge, strict entry requirements, tight regulation of professional practice, all contributed to the status and uniqueness of the professions. As these have been eroded through the increase in paraprofessionals, so the roles of the professionals themselves have changed.

Another issue concerns job 'boundaries' between professional and paraprofessional. Bach *et al.* (2004) and Kessler *et al.* (2005) have focused on these issues across three public service sectors in the UK: health, social care and education. They highlight the notion of 'boundary' to draw attention to the fact that as the roles are analysed and their tasks listed and categorised, the process of separating out 'core professional tasks' from other tasks could lead to disputes over demarcation. There may well be disagreement between individual members of a particular profession about where the boundary line should be drawn, which mark out their roles from those of paraprofessionals in the same field. It seems almost inevitable, as we saw earlier in relation to the National Agreement, that when governments press ahead with policies that would lead to greater roles for paraprofessionals, clashes with the trade unions representing professional groups will follow.

Disputes over boundaries between professional and paraprofessionals are not confined to education. In 2007, the bodies representing the medical profession in the UK proposed that senior nursing staff should be allowed to make clinical decisions regarding the resuscitation of patients, independently of a doctor. This is one more example of a task previously thought to require the skills and knowledge of physicians, being delegated to those working under the supervision and control of a professional group (i.e. doctors).

Another common issue across professions concerns new and growing issues of management. As the numbers of paraprofessionals have increased, the professional groups became drawn into their supervision and management. Professions vary in the extent to which they have progressed in this regard. The legal profession is far behind in this process (Sherr 2007). We shall see in this book that there are also concerns about how far professionals in education are prepared for this widening responsibility in relation to TAs.

Even at the early stages of the evolution of classroom support staff, Barber and Brighouse (1992) addressed the 'increased professionalism' of teachers being asked to manage other staff. They argued that the number of TAs in primary education, and the ad hoc manner in which so many of them were employed and deployed, had reached a point where policy debate needed to be more widespread, open and informed by research evidence. Long before the National Agreement and the DISS project, they argued that almost nothing was known about: 1) the ways in which existing professional boundaries between TAs and teachers were defined and maintained in schools; 2) the terms and conditions of TAs' employment; and 3) the ways in which schools deployed TAs. They felt this was needed in order to avoid policy development being inhibited by the defensiveness of the teaching profession and government agencies' ignorance of the realities of classroom life.

At the time of writing (2011) the future for TAs is not clear. The present government has disbanded the TDA and organisations like WAMG concerned with workforce remodelling, and policy announcements have avoided dealing directly with support staff in schools. We shall see later that a recent Green Paper on the education of pupils with SEN makes many radical suggestions, but to a large extent also fails to address the deployment and impact of TAs. We come back to policy implications in the last chapter (Chapter 7).

1.5 The DISS project

Despite the large increase in TAs and other support staff, it was recognised in the early 2000s by the English and Welsh governments, and by researchers, that there were significant gaps in knowledge about many aspects of support staff in schools. Previous research provided only limited information on the deployment and impact of support staff, and on the school processes through which their impact was maximised or inhibited. The DISS study was designed to help fill these gaps in research. It was the first to systematically address the deployment and impact of all categories of support staff, across all school sectors (primary, secondary and special). It covered the key period between 2003 and 2008, after the National Agreement was signed and implemented over the academic years 2003–2004 to 2005–2006. The study was not restricted to pupils with SEN or other pupils receiving the highest levels of TA support, but covered all pupils who received any amount of TA support.

The two main aims of the project were:

1   To provide an accurate, systematic and representative description of the types of support staff in school, and their characteristics and deployment in schools, and how these changed over time
2   To assess the impact or effect of support staff on teachers, teaching and pupil learning and behaviour.

In contrast to much previous research in the area of TAs, the DISS project was conducted on a much larger, previously unseen, scale. It was naturalistic in design and sought to capture everyday circumstances in schools, allowing an analysis of differences over time, by school type and by support staff category. It should be made clear to the reader that this was not an intervention study: it did not seek to change the situation in schools but to report what happens in everyday settings. Interventions have value, but it was thought more useful and strategic to first find out what the situation was like more generally across many schools, rather than examining what might be possible under certain circumstances. There were two strands.

Strand 1 addressed the first main aim and involved three biennial questionnaire surveys – the Main School Questionnaire (MSQ), the Support Staff Questionnaire (SSQ) and the Teacher Questionnaire (TQ) – which aimed to provide a systematic account of basic information on support staff in schools and changes over the key five-year period (2003–2008). Information collected from the Strand 1 questionnaires included:

- numbers and estimated FTE of support staff
- vacancies and problems of turnover and recruitment
- characteristics of support staff, in terms of their gender, age, ethnicity, qualifications and experience
- support staff's contractual arrangements, working hours and wages
- job descriptions, appraisal, supervision and line management for support staff
- support staff training
- extent to which support staff support pupils and teachers, and have planning and feedback time with teachers
- job satisfaction; and for teachers, levels of workload and stress.

This was a very extensive survey; over the three survey waves, a total of just under 18,000 questionnaires were completed and returned.

The Strand 1 Wave 2 SSQ also collected over 1,600 detailed timelogs (a type of work pattern diary), completed by support staff, to show the type and extent of their various activities over a school day.

Strand 2 used a multi-method approach, combining quantitative and qualitative methods, to obtain a detailed and integrated account of the deployment and impact of support staff. A main aim of Strand 2 was to address the impact of support staff. This is one of the most important yet problematic aspects of research in this area. Lee (2002), among others, concluded that 'relatively few studies provided good evidence on which to base conclusions about impact'. There are a number of limitations to previous studies that make it difficult to draw clear conclusions. Evidence is patchy, with claims often based on anecdotal and informal comments. In particular, there are huge challenges for research seeking to measure effects of TAs on pupil outcomes, in the context of normal school conditions. One limitation of the analyses of the impact of TAs, conducted as part of the earlier Class Size and Pupil Adult Ratio (CSPAR) KS2 study (Blatchford *et al.* 2007), was that relationships between TAs and outcomes were examined for the whole class. It was recognised that future research in this area would need to target more precisely the connections between TAs and the specific pupils they support, and this was a main challenge for the DISS project team. It was decided to address the impact of TAs in terms of pupil learning and attainment, but also in relation to aspects such as confidence, concentration, working independently and the ability to complete assigned work, as well as interactions between teachers and pupils in the classroom. There is only relatively anecdotal evidence on these dimensions, and so we also wanted to collect systematic evidence in order to provide a more comprehensive and reliable account of the effect of TAs.

Strand 2 Wave 1 took place in 2005/2006 and had three main components:

1   The first wave of the Main Pupil Support Survey (MPSS) involved a sample of 2,528 pupils across Years 1, 3, 7 and 10 in 76 schools, and analysed effects of the amount of TA support across the school year (through teacher ratings and data from systematic observations) on pupils' academic progress over the year (based on National Curriculum levels and key stage test results), and 'Positive Approaches to Learning' (PAL), controlling for other factors likely to confound this relationship (e.g. prior attainment, SEN status, gender, income deprivation, ethnic group, pupil age and English as an additional language).
2   A systematic observation component, which resulted in 34,420 separate data points on the nature and contexts of TA–pupil interactions.
3   A set of case studies that focused on the school processes connected to the deployment of support staff, based on observations and interviews with around 500 staff and pupils in 47 schools.

Strand 2 Wave 2 took place in 2007/2008 and had two components:

1   The second wave of the MPSS, involving an increased sample of 5,672 pupils across Years 2, 6 and 9 in 77 schools.
2   A second set of case studies, this time focusing principally on TAs. There were 95 interviews conducted with staff in 18 schools; plus structured observations (1,500 separate data points) and transcripts of the interactions between teachers and pupils and TAs and pupils in the same classrooms.

For ease of reference, further details on methods of data collection and sample sizes are given in Table 1 in Appendix 1. In this book we will be referring the reader to these sources of data collection as we present results.

1.6 This book

When we first looked at the results from the study on pupils' academic attainment, there was surprise expressed within the research team. Our funders and the DISS project steering group also shared this surprise and found the results disappointing and counter-intuitive. When these results were reported at a keynote symposium at the British Educational Research Association Annual Conference in September 2009, there was an understandable public and media interest, with articles in the *Times Educational Supplement*, *The Economist*, and national print and online media, plus radio interviews. There was an understandable concern about the findings and their implications. This book is an attempt to explain the findings and address the implications for practice and policy.

We have written five reports on the DISS project, which were published by the government, along with research briefs to summarise results. We have published a number of peer-reviewed journal papers, and a number of other publications for a practitioner readership. Details on these publications can be found through the project website: www.schoolsupportstaff.net.

However, we felt that only a book-length treatment would allow us to pull together the separate strands and provide in one place a full narrative and explanation. Although the research was sophisticated in terms of research design and statistical analyses, this book is primarily aimed at the non-technical reader. We have tried to make it as accessible as possible, while at the same time adhering to what we hope are high standards of evidence, which allow us to feel confident about the veracity of the findings.

We stress that this is not meant to be a practical guide for schools in how to use their TAs. This is the task of a separate publication.[7] This book provides for the first time a picture of who TAs are, what they do and what impact they have on teachers and pupils. We identify the serious problems that have emerged with the current arrangements for TA deployment and in the last chapter argue that a fundamental change in policy and practice is needed.

Throughout the project, our research managers at the then DCSF gave us valuable support, as did a steering group set up to help the project. The steering group comprised representatives from many of the organisations that had signed the National Agreement. At an early stage it was agreed that the best strategy, and the one likely to have the most credibility for participating schools, was to make it clear that, though funded by the English and Welsh governments, this was an independent research project, based at the Institute of Education, London. We are pleased to say that although there was sometimes disagreement and inevitably a lot of scrutiny about the findings, especially concerning pupils' educational progress, it was always clear that the results would be published. The views expressed in this book are those of the research team, and may not necessarily reflect those of the members of the steering group or our research managers, or the present coalition government.

The DISS project covered all categories of support staff, but this book is primarily about classroom- or pupil-based support staff, whom we refer to throughout as 'teaching assistants', or 'TAs' for convenience. (In the UK, TAs are variously known by other common terms including 'learning support assistant' and 'classroom assistant'. We should also point out when we refer to TAs generally, we include in this definition higher level

TAs, or HLTAs). It is with regard to this category of support staff that many of the issues and tensions described previously are most evident. Of all the different types of support staff in schools it is the TA role that has undergone the most considerable change and as we shall see they have the most direct role of any support staff type in affecting pupil learning.

Shortly, in Chapter 2, we will describe in detail the findings from the DISS project on the impact of TAs and other support staff. The chapter addresses the impact of support staff on two main outcomes:

1   On teachers and teaching, in terms of: teachers' views on the effects of support staff, on their job satisfaction, stress and workloads, and on their teaching; and a systematic breakdown of activities passed from teachers to support staff.

2   On pupils, in terms of the effect of support staff on: pupil learning and behaviour, based on teachers' views; 'positive approaches to learning' (e.g. confidence, motivation and ability to work independently and complete assigned work), based on teacher ratings; and pupils' academic attainment, in terms of the effect of the amount of TA support they receive on end of year attainment, controlling for other factors likely to confound this relationship (e.g. prior attainment and SEN status).

We conducted complementary studies, involving the views of teachers, TAs and other support staff, and schools (via school leaders), as well as detailed documentation of support staff activities and observations of interactions between TAs and pupils. These provided the bases for an analysis of what we call the 'preparedness', the 'deployment' and the 'practice' of TAs, and these in turn help us understand the results on impact. They also provide the basis for the 'Wider Pedagogical Role' (WPR) model, which we develop in each chapter of the book, and also recommendations concerning policy and practice.

First though, in Chapter 3, we give further context to the findings by providing details on the characteristics and conditions of employment of TAs and other support staff. We address the numbers of support staff in schools, their roles and responsibilities, and present a new typology of categories of support staff. We also describe who support staff are – in terms of their gender, age, ethnicity, qualifications and experience – and describe aspects of their conditions of employment (e.g. pay and contracts), hours of work and 'goodwill', supervision and appraisal arrangements, and job satisfaction. Results from the DISS study grouped under 'characteristics' and 'conditions of employment' form part of the WPR model, but as we shall see, these components are not as strongly connected to our broader explanation for the attainment results as the findings from other components, though they do add some useful context.

In Chapter 4, we start to address the first of these core components. We show how the 'preparedness' of teachers and TAs plays a sizeable role in maximising and inhibiting TA effectiveness. We draw on the DISS findings to examine, first, the training and professional development of teachers and TAs in terms of how teachers manage and organise the work of TAs, and how TAs are trained to support learning; and, second, day-to-day preparation in terms of time for joint planning, preparation and feedback between teachers and TAs, before and after lessons.

Chapter 5 provides detailed and systematic descriptive information on just how TAs are used and what their everyday role looks like. We call this the 'deployment' of TAs. We first look at the views and debate about the roles taken by TAs, drawing on the interview material from the case studies. The second section is the heart of the chapter, in which we examine the evidence arising out of the DISS project on: the amount of contact there is between teachers and support staff, including TAs; the general activities of all support staff, including TAs; the contexts in which pupils are supported by teachers and TAs; which pupils are supported by teachers and TAs; and differences in pupil roles in interactions with teachers and TAs. We end with a third section in which we look more closely at the separation of TA-supported pupils from the teacher and the curriculum, as revealed by our results.

In Chapter 6 we use the generic term 'practice' in a pragmatic way to cover the classroom interactions of TAs and teachers with pupils. Study of these interactions is important because they are at the heart of the pupil's educational experience and their learning. There is a good deal of information on how teachers interact with pupils, and characteristics of effective teaching, but very little is known about the interactions of TAs with pupils and their effectiveness. In this chapter, we build on the results in the deployment chapter by exploring the talk between TAs and pupils in more fine-grained detail. We present results from two complementary approaches to the analysis of talk between TAs and pupils and teachers and pupils: first, 'instructional talk analysis' was used to provide a general comparison of the main forms of talk, as they related to everyday, educationally relevant interactions with pupils; and, second, 'conversation analysis' (CA) – an even more closely textured approach – was used to explore in detail ways in which teachers and TAs used language, and the effects of various strategies on learners. CA was used to provide a sequential analysis of talk, which took account of the talk of the pupil as well. Results are illustrated with extracts from the transcripts of teacher-to-pupil and TA-to-pupil talk.

At the end of Chapters 3 to 6, readers will see how the findings explained within each chapter help to develop the Wider Pedagogical Role model. When taken together, we argue that there has been much progress in describing the systemic factors likely to account for the troubling results on the impact of TA support on pupil progress.

In our last chapter (Chapter 7), we address the implications and recommendations for policy and practice, in terms of three key dimensions taken from the WPR model: preparedness, deployment and practice. Finally, we discuss the following in turn: the WPR model and the implications for the education of pupils with SEN in mainstream schools; implications for the National Agreement and allied developments; the need to revise models of school and teacher effectiveness; and the wider context of paraprofessional roles in public services. We end with suggestions for future research.

Whilst existing studies on the deployment and impact of TAs have given us useful information about how to use TAs to good effect, the fact remains that most of what we know about TAs from these studies relates to how they are deployed in specific circumstances, and the impact on pupils this has in somewhat limited terms (e.g. progress in reading over a term). What is less understood is how TAs are deployed in everyday situations and what effect this everyday deployment has on pupil attainment over a school year.

The DISS project is the first research project to provide this data, and has done so on the largest scale seen to date. The study's findings are of the utmost concern, but are, we feel, explainable in a manner that makes clear what needs to change in order to ensure more effective TA deployment in future.

A key aim of this book, therefore, is to highlight not just the problems concerning widespread models of TA deployment, but also the ways in which we can go about rectifying them.

Chapter 2

The impact of TAs

2.1 Introduction

In many ways this is the most important chapter in the book, because it is here that we describe in detail our results on the impact of TAs. As described in Chapter 1, the overall DISS project covered all categories of support staff, but in the case of impact on pupil outcomes, the focus was on TAs. We examined impact on two main types of outcomes:

1   The effects on teachers in terms of first, their workloads, job satisfaction and levels of stress; and, second, their teaching
2   The effects on pupils, in terms of their learning and behaviour; measures of their positive approaches to learning (PAL); and finally, in terms of their academic progress in English, mathematics and science.

Before we present our results, we first give some background to each of the different types of impact we studied. The data sources for this chapter are shown in Table 2.1.

2.1.1 Impact of TAs on teachers and teaching: background

As we saw in the vignette at the start of this book, most teachers feel that TAs have a significant impact on their work. Mark, the teacher, was typical in his summation of TA impact, in terms of how he described the ways in which Mandy (his TA) helped him and his teaching, and the pupils in his class.

As we also saw in Chapter 1, the concern about recruitment and retention in the teaching profession was a main reason for the National Agreement, and the expectation that support staff should release teachers from routine and clerical tasks so that teachers

Table 2.1 Data sources for impact of TAs

	Strand 1				Strand 2				
	MSQ	TQ	SSQ	Work pattern diary	Structured observations	Systematic observations	Case studies	Transcripts	MPSS
Impact of TAs		•				•	•		•

could focus on core teaching tasks. Some studies and commentaries paint a largely positive picture of the impact of TAs and other support staff on teaching (e.g. Mortimore and Mortimore 1992; HMI 2001; Ofsted 2002), though for the most part, evidence is based on teachers' reports. Results from an earlier large-scale study by the authors (Blatchford *et al.* 2007) found that teachers were largely positive about the contribution of TAs in schools. This was seen in terms of increased attention and support for learning (e.g. more one-to-one attention, support for pupils with SEN and support for teaching of literacy), increased teaching effectiveness (e.g. in terms of productive group work, productive creative and practical activities, lesson delivery and curriculum coverage), effective classroom management, and effects on pupils' learning outcomes.

In this book we address the effects on teachers and teaching in a more extensive, multi-method and systematic way. We present results from the three waves of Strand 1 questionnaires returned by teachers, extracts from the case studies and results from the extensive systematic observation study conducted as part of Strand 2 Wave 1.

2.1.2 Impact on pupil behaviour, positive approaches to learning and academic attainment: background

2.1.2.1 Impact on pupil behaviour

Effects on teacher workloads, job satisfaction, stress and teaching (by the teacher) can be seen as evidence that TAs, and some other categories of support staff, have an *indirect* effect on pupil standards. But as we have seen in Chapter 1, the government at the time also proposed that TAs should have a *direct* impact on pupil attainment, through overtly pedagogical input (DfES 2002). In this chapter we present results from the Strand 1 Waves 1–3 Teacher Questionnaire (TQ) on teachers' views on the impact of TAs and other support staff on pupil behaviour and learning. We also present results from the Strand 2 Wave 1 systematic observations on the effect of TAs on pupils' classroom behaviour.

2.1.2.2 Impact on pupils' positive approaches to learning

It would seem to follow from reports of teachers that assigning TAs to particular pupils, usually those with problems of learning, behaviour or attention, would give the pupils more individual attention and help them develop confidence and motivation in their work, good working habits and the willingness to finish off tasks. These are facets separable from academic performance and learning. Schlapp *et al.* (2003) identify the benefits of TAs more in terms of the range of learning experiences provided and effects on pupil motivation, confidence and self-esteem, and found less effect on pupil behaviour. On the other hand, there is a well-established concern that such an arrangement can result in pupils becoming too dependent on staff who support them (Giangreco *et al.* 1997; Moyles and Suschitsky 1997). One aim of the DISS project was to address the impact of TAs on these aspects of pupil development – what we called 'positive approaches to learning' (PAL).

2.1.2.3 Impact on pupils' academic progress

There is a general recognition that we have too little systematic data on the impact of TAs on pupils' academic progress (Alborz *et al.* 2009). The findings from the few studies that have been published are mixed. Positive findings have come from studies of the effectiveness of specific curriculum interventions given by TAs – mainly for literacy (Alborz *et al.* 2009; Savage and Carless 2008). Slavin *et al.* (2009) reviewed the evidence of different kinds of intervention with poor readers and found a generally positive effect for structured interventions from trained TAs.

But other studies report negative results. Finn *et al.* (2000), on the basis of data from the often-cited Tennessee Student Teacher Achievement Ratio (STAR) project, found that there was no beneficial effect on pupil attainment of having a teacher aide, as well as a teacher, in a class. Klassen (2001) found that pupils with SEN who were assigned additional support for literacy made less progress than their unsupported peers; a result similar to that of Reynolds and Muijs (2003) in relation to maths. Gerber *et al.* (2001) reported on the impact of TAs in the USA on the academic achievement of pupils in kindergarten to grade 3, and concluded that TAs had little, if any, positive effect on pupils' academic achievement. Giangreco and colleagues, in a series of publications, have argued that over-reliance on one-to-one paraprofessional support leads to a wide range of detrimental effects on pupils (e.g. Giangreco *et al.* 2005).

As noted in Chapter 1, Ofsted (2006) concluded that support from TAs did not necessarily ensure good quality intervention or 'adequate progress' for pupils. But, in 2008, the inspectorate reported that some schools believed they could make causal links between effective support staff deployment and training, and improved end of year test results. However, this link was impressionistic and not based on systematic evidence (Ofsted 2008).

Given the ubiquity of TAs in classrooms, this lack of clear educational benefits for pupils is troubling. But a main limitation of research in this field, and a key reason for the DISS study, is the lack of rigorous empirical studies of the impact of TAs on pupils working in everyday classroom conditions. We therefore conducted a large-scale systematic analysis of the effects of TAs on pupils' approaches to learning and their academic progress.

2.2 Impact of TAs on teachers: results

2.2.1 Workloads, job satisfaction and levels of stress

2.2.1.1 Impact on teacher workloads

One of the most notable results from the DISS study was the positive effect of TAs and other support staff on teachers' workloads. This was evident in several different sources of data.

2.2.1.1.1 IMPACT ON ROUTINE ADMINISTRATIVE AND CLERICAL TASKS

One method of assessing the impact of support staff on teachers was to see how many of the routine administrative and clerical tasks (as identified in the National Agreement guidance) had been transferred from teachers, especially given that Phase 1 of the Agreement's implementation required that these tasks be transferred to support staff from September 2003. In the TQ, teachers were presented with a list of 26 routine and clerical tasks and asked to say, for each task, which they still performed themselves, which were performed by other staff, and to also give the post title of the staff now carrying out the tasks.

The main finding was that while at Wave 1 most of the tasks were conducted by teachers, by Wave 2, there had been a marked transfer to support staff; a trend that continued through to Wave 3. As we highlighted in the vignette, tasks that were once performed by teachers are now largely performed by TAs, such as Mandy, and other support staff, such as Crystal, Dalebrook's finance officer. Support staff at Wave 3 were now collecting money, chasing absences, bulk photocopying, copy typing, producing standard letters, producing class lists, analysing attendance figures, processing exam results, administering work experience, administering teacher cover, ICT trouble shooting, commissioning new ICT equipment, stocktaking, preparing/maintaining equipment and inputting pupil data (reflected in the fact that more than 60 per cent of teachers reported TAs had taken on each of these tasks). The drop in numbers of teachers now performing these tasks was in many cases very marked, with the number of teachers performing them more than halving. At Wave 3, only record keeping, classroom displays, administering and invigilating examinations, and giving personal advice were tasks still mostly done by teachers (i.e. more than 60 per cent of teachers).

We found that the transfer of tasks was not even across support staff categories. It was administrative staff, like Crystal, who were far more likely than any other support staff category to perform these tasks previously undertaken by teachers. By Wave 3, they had largely taken main responsibility for half of the 26 tasks. TAs at Waves 2 and 3 were said to have taken on classroom displays (this does not necessarily contradict the fact that classroom displays are still, for the most part, undertaken by teachers).

2.2.1.1.2 EFFECT OF TAS ON TEACHERS' WORKLOADS: TEACHER RATINGS

The positive effect of support staff on teachers' workloads was also seen in answers to closed questions in the TQ. Teachers were asked to give information on two different types of support staff with whom they had worked in the last week, and asked to describe how these people had affected their job satisfaction, level of stress and workload. Answers were expressed in terms of a five-point scale, but to simplify results, they were combined into three levels: a decrease; no change; and an increase. The results for Wave 3 are presented in Figure 2.1.

Results showed that at Wave 3, over half of teachers (53 per cent) said these members of support staff had caused a decrease in workload, over a third (36 per cent) said they had led to no change in workloads, and just 12 per cent said they had caused an increase. There was a very similar picture at Wave 1 and 2. TAs (as well as administrative staff and technicians) had the greatest effect on workloads.

As we saw in our vignette, it was not just teachers like Mark who felt that their workload had benefited from support staff; in her response to the survey, Liz, the headteacher at Dalebrook, acknowledged how Crystal had taken on much of the school's financial administration with which the headteacher previously dealt. In the third MSQ (Wave 3), headteachers were asked about the extent to which remodelling had affected the workload of teachers, headteachers and leadership team, and support staff in the school. Of these four groups, it was only teachers who were said to have experienced a decrease in workloads, with three-quarters of headteachers saying that teachers had experienced a decrease. It is appreciated that school workforce remodelling involves more than just support staff, but the deployment of support staff is a large component of remodelling within schools.

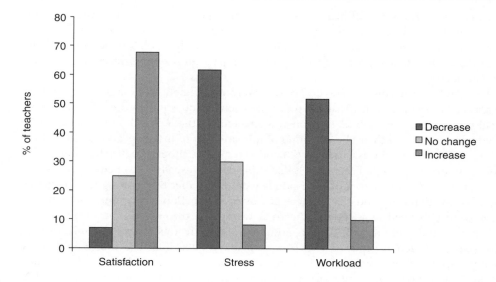

Figure 2.1 Effect of support staff on teachers' job satisfaction, stress and workloads (Wave 3)

Teachers' answers to an open-ended question in the TQ gave further details on the ways in which TAs and other support staff had helped to reduce workloads. Teachers were asked to comment on how the members of support staff they had worked with in the last week had affected their workload, if at all. There were 605 teacher responses at Wave 2 and 468 at Wave 3. As with the other open-ended responses answers, restrictions were not put on which categories of support staff teachers could refer to, but the majority of comments related to TAs. It was clear from the teachers' comments in Wave 2 and 3 that for many of them, the presence of support staff had a positive impact on their workload. In line with the questions about the transfer of routine activities, teachers often listed the tasks they no longer had to perform, or at least carried out less frequently, because support staff were doing them instead. This helped give teachers more time for other areas of their work, particularly teaching and attending to pupils. For others, it brought about the pleasure of a good working relationship, a reduction in pressure and making the job easier.

At each wave there were a minority of teachers who said that some aspects of their workload had increased as a result of having support staff work for them. The reason was usually due to the increased amount of planning and preparation that was required in order for the support staff to be able to carry out their work. However, the time taken up with this extra work was still considered by some to be worthwhile, in terms of it helping support staff work more effectively.

2.2.1.2 Job satisfaction

Teachers were also clear that their job satisfaction was positively affected by support staff. Results, again shown in Figure 2.1, reveal that about two-thirds of teachers at each wave (68 per cent, 65 per cent and 66 per cent for Waves 1, 2 and 3 respectively) said that this member of support staff had led to a slight or large increase in job satisfaction, and only a small percentage at each wave (7 per cent, 5 per cent and 7 per cent for Waves 1, 2 and 3 respectively) said that support staff had decreased their job satisfaction. As Mark indicated in the vignette, Mandy had a positive impact on his job satisfaction, as well as his workload.

TAs (and technicians) at Waves 2 and 3 were most likely to be associated with an increase in job satisfaction. Answers to an open-ended question in the TQ gave more detail on why teachers' job satisfaction was affected. In the Wave 3 TQ, teachers were asked to comment on their chosen rating of job satisfaction. Just over 500 teachers chose to comment, and there was a total of 720 coded responses altogether (teachers could give more than one response). Teachers felt that support staff (usually TAs) helped ensure that more of the individual needs of their pupils were being met by ensuring that particular pupils were supported and that none were overlooked. Pupils' learning and achievement were enhanced (e.g. lesson objectives were met) through the personal qualities and skills of the support staff (such as positive attitudes to their work and relationships with pupils). Teachers reported that time available for teaching had increased and the quality improved; they were able to focus more on teaching, teach better lessons and devote more time to that core role. Here is a typical quote from a teacher about her TA: 'Through quality support accompanied by constant communication between myself and the HLTA, I can quickly target work at the correct level to the targeted group.'

2.2.1.3 Levels of teacher stress

A question in the TQ asked teachers how TAs and other support staff affected their level of stress; the results are displayed in Figure 2.1. The results showed that support staff had a positive impact on teachers' stress levels, with about two-thirds of teachers saying that support staff led to a decrease in stress in Wave 3 (65 per cent) and only 8 per cent saying it led to an increase. A similar picture was found in Waves 1 and 2. As with the two previous waves, different support staff categories had a differing impact on teachers' stress. In Wave 3, TAs (as well as pupil welfare, technicians and administrative support staff) were most likely to cause a decrease in teacher stress, as recognised by our teacher, Mark, in the vignette.

As with workload and job satisfaction, teachers in Waves 2 and 3 were given the option of writing comments to explain their rating of the impact of support staff on levels of stress. In Wave 2, 629 teachers responded, producing a total of 756 responses; and in Wave 3, there were responses from 105 teachers, producing a total of 233 comments. Teachers' comments showed that the impact on teachers' stress levels was linked to the reduction in workload brought about by the transferring of routine tasks to TAs and others. Teaching had changed due to working with support staff: more pupils were being supported or were able to take part due to the extra help in the classroom, and the behaviour of supported pupils improved. Here is a typical quote from a teacher about their TA: 'The role of the teacher has changed over the years. I spend a very long time working each week (60+hours). Without a teaching assistant/learning support assistant to shoulder some of the burden, life would be impossible.'

Once again, as with workloads, in a minority of cases, support staff had led to decreases in satisfaction and increased levels of stress; teachers explained that they felt they had to do more planning and preparation. Some teachers also said that the personal qualities of support staff, such as a reluctance to do tasks and a lack of initiative, could cause problems for the teacher. However, whilst an increase in workload may have a negative impact on job satisfaction and stress, the positive effects of support staff seem, from a teacher's perspective, far outweigh this.

2.3 Effect of TAs on teaching

The effect of TAs and other support staff on teachers in terms of workloads, job satisfaction and levels of stress can be distinguished from their effects on teaching more directly. This was addressed in two different ways in the DISS study: 1) through teachers' experiences, as expressed in answers to open-ended questions in the TQ; and 2) through systematic observations, carried out as part of Strand 2 Wave 1. We now look at results from these two forms of data collection, starting with responses to the TQ questions.

2.3.1 Teachers' views on how TAs had affected their own teaching

In the TQ, at each wave, teachers were asked to identify a member of support staff, and describe how the support they provided affected their teaching, if at all. Analysis of the answers showed that at Wave 2, teachers felt that the main benefits of support staff for their own teaching were because they brought specialist help to the classroom, they allowed more teaching, they had a positive effect on the curriculum, tasks and activities offered, and because they could take on specific pupils. There were similar reasons given at Wave 3: bringing specialist help; allowing more teaching; removing administrative and routine tasks; and allowing more time for planning and preparation. This question, like the other open-ended questions, concerned all categories of support staff. The value for teaching, in terms of bringing specialist help, was provided by bilingual support assistants, librarians and technicians. TAs were of more general help in increasing the amount of teaching, taking on administrative and routine activities, and taking on particular pupils – usually those who have difficulties – thus allowing more individual attention.

It is interesting to note that the benefits of support staff to teaching were seen not so much in terms of enhancing teachers' own interactions with pupils in need of support, but rather in terms of allowing more time with the rest of the class. We return to this point in Chapter 5.

2.3.2 Effect of TAs on teaching: systematic observation results

The results describing teachers' experience of the impact of TAs on teaching were systematically collected and analysed, but still relied on the reports of teachers. While there is no reason to think the reports are unreliable, they are still based on subjective judgments. In Strand 2 Wave 1 we were also able to address the impact of TAs on teaching through the use of detailed systematic observations, using an observation schedule of proven reliability and set time intervals within which observations were coded.

One of the benefits of this form of data collection was that for each ten-second time interval, we were able to code whether the TA was present in the classroom, while at the same time code the teacher and pupil behaviours that occurred in the same time interval. When examined across all the many time intervals in the study, this enables us to determine the overall extent to which TA presence was associated with the likelihood of particular teacher and pupil behaviours occurring at the same time. This is a much more powerful form of analysis than just looking at totals of types of behaviour. Essentially, it is capturing the co-occurrence in time of TA presence and particular behaviours. In this section we look at relationships with adult behaviours, and later in the chapter we look at relationships with pupil behaviours.

The results showed that the presence of TAs had two general beneficial effects on teaching. First, TA presence was associated with a greater amount of adult (teachers and TAs) individual attention toward pupils (a category that was called 'focus'; we look at this in more detail in Chapter 5). It seems fair to conclude, therefore, that TA presence led to more *individualisation of attention from adults*.

Second, there seemed to be benefits in terms of *classroom control*, with the presence of TAs leading to reductions in the amount of talk from adults (teachers and TAs) that dealt with negative behaviour. These benefits are similar to those found in studies of the effect of class size reductions on pupil behaviour (Blatchford *et al.* 2005). This is an important contribution by TAs and should not be underestimated. Visits to schools showed that pupil behaviour was not always acceptable, and could interfere with concentration and learning in the classroom. Some schools worked in very difficult circumstances and pupil behaviour was particularly problematic. Having an extra, sometimes very experienced, adult in the classroom could help greatly with order and discipline.

One particular aspect of TAs' behaviour management practice to emerge in the Strand 2 Wave 2 case studies was the way in which they acted swiftly and discreetly to deal with off-task behaviour, so that the teacher did not have to interrupt their whole class delivery. Some teachers and TAs we interviewed described this as 'having a quiet word'.

> We say to staff that if a child goes to amber, to get them back to green as quickly as possible, so that they don't then go on to red ... And very much you find that teachers rely on their TAs to get the children back down.
>
> (Primary headteacher)

> I would never undermine the teacher, but often I will just lean across and say, 'sit still', in a very low tone ... Or what will often happen is, I will make eye contact with the teacher, so she knows what's happening, and then it's up to her to do the disciplining.
>
> (Secondary TA)

But perhaps the most notable result from the systematic observation study was that the overall increase in individual attention, as a result of the presence of TAs, is explained entirely by the increase in individual interactions with TAs themselves. When we looked separately at just teacher-to-pupil interactions, we found that at primary level, the presence of TA support led to less overall interaction with the teacher, and at secondary level, the presence of TAs led to less contact with teachers and less individual attention from them. In general, the effect of TAs was strongest in pupils with a higher level of SEN status, and, though present, was less strong for pupils with lower levels of, or no, SEN. This means that individual attention is provided by TAs, but this is *instead of* individual attention from teachers. This also means that, contrary to the notion that TAs provide 'additional' support, they in fact provide an *alternative* or *replacement* form of support.

This is one of the most important results from the study, with very important consequences, and we return to this in later chapters, notably in Chapter 5.

2.4 The impact of TAs on pupils

2.4.1 The effect of TAs on pupil behaviour and learning

We now turn to the impact of TAs on pupils. First, we look at the views of teachers on the impact of TAs on pupil behaviour and learning. We analysed around 4,000 teacher questionnaires over the three waves and the comments teachers made were mostly positive. At Wave 2, the four most common ways that pupils were seen to benefit from support staff were in terms of: 1) taking on specific pupils; 2) bringing specialist help to the teacher and classroom (e.g. technology skills, counselling, careers advice); 3) having a positive impact on the pupils' behaviour, discipline or social skills; and 4) by allowing individualisation and differentiation.

At Wave 3, the responses of 419 teachers (a random sample of approximately 25 per cent of the total sample of respondents) were used in the analysis, and there were 631 comments altogether. The main ways TAs benefited pupils was in terms of: 1) improving pupils' attitudes and motivation to work; 2) encouraging a general positive effect on learning and behaviour; 3) having an indirect effect on learning and behaviour; and 4) allowing more individualisation and differentiation. There was a good deal of similarity across Waves 2 and 3. Here are some quotes from teachers about their TAs:

> I have my TA for two mornings and one afternoon a week. During the mornings when she works with pupils I use her to support my lower ability groups in literacy and maths and she has a positive support on the learning and behaviour of the group.

> Gives one-to-one support with three children on reading and spelling three times a week. Big impact on their participation and completion of tasks.

One can see again that the benefits of TAs, from a teacher's point of view, stem largely from their function of taking on particular pupils, and therefore allowing individualisation and differentiation, while the teacher can then spend more time with the rest of the class and devote more time to teaching.

Despite the quotes above, it was noticeable that in general teachers tended not to refer to attainment and learning when addressing the benefits and effects of TAs on pupils, even when they were specifically asked to consider effects on pupil behaviour and learning. Instead, we found that most answers were more about effects on *teachers* and *teaching* than on pupil outcomes. When teachers did mention effects on pupils, the main benefits were not so much on learning or attainment, but on motivation, social skills and behaviour. This trend was confirmed in the Strand 2 Wave 2 case studies. This is not to argue that these aspects are unimportant, but we have found in this study, and in previous research (Blatchford *et al.* 2004; 2006), that there is a general tendency for headteachers and teachers to voice a generally positive, but largely impressionistic view of the benefits of TAs for pupil learning and attainment, rather than one based on hard or specific evidence.

2.4.2 Impact of TAs on pupil engagement and active interaction with adults: systematic observations

We also used data from the systematic observation study to examine effects of the presence of TAs on pupil behaviour (rather than on adult behaviour, as discussed previously). The same logic underpinned these data; that is, interest was in whether the presence of a TA in the classroom was associated with a greater likelihood of certain pupil behaviours occurring in the same time interval. These results indicated that the presence of TAs had a seemingly beneficial effect on pupils in terms of two main behaviours. First, the presence of TAs was associated with an increase in the amount of pupil *classroom engagement*. This was seen in an increase in pupil on-task behaviour, and a simultaneous reduction in off-task behaviour. The second effect of TA presence was that it led to pupils having a more *active role in interactions with adults* (i.e. teachers and TAs), as seen in an increase in the extent pupils began, responded to and sustained interactions with adults over ten seconds.

But, to return to the systematic observation results above, this increase in active involvement with adults was actually with TAs; indeed, the amount of active interaction with the teacher *decreased* because of the TAs' presence.

2.4.3 The impact of TAs on pupil positive approaches to learning and academic attainment

The key task of the DISS project was to establish whether there is a causal role of TA support on pupils' positive approaches to learning and attainment. A traditional approach would be to use an experimental design, contrasting groups with and without TA support, but experimental manipulations can have a narrow range of applicability and do not always capture the range of ways that adults are normally used and deployed in schools (Goldstein and Blatchford 1998).

As explained in Chapter 1, in this study an alternative naturalistic design was therefore used that sought to measure TA support received by pupils under normal circumstances and then examine relationships with academic and behaviour outcomes. The well-established difficulty with this sort of design is that it results in correlations between the main predictor variable (in this case, TA support) and outcomes (in this study, scores at the end of the school year), which are then difficult to interpret in terms of causal direction. To overcome this problem, a longitudinal design is required within which effects of TA support on pupil end of year outcomes can be assessed, while controlling for other carefully selected factors, including pupil characteristics (such as prior attainment and SEN status and severity) which might potentially confound the relationship. If one still finds a significant relationship between TA support and the outcome (i.e. pupil attainment or positive approaches to learning), having factored in these other variables, then one can be more confident that a real, independent effect of TA support has been found; that is, an effect that is unlikely to be explained by another factor. When controlling for prior attainment, one is essentially looking at the effects of TA support on academic progress, a much more useful approach than a simple cross sectional study of attainment (that is, an analysis looking at associations at one point in time).

2.4.3.1 Research design

The DISS study covered both primary and secondary school phases. There were two cohorts: Wave 1 took place in 2005–2006 and focused on pupils in 76 schools in Years 1, 3, 7 and 10; and Wave 2 took place in 2007–2008 and involved an increased sample of pupils in 77 schools in Years 2, 6 and 9.[1]

2.4.3.2 Information on pupils

Data on pupil characteristics at Waves 1 and 2 was obtained through the School Census (formerly PLASC – Pupil Level Annual School Census) supplemented by information from schools. Information was collected on:

- baseline attainment in English
- SEN status (four-point scale: non-SEN; School Action; School Action Plus; and SEN statemented)
- gender
- eligibility for free school meals (FSM)
- ethnic group (grouped as white, or other than white)[2]
- IDACI (Income Deprivation Affecting Children Index) (Wave 2 and England only)
- English as an additional language (EAL) (Wave 2 and England only)
- pupil age (Wave 2, Year 2 only).

2.4.3.3 Amount of support

2.4.3.3.1 HOURS OF TA SUPPORT – TEACHER RATINGS (WAVES 1 AND 2)

The first, main measure of the amount of TA support was teacher estimates of the amount of TA support in English (in and away from the classroom), expressed as a percentage of time. Teachers were asked to select from six categories denoting the amount of TA support: 0 per cent; 1–10 per cent; 11–25 per cent; 26–50 per cent; 51–75 per cent; and 76 per cent and above. For the smaller sample size in Wave 1, these categories were combined to form a three-point scale for the purposes of analysis. These were low TA support (supported 0–10 per cent of the time), medium TA support (11–50 per cent) and high TA support (51 per cent and above). With the bigger sample at Wave 2, five categories of support were used for the analysis: 0 per cent; 1–10 per cent; 11–25 per cent; 26–50 per cent; 51 per cent and above. This is shown in Table 2.2.

2.4.3.3.2 LEVEL OF TA SUPPORT – SYSTEMATIC OBSERVATIONS (WAVE 1)

In addition to the main teacher rating measure, there were four other measures of the amount of TA support received by a pupil, taken from the systematic observation data. These were measures of the percentage of time TAs were observed in certain 'states':

- *TA presence*: when a TA was present in the classroom during observations
- *TA proximity*: when pupil supervision by a TA was either one-to-one or as part of a group
- *TA interaction*: when the pupil was interacting with a TA
- *TA attention*: when the pupil interacted with a TA, and in addition, the pupil was the focus of the TA's attention.

Table 2.2 The measure of the amount of TA support from teacher estimates of the amount of TA support in English (in and away from the classroom), expressed as a percentage of time. Wave 1 and Wave 2

Amount of support	% time TA support provided in English	
	Wave 1	*Wave 2*
Low	0–10%	0%
		1–10%
Medium	11–50%	11–25%
		26–50%
High	51% +	51% +

These measures of TA support represented a hierarchy with different levels closer or further away from the pupil; that is, they ranged from a simple tally of hours of TA support, through to TA individual attention on the pupil.

The majority of these measures had highly uneven, skewed distributions, and so for most analyses, pupils were divided into two groups: those with a high occurrence of each measure; and those with a lower occurrence (the exact cut-off varied for each measure as described in Appendix 2).

2.4.3.4 Pupil outcomes: positive approaches to learning (PAL)

Teacher-completed rating scales were developed, based on an amended version of the Pupil Behaviour Rating Scale, as developed in the CSPAR study (Blatchford *et al.* 2003). For the purposes of the DISS project, the form was adapted to produce one item and scale for each dimension. Dimensions were representative of those previously developed, which had proven reliability. The eight dimensions were:

- *Distracted*: pupil was easily distracted
- *Confident*: pupil was confident about doing the tasks they are set
- *Motivated*: pupil was motivated to learn
- *Disruptive*: pupil was disruptive
- *Independent*: pupil worked independently
- *Relationship*: pupil had good relationships with other pupils
- *Completed*: pupil completed assigned work
- *Instructions*: pupil followed instructions from adults.

For each dimension, teachers were asked near the end of the school year to say whether the pupil's behaviour had 'improved', 'stayed the same' or 'deteriorated' over the year. In both waves there were a few responses (2–3 per cent) that indicated that the pupil's attitude to learning had deteriorated over the year, and so the 'deteriorated' and 'stayed the same' categories were combined. As a result, the PAL outcome measure was a two-point scale.

2.4.3.5 Pupil outcomes: academic attainment

Measures of pupil attainment were collected at the end of the year (so-called 'outcome' scores) and at the beginning of the year (baseline scores). This was repeated for each of the three subjects in each of the seven year groups in the study, and so different measures had to be used to cover the wide age range involved. In England and Wales, at the time of the study, there was an extensive series of assessments of English, maths and science set in place by government. These involved end of key stage assessments, optional tests and also teacher assessments. One advantage of these measures over separate tests in the three areas is that they were readily available for all the pupils in the schools. A separate testing programme, for example using standardised tests, would have been refused by schools; many in schools already felt they were devoting too much time to government-set assessments. But another advantage of the assessments we used is that they related very closely to the curriculum areas covered in schools, and so were a fair reflection of pupils' attainments in these subjects. As we shall see, for the purposes of the research all the measures collected were expressed in terms of a common metric: National Curriculum levels and sublevels.

For Wave 1, start of year attainment scores came from Foundation Stage profiles (for start of Year 1) or end of previous year key stage test scores (SATs) (for Year 3, 7 and 10). Attainment scores at the end of year came from assessments already used in schools and were teacher-rated National Curriculum levels, except for Year 10, where scores were predicted GCSE grades.

Wave 2 involved Years 2, 6 and 9. The start of year scores came from assessments at the end of the previous school year. Where possible, these data came from optional tests, but if they were not available then teacher assessments were used. Again the data collected was in terms of National Curriculum levels and sublevels. Pupil attainment at the end of the school year came from end of year key stage tests and took several forms. In Year 2, attainment took the form of National Curriculum levels, which for English schools, were reported as a main level and a sublevel (split into three categories A, B and C; e.g. 1C, 2B, etc). For Wales, only the main numeric levels were available (e.g. 1, 2), and for Welsh data it was assumed that each pupil took the middle sublevel within each category. The main National Curriculum levels were also used in Year 6, as were fine grade levels, which gave a greater distinction between pupils. Raw attainment scores were also analysed in Year 6. End of year attainment in Year 9 took the form of National Curriculum levels for all subjects, and also raw scores for English only.

Using guidelines from the DCSF, National Curriculum levels were converted into a numerical score. One whole level represents six points on this numerical scale, whilst a sublevel represents two points. The exception was for Year 10 in Wave 1, where the predicted GCSE scores were also converted to numerical scores, with one point representing one GCSE grade. More details on the scores used and how they can be interpreted is given shortly in our presentation of results from the study.

2.4.3.6 Statistical methods

As described previously, in order to control for possibly confounding factors that are known to influence pupil attainment and TA support, additional pupil characteristics from the School Census (listed earlier) were included in the analyses.

Statistical analyses of the effect of TA support on PAL and attainment scores were performed in a number of stages, starting with a simple, unadjusted analysis of the effect of TA support, followed by an examination of the effect of TA support after adjustments for the potentially confounding factors. In the interests of brevity only results from the most complete analysis are used, which adjusted for the greatest number of potentially confounding variables.[3]

2.4.3.7 Results on associations between the amount of TA support and pupils' positive approaches to learning

We summarise the results in Table 2.3. It can be seen that there were few significant effects for Wave 1 in Years 1 and 3, and no effects at all in Years 7 and 10. There were also no effects for Years 2 and 6 in Wave 2. For six of the seven age groups, there was therefore little sign of a consistent effect.

Table 2.3 shows, however, that in Year 9 in Wave 2 there was a highly significant effect of the level of TA support on all eight of the PAL outcomes. With the exception of pupil motivation and independence, there was little evidence of a statistically significant difference

Table 2.3 Summary of findings of effects of TA support on pupils' positive approaches to learning

Wave	Year group	Not distracted	Confident	Motivated	Not disruptive	Independent	Relationship with peers	Completes work	Follows instruction
1	1	✗	✗	✗	✗	✓n	✗	✗	✗
	3	✗	✗	✗	✗	✓n	✗	✓n	✗
	7	✗	✗	✗	✗	✗	✗	✗	✗
	10	✗	✗	✗	✗	✗	✗	✗	✗
2	2	✗	✗	✗	✗	✗	✗	✗	✗
	6	✗	✗	✗	✗	✗	✗	✗	✗
	9	✓p	✓p	✓p	✓p	✓p	✓p	✓p	✓p

✗ = No significant effect of TA support
✓n = Significant negative effect of TA support
✓p = Significant positive effect of TA support

between pupils with a low and medium level of TA support. The main effects were between the pupils with a high level of TA support and those with a lower level of TA support. The largest effect was a change toward being less distracted, which was 11 times more likely with high levels of TA support compared to low levels of TA support. High levels of TA support led to pupils being nine times more likely to develop good relationships with peers, become more independent and become less disruptive. Pupils were seven times more likely to become more confident, six times more likely to follow instructions, four times more likely to become motivated and three times more likely to complete work.

These results were found even when potentially confounding factors like prior attainment, SEN status and gender were accounted for. The main effects were between the pupils with a high level of TA support and those with a low level of TA support. There was no evidence for any age group or either wave that the effect of TA support on the PAL scores varied for those pupils with and without SEN.

We therefore found little support in our results for the view from some studies (e.g. Giangreco *et al.* 1997; Moyles and Suschitsky 1997) that one consequence of TA support may be that pupils become reliant on the TA and less willing to engage in independent work. There was also little support in the results for the suggestion from Ofsted (2004a) that TA individual attention can help pupil engagement, but adversely affect independent work, because we found that for most year groups there were no effects at all, and at Year 9 effects were in the same direction for these two outcomes. It was only at secondary level, at the end of Key Stage 3, that the support provided by TAs is having a positive effect, consistent with teachers' views on supported pupils' motivation, independence, etc. That this effect is found in Wave 2 at secondary only suggests that the explanatory processes at work differ between primary and secondary sectors. In one respect these results are unexpected, because in Wave 1 we found little evidence of any effect on the nearest equivalent age level – Year 10. The disparity in results between Year 10 and Year 9 is not easy to explain, but may be connected to the larger sample in Year 9 (in Wave 2), and hence a greater likelihood of showing effects of TA support, should they be there.

The strong positive result for Year 9 in Wave 2 may be connected to other findings from the study. As we shall see in Chapter 5, while TAs in primary schools were more likely to be classroom based and interact with other pupils in a group, as well as those they were supporting, in secondary schools TAs tended to interact more exclusively with the pupil they were supporting. It may therefore come as no surprise if the TA-supported pupils showed most effects in terms of the PAL dimensions. Though we cannot be sure, it may also be that our results are picking up something connected to Year 9 being the end of Key Stage 3, and the first year in the secondary years when pupils had to take end of key stage tests (these tests for Year 9 pupils stopped in 2008). It is possible that targeted TA support in this year was specifically directed at ensuring that each pupil learned to work independently, with confidence and motivation, to help them do well in their end of year tests, and this may have had a beneficial effect, in terms of teachers' judgements about pupils' attitudes to learning.

2.4.3.8 Results on associations between the amount of TA support and pupils' academic progress

In this section we present the most important results in the book: those on the relationship between the amount of support pupils received from TAs and their academic progress over a school year.

2.4.3.8.1 TEACHER RATING OF TA SUPPORT – WAVE I

As described previously, at Wave 1 the amount of TA support was divided into three groups: low (supported 0–10 per cent of the time), medium (11–50 per cent) and high (51 per cent and above). Results for all four year groups in Wave 1 are summarised in Table 2.4. (We present full results from the statistical analyses in Appendix 2 for interested readers.)

It can be seen in Table 2.4 that in Wave 1, there were 12 analyses conducted (i.e. three school subjects at four age levels). Of these 12, there were seven significant effects of TA support on academic outcomes. There was a significant effect of TA support on pupil attainment in English and mathematics in Years 1, 3 and 7, and for English in Year 10. In every case, the higher the level of TA support, the lower the level of attainment.

To take English in Year 1 as an example, and by referring to figures shown in Table 1 in Appendix 2, there was a difference of roughly three units between the pupils with most and least TA support, which is equivalent to one and a half National Curriculum sub-levels. Those pupils with a medium level of TA support obtained attainment scores that were almost two points less than those with a low level of TA support. Two points equate to one sublevel of the main National Curriculum levels (e.g. the difference between level 1B and 1C). There was an even greater effect for Years 3, 7 and 10, with a difference between pupils with the most and least TA support of about four points, or two National Curriculum sublevels. Over the four years of Key Stage 2, pupils are expected to make two National Curriculum levels of progress. As there are three sublevels for every level, one can see that a sublevel equates to about eight months more progress. Two sublevels is therefore equivalent to 16 months. Great care should be taken over the accuracy of this kind of age equivalent calculation – not least because it depends on some questionable, general assumptions – but it does help the reader get some measure of the scale of the difference in attainment between those with most and least TA support.

Table 2.4 Summary of associations between the amount of TA support and pupils' academic progress: teacher rating measure of amount of TA support

Wave	Year	English	Mathematics	Science
I	I	✓n	✓n	✗
	3	✓n	✓n	✗
	7	✓n	✓n	✗
	10	✓n	✗	✗
2	2	✓n	✓n	✓n
	6	✓n	✓n	✓n
	9	✓n	✓n	✓n

✗ = No significant effect of TA support
✓n = Significant negative effect of TA support

There were similar and significant, negative effects for mathematics at Years 1, 3 and 7, with differences between those with most and least TA support being two to four points, which equates to between one and two National Curriculum sublevels. There was no effect of TA support on progress for mathematics in Year 10, and none for science at any age at Wave 1.

For Wave 1, there was little sign that this relationship varied between pupils with and without SEN.

For ease of reference, Table 2.5 summarises effects for Waves 1 and 2 in terms of National Curriculum sublevels.

2.4.3.8.2 TEACHER RATING OF TA SUPPORT – WAVE 2

What does not come across from this factual description of the results from Wave 1 is the surprise of the research team and the managers of the project when we first saw the figures. Given that this was not a controlled experiment, in which there was control over the amount of contact and type of training provided for TAs, there was perhaps little confidence that the results would result in a clear finding. It is probably true to say that the general expectation of the research team prior to the statistical analysis was that there might be a small positive relationship between the amount of TA support and pupils' progress. But to find a consistent negative finding like this was quite unexpected and counter intuitive.

Much time was spent checking and re-analysing to be sure the results stood up. As we shall see later in the chapter, the results did not appear to reflect the low rate of progress that would be expected in any case for pupils receiving extra support, and they most likely represented an independent effect of the amount of TA support. It was felt that the

Table 2.5 Size of effects of TA support on progress quantified in terms of National Curriculum sublevels

Wave	Year	National Curriculum sublevel		
		English	Maths	Science
1	1	1.5	1	
	3	2	2	
	7	2	1.5	
	10	1*		
2	2	1.5	1	1
	6	1	0.75	1
	9	1	0.75	1

* At Year 10 results are expressed as 1 GCSE grade

Note: Figures are the difference in attainment between pupils with least and most TA support.

research design and data collection were strong enough to draw valid conclusions from the statistical analysis, but there were some limitations at Wave 1 (e.g. in terms of the sample size) and so we decided, along with the project steering group, that we would repeat the study, this time with a bigger sample and with a few other refinements, in order to be as confident as possible about the results. This replication study also allowed us to include a couple of extra design features not possible with Wave 1. These included the effects of TA support on the rest of the class, which we address below.

The results for Wave 2 are also summarised in Table 2.4 (full results are again in Table 2 in Appendix 2) which also shows results for the three year groups, for all pupils combined, and also separately by SEN status when there were significant differences between levels of SEN and those pupils without SEN.

The results for Wave 2 were even clearer than those for Wave 1. This time there were significant results for all nine of the analyses (i.e. three year groups and three school subjects). There were significant effects of the amount of TA support on pupil progress in English, mathematics and this time for science, as well at each of the three age levels in Wave 2. Differences between those with the most and least TA support varied from 1.3–2.9 points; about one and a half National Curriculum sublevels, as can be seen in Table 2.5.

Across both waves there was a tendency for a linear stepped increase in effects with each level of TA support (as can be seen in Table 2 in Appendix 2), though this was less clear in some cases.

In comparison to Wave 1, in Wave 2 there was evidence of a difference in this effect between pupils with and without SEN. There was a tendency for the relationship between the amount of TA support and poorer progress to be most marked for pupils with higher levels of need, as can be seen in Table 2 in Appendix 2 (there were significant interactions with the level of SEN for maths in Year 2, all three subjects in Year 6 and English in Year 9). However, the effect of TA support on progress was in a similar, negative, significant direction for each of the three pupil groups.

2.4.3.8.3 OBSERVATION MEASURES OF TA SUPPORT (WAVE 1)

As described above, the main teacher rating of TA support over the school year was supplemented by four additional measures of the amount of TA support taken from the systematic observation analysis, conducted at Wave 1. Table 2.6 shows the significant results for all four observation variables used at each of the four year groups. The full results are shown in Table 3 in Appendix 2.

Statistical analyses compared those with high and low amounts of TA support (see notes at foot of Table 3 in Appendix 2 for exact definitions for each type of measure). As we saw earlier in this chapter, the four observation categories measured the amount of moment-by-moment TA support received by pupils, ranging from the TA simply being present in the classroom, through to the pupil receiving individual attention from the TA. As with the results involving the teacher rating of the amount of TA support over the school year, just presented, there was a similar trend for a negative relationship between the amount of TA support and pupil progress, though this was less consistent, and sometimes varied for pupils with and without SEN. The strongest effects were in Year 3, though results for Years 1, 7 and 10 were generally in the same negative direction. Significant negative effects varied from one to four points; around a half to two National Curriculum sublevels.

Table 2.6 Significant results from analysis of relationships between systematic observation TA support measures and pupil attainment. Wave 1

Year	Support measure	Subject	Pupil group with significant effect
1	Presence	English	SEN
	Presence	Science	All
3	Presence	Science	Non-SEN
	Proximity	English	All
	Proximity	Maths	All
	Proximity	Science	All
	Interaction	English	Non-SEN
	Interaction	Maths	All
	Interaction	Science	All
	Attention	English	Non-SEN
7	Presence	English	All
	Interaction	English	Non-SEN
10	Proximity	English	All

Note: Each analysis controls for pupil characteristics, baseline attainment, SEN status, gender, eligibility for FSM, ethnic group.

2.4.3.8.4 BENEFITS FOR NON-SUPPORTED PUPILS?

We have seen that a consistent view of teachers, when they considered the benefits of TAs for their own teaching and pupils' learning and behaviour, is that the TA's presence allows more teacher attention to the rest of the class and therefore better progress for the rest of the class. We captured this commonly held view in the vignette at the start of this book. The teacher, Mark, felt free to teach the rest of class, whilst Mandy provided individualised help to Reece and the other pupils with SEN, which was seen as beneficial to their learning.

One of the extra features in the Wave 2 analyses was that information on academic attainment was collected for all the pupils in the class, and so we could examine whether this perception was true. This is actually not an easy thing to analyse statistically and it is not possible to go into the full details here (see Blatchford *et al.* 2009 for a full explanation). The main question was whether otherwise similar pupils who received no or very little support made better progress in classes where there was a lot of support given to some pupils (but not them) compared to classes within which there was little or no support given by TAs to anyone. The way we approached this statistically was to compare the difference in attainment between low TA-supported pupils in classes where the rest of the class received little TA support, and low TA-supported pupils in classes where the rest of the class received more TA support. Interest was therefore in whether the rest of the class benefited when some pupils received a lot of support.

The results at Year 2 showed different results for the three subjects. In English, TA support for other pupils in the class had little impact on the unsupported pupils; in science, the effect was positive; and in mathematics the effect was negative on attainment for pupils who received little TA support.

At the end of the primary school stage – in Year 6 – there was no effect at all on the non- or low TA-supported pupils. However, in Year 9, by the end of Key Stage 3, unsupported pupils or those with little TA support made less progress in mathematics, English and science when a larger proportion of pupils in the class were supported by a TA, compared to when fewer pupils in the class were supported by a TA. It therefore seems that increased TA support had a detrimental effect on the progress of pupils who had little or no support from TAs in all three subjects.

So, contrary to teachers' views about the effects of TA support, as expressed in the vignette and in responses to our Teacher Questionnaire, there is little sign in our results of a positive effect of TA support on the other non-supported pupils in the class. The results further suggest that there is a change between primary and secondary stages in the effects on unsupported pupils, in classes where other pupils receive TA support. It is difficult on the basis of data collected in the DISS project to account for these results. It is also difficult to know what part the setting of pupils (i.e. when pupils are allocated to classes based on attainment), which might be expected in mathematics and science at Year 9, might have played on the results. Further exploration of effects of TA support on non-supported pupils is needed.

2.5 Conclusions

2.5.1 Accounting for the results on the impact of TA support on pupil attainment

The DISS study has been the first in the UK to address the impact of TAs on pupil outcomes in a systematic way, under normal classroom conditions, across multiple outcomes.

There were positive effects of TAs on teachers and teaching, in terms of teacher job satisfaction, stress and workloads; activities passed from teachers to support staff; and teacher views on effects of TAs on their teaching. To these positive results we should add the positive effect of TAs on classroom control, as found in systematic observation findings and also case studies; and on pupils in terms of the effect of TAs on pupil learning and behaviour (from teacher views), PAL (in Year 9) and pupil active involvement in interactions with adults and classroom engagement (from the systematic observations).

On the other hand, we found consistent negative relationships between the amount of support from TAs and pupils' academic progress. To summarise: for Wave 1, the strongest effect was found for the overall measure of TA support. In Years 1, 3 and 7 in English and mathematics, there was a consistent negative relationship between the amount of TA support a pupil received and the progress they made; the more support they received from a TA, the less progress made, even when the eight potentially confounding factors (like prior attainment and SEN status) were taken into account. As we have said, given the important nature of these findings on attainment, the study was repeated on a separate and larger sample (Wave 2). This was conducted at the end of Key Stages 1, 2 and 3, with end of year assessments in Year 2, 6 and 9, and this again showed a negative relationship between the amount of TA support and progress in English and mathematics, and this time for science as well, even after carefully controlling for the eight potentially confounding factors. The negative relationship between TA support and academic progress was therefore replicated across two waves and seven different year groups, across both primary and secondary stages, and so the finding seems to be a clear one. There was some evidence that the effect was more marked for pupils with a higher level of SEN, but it was still generally evident for pupils with no SEN.

The other four measures of TA support used were drawn from the systematic observation study at Wave 1. These had the advantage of being a more precise account of the contact between pupils and TAs. Though the aim was for the observations to provide a representative picture, it was still only a relatively small window on pupils' classroom experiences over a school year (between two to four days). Once again, we found a general trend towards a negative relationship between TA contact and pupils' academic progress over the year, though the results varied to some extent according to the level of SEN.

The study was longitudinal and not just cross sectional, and we can therefore say that the statistical analysis examined relationships between the amount of TA support and pupils' educational progress, but we still found an independent effect of the amount of TA support.

2.5.2 Explanations of the findings on academic attainment: pupil explanations

What might explain this negative result? Perhaps the most obvious explanation is that results are attributable to the pupil rather than the support they receive from TAs; that is, pupils are likely to receive TA support because they are performing less well or have a particular learning or behavioural problem, and it is this that explains the relationship between TA support and attainment. From this point of view, the support from TAs therefore reflects the underlying correlation between pupil characteristics and progress, but does not itself affect progress. Unsurprisingly, the data do suggest that lower attaining pupils or those with SEN tended to have more support from TAs than those with higher baseline attainment. This was expected, as both case studies and questionnaire responses from the DISS study indicated that the allocation of TA support is usually on the basis of how well the pupil is doing academically or because they are considered to have SEN. However, it is unlikely that this explanation accounts for the relationship between TA support and pupil attainment, because the pupil characteristics that are likely to be the basis for the provision of TA support were included in the statistical analysis. The following variables were included: prior attainment (collected at the beginning of the year), the severity of SEN on a four-point scale (non-SEN; School Action; School Action Plus; or SEN statemented), gender, income deprivation, ethnic group, pupil age and English as an additional language. We therefore examined as far as possible the *independent* effect of TA support over and above these pupil characteristics.

It is important to realise that in order to explain the relationship between TA support and attainment, additional pupil characteristics would need to be related not only to progress, but also to TA support. They would need, therefore, to inform (or at least be related to) the decision to give TA support, and this would need to be over and above anything captured by the eight measures already included in the analysis. As part of the systematic observation study, SENCos and teachers filled in a form asking them to indicate the main reason for assigning TA support. The responses suggested that this was almost always due to the pupil not making expected levels of progress (because of learning difficulties, problems with literacy or numeracy, and/or low attainment or SEN status), most of which would have been captured in the variables included in the statistical analysis.

Nevertheless, the measures of SEN status (School Action, School Action Plus and SEN statemented) were relatively strict and might have excluded some pupils who had behavioural or learning difficulties, for which they were assigned TA support, not revealed in these categories. To address this, pupils identified in this way on the forms completed by SENCos (there were 50 such pupils) were included with the SEN pupil group, but even when the analysis was redone with this larger group, the relationship between TA support and attainment was very largely unchanged. The results, therefore, suggest that the negative effect of TA support cannot easily be explained by the fact that there are pupils over and above those we have previously identified as making less progress (especially those with SEN) who were picked out for TA support for a particular reason related to their anticipated progress.

Another approach to the possibility that it is pupil characteristics which account for the relationship between TA support and progress is to see whether the relationship holds for other pupil outcomes. We have already seen that the effect of TA support on PAL generally showed either no effect of TA support on these measures over the year, or, in the case of Wave 2 Year 9, a clear positive effect. If there were underlying constructs which were somehow biasing the results in the direction of less progress for the most TA supported pupils, then it would be expected that the PAL results would mirror those of the attainment outcomes. The fact that this was not the case gives further validity to the attainment results.

One last way of viewing the relationship between TA support and attainment, couched in terms of pupil characteristics, might be that a pupil's difficulties begin in a school year and slow up progress, for reasons we do not know, and which were not shown in previous years (they would then have been picked up in the other measures included), and TA support is then allocated to such pupils. In the study, the main measure of TA support used was an estimate over the school year, but it might be argued that this would miss effects revealed by a change in TA support over the year, (e.g. as staff came to feel a pupil needed more TA support). But even this does not seem to explain the results. Further statistical analyses at Wave 2 showed that the introduction of a measure of change in TA support over the year did not affect the relationship between TA support received and progress over the year. Moreover, the Strand 2 Wave 1 case studies and the CSPAR study (Blatchford *et al.* 2004) indicate that change in TA support over the year tends not to happen with any frequency. This is because resources are rarely available to give to previously untargeted pupils. In order to explain the negative effect, this mid-year change of TA support would also need to be happening in a systematic way across all years and school subjects. It also needs to be remembered that for a number of analyses conducted, the effect is not restricted to pupils in need.

The scale and rigour of the study make the DISS project unique in addressing, in a systematic way, whether or not TAs have a positive effect on pupils, and so we make no apologies for expressing in some detail the results on attainment and also the working through of other possible explanations of the findings. The longitudinal design adopted in the DISS study has gone a long way with a naturalistic, non-experimental design to establish grounds for the effect of the amount of TA support on pupil attainment. We have seen that it is possible that there is other information about pupils, used by teachers and schools, which is not captured by the variables listed earlier, and which explains the systemic relationship between TA support and attainment, but, as we have said, it is very difficult to think what this might be.

2.5.3 Other explanations for the effect of TA support on pupil progress

Another possible explanation for the negative relationship is that it may be due to the different levels of TAs' qualifications relative to teachers. We note, however, that research has not found that teachers' or TAs' level of qualification are related to their effectiveness (Blatchford *et al.* 2004; Muijs and Reynolds 2001; Wiliam 2010).

So, if pupil factors and TA qualifications do not appear to be explaining the negative relationship between TA support and pupil progress, what might account for it?

We feel it is important to make very clear at this point that a consideration of the effectiveness of TA support should not be personalised or individualised just to characteristics of individual TAs (e.g. in terms of their experience or practice), because to do so would be to seriously underplay the situational and structural factors within which TAs have to work. We argue in this book that it is likely that the organisational factors governing TAs' employment and deployment offer the most fruitful answers to questions about the effectiveness of TAs, starkly highlighted by the findings on pupils' learning outcomes. We have developed a model of the 'Wider Pedagogical Role' (WPR) of TAs to both summarise findings from the DISS project and to suggest possible explanations for the results on academic progress. The basic components of the model are shown in Figure 2.2. The model enables us to interpret the impact of TA support on pupils' academic progress within the wider context of the factors within which TAs work, and which, we argue, maximises or inhibits their effectiveness, and over which they have little or no control. This is also reflected in the vignette at the beginning of the book, where we begin to see the multiple and interconnected factors related to support provided by TAs.

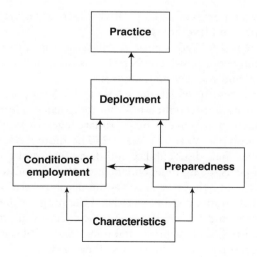

Figure 2.2 The Wider Pedagogical Role model

The WPR model has three main components: first, the *preparedness* of TAs and teachers, in terms of their training for the role (which will influence pedagogical and subject understanding) and the amount of planning, preparation and debriefing/feedback time with teachers; second, the *deployment* of TAs by teachers and headteachers, which are outside their control; and third, the *practice* of TAs, in terms of the nature and quality of their interactions with pupils. From this point in the book, we will work through each component, and as we do so, we narrow our focus from the school level, through the classroom level, getting closer to the pupil-level experience of TA support. In this way, we seek to explain the negative effect of TA support and pupil progress.

These themes, though not made explicit, echo in the descriptions of classroom practices and the relationship between teacher and TA set out in the vignette in Chapter 1: the way Mark deploys Mandy to work with pupils with SEN on red table, thus (inadvertently) separating himself somewhat from their educational experience; the lack of time for pre-lesson communication and post-less feedback; the limited opportunity for the type of training that could make for a more effective partnership; and Mandy's misunderstanding of mathematical concepts revealed in her talk to Reece.

This WPR model will act as the basis for the rest of this book, with each chapter describing a different component and in the process identifying key results that will be added to each box in the model. These will help summarise our results overall, explain the findings on impact, and also identify our key recommendations for practice and policy. Accordingly, in Chapters 4, 5 and 6, we address the preparedness of TAs and teachers, the deployment and then the practice of TAs respectively. In the final chapter we present the full WPR model and show how it can be used to reconceptualise the work and role of TAs, and inform models of educational effectiveness. But first, in Chapter 3, we describe the main findings on the two remaining components of the WPR model.

Key findings

The impact of TAs

- TAs and other support staff had a positive effect on teachers' workload, level of job satisfaction and levels of stress.
- Teachers felt that TAs had a positive effect on the quality of teaching and observations showed a positive effect of TAs on the overall amount of individual attention and on classroom control.
- Analysis of the extent to which the amount of TA support received by pupils over a school year improved their positive approaches to learning showed little evidence of an effect at Wave 1, or at primary level for Wave 2, but there was a strong relationship at Year 9 at Wave 2. The more TA support received by pupils, the lower their distractibility and disruption, and the better their relationships with peers, being independent and following instructions.
- At both Wave 1 and 2 there was a consistent negative relationship between the amount of TA support a pupil received and the progress they made in English and mathematics, and also at Wave 2 in science, even after controlling for pupil characteristics, such as prior attainment and SEN status. The more TA support pupils received, the less progress they made.

Chapter 3

Characteristics of TAs and their conditions of employment

3.1 Introduction

In this chapter we provide information on the characteristics of TAs and other support staff, and their conditions of employment, during the period 2003 to 2008, when the school workforce remodelling and teacher workload reduction policies were implemented in English and Welsh schools.

We begin by presenting a new typology of support staff, which, compared to previous categorisations, more accurately reflects the effect the workforce reforms have had on shaping new and existing support roles. We go on to provide some broad descriptors of support staff characteristics, in terms of their number, gender, age and ethnicity, and then we will begin to concentrate our focus on one category of support staff: teaching assistants. We will look at data on the qualifications and experience of TAs, before looking at elements of their conditions of employment (e.g. pay and appraisal), and how this affects how they feel about their job. This chapter will conclude by examining TAs' hours of work – both paid and unpaid – which, together with the findings on TAs' qualifications, provide the first component of the WPR model, which we use to explain the findings on TA impact described in Chapter 2.

Table 3.1 shows the sources of data on which we draw for this chapter: the Strand 1 surveys (of which there were three biennial waves) and the more fine-grained data from the Strand 2 case studies.

Table 3.1 Data sources for characteristics and conditions of employment

	Strand 1				Strand 2				
	MSQ	TQ	SSQ	Work pattern diary	Structured observations	Systematic observations	Case studies	Transcripts	MPSS
Characteristics and conditions of employment	•	•	•				•		

3.2 Support staff characteristics

3.2.1 The number of support staff in schools

We saw in Chapter 1 that there has been an unprecedented increase in the number of support staff in mainstream schools in England and Wales. Data from the Strand 1 surveys allows us to map the rise in TA numbers in terms of the way English and Welsh schools expanded their individual workforces over the period 2003–2008. Table 3.2 shows how schools increased at each survey point the number of TAs they employed (the table shows primary, secondary and special schools combined). For comparison, we include in the second column of Table 3.2 government figures on the number of TAs in the school workforce in the maintained sector for the year each DISS survey wave was conducted (DfE 2010a; Statistics for Wales 2009). It can be seen that the proportion of schools employing 11 or more TAs almost doubled over the course of the DISS project, from 25 per cent at Wave 1 to 47 per cent at Wave 3. At Wave 2, 41 per cent of schools employed 11 or more TAs, showing the extent to which, even by 2005/2006, the effects of workforce remodelling were apparent in staff numbers alone.

As we described in Chapter 1, a number of key developments (the introduction of literacy and numeracy strategies, the school workforce remodelling agenda and greater numbers of pupils with SEN) have been instrumental in driving both the growth of support staff and the expansion of their roles and responsibilities; this was reflected in the DISS project data.

The Strand 1 surveys found significant increases in the number of all support staff roles, noting a rise in the specific roles created as part of the workforce reforms (e.g. HLTAs, cover supervisors, examination officers, data managers/analysts and ICT support staff).

Table 3.2 Numbers of TAs at each wave

Strand 1 survey wave and year	No. of TAs (England and Wales)		No TAs		1–5 TAs		6–10 TAs		11–20 TAs		21+ TAs	
			n	%	n	%	n	%	n	%	n	%
Wave 1 (2004)	Eng	132,200										
	Wales	8,284	260	11%	856	37%	613	26%	444	19%	145	6%
	Total	140,484										
Wave 2 (2006)	Eng	153,100										
	Wales	10,225	73	4%	497	24%	653	32%	595	29%	253	12%
	Total	163,325										
Wave 3 (2008)	Eng	175,700										
	Wales	11,938	50	3%	365	22%	490	29%	533	32%	249	15%
	Total	187,638										

Note: Number of schools in each survey: Wave 1 = 2,318; Wave 2 = 2,071; Wave 3 = 1,687.

HLTAs and cover supervisors in particular were created with the specific purpose of easing teachers' teaching and lesson cover responsibilities, which includes leading lessons in the absence of the teacher.[1] Other support roles (e.g. administrative roles) were instrumental in absorbing teachers' non-teaching tasks and tackling workload, as we saw in Chapter 2. An overall aim of workforce remodelling was to employ and deploy a greater number of support staff to take on certain 'non-teaching' duties in order to enable teachers to spend more time planning and preparing lessons and assessing pupil work.

The DISS survey was able to ask school staff directly about the key factors accounting for any growth in support staff. We found that the main reason for the growth in TAs and other support staff, according to the headteacher or other senior staff, was due less to the implementation of the National Agreement and more to the increase in the number of children classified as having SEN being taught in mainstream settings, the accompanying funds making it possible to employ additional staff to support them.

The influence of other initiatives that had come on-stream during the lifetime of the DISS project, such as Extended Schools and Every Child Matters, was also evident in the responses: at Wave 3, 17 per cent of schools indicated that the introduction of extended services for pupils was a reason for a change in support staff numbers. It is worth noting that the increase in TAs in Wales in 2009 is mainly due to recruitment for the Foundation Phase for three- to seven-year-olds – a curriculum that places a greater emphasis on experiential learning – introduced by the Welsh Assembly Government in September 2008 (Statistics for Wales 2009).

3.3 Support staff roles and responsibilities: a new typology

A main point to arise out of previous studies (e.g. Kerry 2005) is that there were a large number of terms applied to different support staff, and sometimes different terms applied to staff with the same role. For example, on our case study visits we encountered people working in cover supervision roles who were called 'learning mentors'; in other schools, 'learning mentors' had pastoral, but not learning-related, responsibilities. There were also a number of new types of support staff beginning to work in schools, such as HLTAs, business managers, bursars and so on. One first basic aim of the research was therefore to document and then find a method for categorising the types of support staff working in schools at the beginning of the project in 2003. This would then provide a framework for the research and its findings.

There have been a number of previous methods for classifying different types of support staff, but they differed from each other in a number of respects, and we did not assume in advance the validity of one over another. The National Joint Council for Local Government Services (NJC) – which includes local government employers' organisations and support staff unions – devised one such system with four main categories of support staff and indicative tasks appropriate to each (NJC 2003). The DfES, in its reporting of annually collected data, used the main headings 'teaching assistants', 'administrative staff', 'technicians' and 'other staff'. In an earlier study, Mortimore and Mortimore (1992) identified eight categories: finance; administration; site and services; in-class support; pupil support; IT/resources; librarian/resources; and technician.

Our classification of support staff is presented in Table 3.3. It goes beyond previous approaches in that it was based on a systematic grouping of post titles in terms of similarities in their activities, rather than a more impressionistic grouping of post titles. In the first Support Staff Questionnaire (SSQ), respondents were given a list of 91 tasks and asked to tick which of the tasks they carried out in their posts. If they carried out any tasks not listed they were asked to add them in a space at the end of the list. The list of tasks was based on the NJC system described previously, and refined after a pilot postal questionnaire survey.

The support staff post titles were classified into groups using the statistical method of 'cluster analysis' which allocates post titles to the same group on the basis of being more alike in terms of activities undertaken, in comparison to those allocated to different groups. It is therefore exactly measured similarities in support staff activities that determines the clusters rather than assumptions about which titles should go together. Using this procedure, support staff in mainstream and special schools were classified into seven groups: TA equivalent; pupil welfare; technicians; other pupil support; administrative; facilities; and site. The classification enabled a comparison of changes over time across the three survey waves, in terms of their overall number and widening range of roles titles and responsibilities.

We conducted a second grouping of post titles at Wave 3, using the same statistical procedures, to see whether new support roles created by workforce remodelling had changed the situation. Whilst there were some differences, these were relatively minor, and so for the purposes of analysis, and in order to allow meaningful comparisons over time between waves, we used the Wave 1 typology. This is presented in Table 3.3. The DISS typology can be considered the most representative, up-to-date and accurate classification support staff working in English and Welsh schools.

Table 3.3 A new typology of support staff

TA equivalent	Pupil welfare	Technicians	Other pupil support
Teaching assistant	Learning mentor	ICT manager	Bilingual support
Higher level teaching assistant	Education welfare officer	ICT technician	Cover supervisor
Classroom assistant	Welfare assistant	Librarian	Escort
Learning support assistant (LSA)	Connexions advisor	Technology technician	Midday supervisor
LSA for SEN	Nurse	Science technician	Midday assistant
Nursery nurse	Home-liaison		Language assistant
Therapist			Exam invigilator

Administrative staff		Facilities staff	Site staff
Administrator	Secretary	Cleaner	Caretaker
Office manager	PA to Head	Cook	Premises manager
Finance officer	Data manager	Other catering	
Bursar	Exam officer		
Attendance officer			

Of particular interest to this book is the TA equivalent group. It can be seen that there were seven post titles included: teaching assistant; higher level teaching assistant; classroom assistant; learning support assistant (LSA); LSA for SEN; nursery nurse; and therapist. These post titles were found to be similar in terms of the activities they engaged in. The vast majority of this group were teaching assistants. It is the TA equivalent group we are referring to when citing 'TAs' in this book.

3.4 Gender, age and ethnicity of support staff

The DISS Strand 1 surveys collected data on the broad characteristics of all school support staff. The vast majority of all support staff were female, of white ethnic origin, and aged 36 or over. Most TAs also fitted this description, and these findings were in line with those of the TDA's Support Staff Survey for England (Teeman *et al.* 2008). We found proportionately more men working in school site support roles (76 per cent at Wave 3) and relatively high numbers of male technicians (41 per cent), but men are hugely under-represented in classroom roles (only around 2 per cent of TAs were men).

At this point in the book, we narrow our focus from all categories of support staff covered in the DISS project, to pay particular attention to teaching assistants.

3.5 TAs' qualifications and experience

3.5.1 Qualifications

As would be expected, TAs tend to have lower qualifications than teachers. Unlike teaching – which is a graduate profession – there is no minimum entry-level qualification required for working as a TA. To be as clear as possible about qualifications, TAs were asked to tick from a list all academic qualifications they held, and to also note pass grades in GCSE or GCSE equivalent English, mathematics and science, Level 2 skills, and certificates in adult numeracy and literacy, and also vocational awards (e.g. NVQ).

The results for Wave 3, shown in Table 3.4, revealed a range of qualifications. We found only a minority of TAs (13 per cent) had no or low qualifications (e.g. GCSE grades D to G). Just over a quarter of TAs (27 per cent) held at least one AS or A level, and 15 per cent had a degree as their highest qualification.

It can be seen in Table 3.4 that percentages total more than 100 per cent, indicating that respondents could list more than one qualification, as intended, and not just their highest qualification. However, it was also likely that not everyone ticked all their qualifications; those with a degree, for example, did not always note that they had A levels, though this is likely to be the case. For this reason, and for the purposes of more meaningful analyses, qualifications were grouped into two categories: 1) grades up to GCSE or equivalent; and 2) those equivalent to grades above GCSE level (GCSE being the school-leaving age qualification in England and Wales). Using this criterion, further analysis showed that the majority of TAs (59 per cent) had a highest qualification that was at or below GCSE level.

Table 3.4 TA academic qualifications. Wave 3

Qualification	n	%
No qualifications	9	1
GCSE (Grade D–G)	79	12
GCSE (Grade A*–C)	195	29
CSE	293	44
O level	392	59
AS/A level	182	27
Certificate of Education	68	10
Foundation degree	45	7
Undergraduate degree	98	15
Higher degree	17	3
Total	1,333	–

Note: Total percentage more than 100 per cent because respondents could give more than one qualification.

3.5.2 Experience

We also found a spread of experience among TAs. At Wave 3, just over a quarter (27 per cent) were fairly new to the post, having three or less years' experience (again, this reveals something about the increase in TA numbers that occurred over the duration of the study, in line with workforce reform policy); 30 per cent had between four and eight years' experience; and 43 per cent had nine or more years' experience (just under half of this group had been working in schools for 16 or more years). At Wave 3, 32 per cent of TAs had been in the same post in the same school for between 5 and 10 years, and 31 per cent for 10 years or more.

These findings are significant. Evidence from the case studies revealed the extent to which headteachers used the experience of long-serving TAs as a proxy for qualifications; for example, when assessing suitability for roles with enhanced responsibility (e.g. leading a class as part of cover or PPA arrangements). HLTA accreditation lends an interesting angle on the tendency for TAs to 'qualify by experience', as it requires TAs to demonstrate 'higher level' skills picked up on the job in order to obtain HLTA status. In this sense, becoming an HLTA was more a process of formalising existing competencies and less the development of new skills.

Furthermore, in terms of new appointments, case study interviews with headteachers revealed that there was no overall expectation that new staff should be qualified or experienced. Instead, it depended on the particular post and the importance of personal qualities of applicants felt to be essential for it.

It can be seen that Mandy – the TA in our Chapter 1 vignette – is fairly typical of the general picture of TAs' experience emerging from the DISS project surveys.

3.6 TAs' conditions of employment

In the second part of this chapter, we maintain our focus on TAs and look at some aspects of their conditions of employment, revealing some of the school-level processes in operation around them. As a lens for this exploration, we use data on TAs' job satisfaction from the SSQ.

3.6.1 Job satisfaction

TAs were asked to rate their job satisfaction on a five-point scale, together with the extent to which they were satisfied with their contracts and working hours, their participation in line management and performance reviews, and their pay. This was the survey that our TA, Mandy, completed in the vignette.

Ninety-three per cent of TAs were 'very' or 'fairly' satisfied with their jobs. They reported high levels of satisfaction with contracts and working arrangements, job descriptions, and line management and appraisal arrangements. But they were less satisfied with how much they felt appreciated by the school (this declined over three waves from 73 per cent to 69 per cent), and less still with their pay (51 per cent of TAs were dissatisfied). In these respects, TAs were less happy than other categories of support staff.

3.6.2 Pay and contracts

Data from the SSQ showed the aspects of their work that TAs were broadly satisfied with, but there were underlying problems and inconsistencies in, were the contractual arrangements that could affect pay. In 2008, WAMG highlighted the widespread use of 'split contracts': a phenomenon we also found in the DISS case studies in primary and special schools. Some TAs – many of whom were HLTA-accredited – were paid twice their hourly rate when they led classes as part of cover supervision and/or PPA arrangements. Schools did this in preference to paying TAs consistently at a higher hourly rate; a practice 'not in line with the aims of workforce reform and the principles of the National Agreement' (WAMG 2008). Many of the TAs interviewed as part of the case studies recognised how 'split contracts' could be potentially exploitative, but its effects were yet to be fully felt, given that such practice was relatively new.

3.6.3 Supervision and appraisal

Around three-quarters of TAs reported having their work supervised by a teacher, and over half of teachers (54 per cent), some of whom have a responsibility for SEN (e.g. SENCos), line-managed one or more TAs. As with pay and contractual arrangements, on a national scale, opportunities and processes for appraisal were inconsistent. In general, TAs are not subject to the same type of formal performance management review that teachers are, but we found that many schools had some form of annual appraisal in place for TAs: the number of TAs reporting that they had had an appraisal in the previous 12 months increased at each wave of the SSQ, to 69 per cent at Wave 3.

The case studies suggested a tendency for these appraisals to be informally organised. This could result in the likelihood that, whilst there was a sense of working towards targets, achievement was not measured by well-defined standards or by way of a systematic process, as is the case for teachers. There were signs, however, that headteachers seemed to understand the need for a more structured approach, given that not only were there increasing numbers of TAs working in schools, but headteachers recognised that some TAs were occupying a more central role with regard to some pupils.

3.6.4 TAs' hours of work and their 'goodwill'

The view expressed by many TAs – such as Mandy – was that a love for supporting and helping children and young people was a large factor in the high rates of job satisfaction, which goes some way to explaining the disparity between what TAs felt about their pay compared with their job satisfaction.

The DISS study found that TAs were contracted to work an average of 23.6 hours per week, but TAs' dedication to supporting pupils was evident in their willingness to work beyond these stated hours. Support staff overall volunteered to work extra hours three times as often as they were 'required to' by a member of staff (that is, when they were asked by, say, a headteacher to work additional hours for a specific reason, such as assisting at a school event). But TAs were four times more likely to work extra hours voluntarily, typically up to three hours per week.

However, much of this work was unpaid. We found that less than half of TAs (40 per cent) were likely to be paid for working extra hours. One way in which schools routinely benefit from this unpaid work is from TAs readily arriving at school early, or leaving late, in order to have valuable liaison time with teachers. The case studies revealed the extent to which primary school TAs met with teachers, and planned and prepared lessons work in their own unpaid time, out of a strong sense of duty to do the best for the pupils they supported. We also saw this in the case of Mandy.

It was clear from the case study data that the goodwill of TAs and other support staff was clearly indispensable to the remodelling process. Headteachers revealed the extent to which they were aware of, and managed, TAs' goodwill, and some were aware of how excessive extra work could be perceived as exploitation. WAMG (2008) expressed its view on the use of support staff's goodwill, describing the expectation that they undertake unpaid overtime as 'unacceptable'.

3.7 Conclusions

In this chapter we have drawn mostly on data from the DISS Strand 1 surveys to provide some broad descriptors (e.g. age, gender and ethnicity) of support staff and, specifically, TAs. We presented a typology for support staff as a whole, which is the first to capture the myriad roles that have been created through the extensive workforce remodelling schools have performed in the last ten years. In line with the purpose of this book, we narrowed our focus to concentrate on teaching assistants – a position in schools dominated by women like Mandy, the TA we introduced in Chapter 1.

The Strand 1 surveys collected a wealth of data on support staff, but for the purposes of fleshing out the Characteristics component of the Wider Pedagogical Role model prefigured in the previous chapter, we reported on two characteristics of TAs: their qualifications and experience. TAs typically have lower level qualifications than the teachers in whose classes they work, but have spent many years working in the same school.

We also presented data relating to the second component of the WPR model – TAs' conditions of employment. TAs who responded to our questionnaire reported a high level of job satisfaction, regardless of the low pay. The New Labour government's attempts to raise the status of the TA role for experienced practitioners via HLTA accreditation has not been matched with improved pay, and – despite the huge growth in their number and role – there is still no national formal framework for TA appraisal and this seems even less likely under the present coalition government. Finally, we have begun to see how the goodwill of many TAs makes up for the widespread structural failure to provide adequate opportunities for day-to-day preparation (more of which in Chapter 4).

The key findings from the DISS project on TAs' characteristics and their conditions of employment are certainly important, but somewhat 'distal' as an explanation of why it is that TA support has a negative impact on pupils' academic outcomes. The key messages from these two components of the WPR model can be seen below in Figure 3.1, but it is the findings from the remaining components of the WPR model that we argue have a much greater bearing on TA effectiveness, and in the next chapter we begin to expand this explanation by looking at the Preparedness dimension.

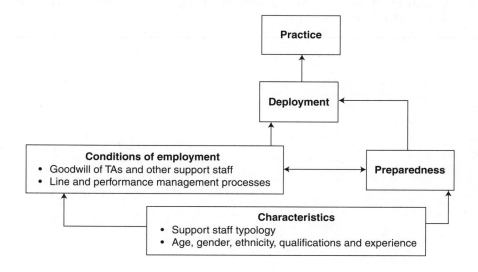

Figure 3.1 The Wider Pedagogical Role with characteristics and conditions of employment

Key findings

Support staff characteristics

- There was a significant increase in the numbers of TAs in schools over the three waves.
- The main reasons for change in TAs and other support staff numbers given by schools was the number of pupils with SEN, new initiatives in school, change in overall school budgets and the implementation of PPA time.
- Most support staff were female, aged 36 and over, and almost all classified themselves as being of white ethnic background. This description is typical of the TA profile.

Conditions of employment

- Over two-thirds of support staff worked extra hours. There was a significant decrease over the three waves in being paid for extra work. TAs were prominent among this group.
- TAs and other support staff were generally positive about their level of job satisfaction, how much they felt appreciated by their school, their contracts, conditions of employment and working arrangements. There was relatively less satisfaction with their pay.

Chapter 4

Preparedness

4.1 Introduction

'Preparedness', as we define it, takes two forms:

1 The training and professional development of teachers and TAs: how teachers manage and organise the work of TAs; and how TAs are trained to support learning.
2 Day-to-day preparation: time for joint planning, preparation and feedback between teachers and TAs, before and after lessons.

In this chapter, we shall see that there is a general lack of preparedness for both teachers and TAs, on both these aspects, and this contributes to our explanation of why TA support negatively affects pupils' academic progress. The DISS project results show that teachers lack training on how to organise and manage TAs, even though more and more are involved directly in their training and line management. The problems in finding enough time for planning and feedback, especially in secondary schools, add to the difficulties faced in terms of the day-to-day preparedness of TAs and the teachers who deploy them. This general picture is not only in line with most other studies (e.g. Butt and Lance 2005; Howes *et al.* 2003; Lee 2002), but extends them; for example, in this chapter we will see how TAs' goodwill (described in the previous chapter) is essential in allowing time for teachers and TAs to meet. As we develop the second expression of day-to-day preparedness, we will note how subject and pedagogical knowledge are important aspects of what it means to be a 'prepared' TA, ready and equipped to support pupil learning in everyday classroom conditions.

The data in this chapter is drawn largely from responses to the teacher and support staff questionnaires (SSQ) (see Table 4.1). The survey data provide the broad detail, but

Table 4.1 Data sources for preparedness

	Strand 1				Strand 2				
	MSQ	TQ	SSQ	Work pattern diary	Structured observations	Systematic observations	Case studies	Transcripts	MPSS
Preparedness	•	•	•				•		

our deeper understanding of how preparedness impacts on TAs' effectiveness in teaching and learning contexts is developed by drawing on the rich case study data. We will look at the two forms of preparedness in turn, beginning with training for TAs.

4.2 Training and development

4.2.1 Training for TAs

Responses to the Strand 1 surveys consistently found that the majority of TAs (and other support staff) attended training events (e.g. in-service training, or Inset). Ninety-five per cent of TAs had attended at least one training event in the previous two years. Attendance was most likely at school-based Inset (around 90 per cent at each wave), with 60 per cent having attended non-school-based training at Wave 3. The number of TAs having attended training that led to a qualification decreased at each wave, from 49 per cent at Wave 1 to 42 per cent at Wave 3. The vast majority of teacher-led training for TAs was described as informal support given on the job (82 per cent at Wave 3).

TAs reported being broadly satisfied with the training they received: at Wave 3, 78 per cent of TAs were either very or fairly satisfied; 7 per cent were fairly or very dissatisfied. However, there was relatively less satisfaction with the opportunities available for training: at Wave 3, 63 per cent of TAs were either fairly or very satisfied; 15 per cent were fairly or very dissatisfied. Training, therefore, was broadly described as good, but opportunities were limited. This was also the experience of Mandy, as we saw in our vignette.

Critics have commented on the patchy nature of TA training and the impact on their professional development (see the systematic review by Cajkler *et al.* 2007). Evidence from the DISS case studies suggests that this patchiness is additionally affected by the difficulties TAs have in attending training and Inset. Schools may have difficulty releasing TAs, or TAs may not be invited to attend. Some schools may have difficulty funding training. TAs themselves may face practical barriers, such as family/childcare commitments, or the times at which courses run may make them inaccessible to TAs working part time (see also Ofsted 2002; P. Smith *et al.* 2004).

The case studies also revealed particular issues with the process through which TAs can seek to become higher level teaching assistants (HLTAs). This new category of TA was instigated by the National Agreement in order to play a greater role in supporting teachers by leading lessons and being more closely involved in pupil learning. Headteachers and TAs commented unfavourably on the HLTA accreditation process, and similar comments were made in response to the open-ended questions in the Strand 1 surveys. We consistently found that some headteachers were willing to provide and support a TA's bid to attain HLTA status, but they offered no guarantees that it would lead to increased pay or promotion. TAs complained that they had found it difficult to get a place with local providers, and that the HLTA process was time consuming and suffered from ineffective administration.[1]

4.2.2 Training for teachers

4.2.2.1 Working with TAs

Given the growth of TAs and their high visibility in classrooms, it might be expected that training to help teachers to work with TAs would form a sizeable part of pre-service training and professional development. However, at each wave of the Strand 1 teacher questionnaire, we found that 75 per cent of teachers reported having had no such training. This was despite the fact that the proportion of teachers involved in directly training TAs and other support staff grew over the duration of the study. By Wave 3, over half of teachers (55 per cent) were involved in training support staff compared to 40 per cent in Wave 1.

The Teacher Questionnaire (TQ) asked teachers an open-ended question about the extent and duration of the training or development they had received on working with TAs. Most teachers had received no more than a short course lasting one day or less. For most teachers, this training had formed part of their initial teacher training (ITT) course or their newly qualified teacher (NQT) training; fewer respondents had received such training via Inset sessions.

We asked teachers to comment on how useful they found the training or development they had received for working with TAs and other support staff. At Wave 3, just under half were positive about it and 11 per cent were negative. We also asked teachers who had *not* been involved in training or developing support staff, whether they would have found such training useful. The majority (74 per cent at Wave 3) said they would have, suggesting a clear desire for preparation of this type.

In terms of what teachers felt they had gained from the training or development they received, they cited an increased understanding of what TAs, and those in other support roles, could be asked to do, learning how to make the most effective use of them, and what both parties may expect from their working relationship.

4.2.2.2 Line managing TAs

As we reported in the previous chapter, around three-quarters of TAs had their work supervised by a teacher, and over half of teachers (54 per cent) line managed TAs. In most cases, these were largely informal arrangements. Yet, again, we found a high proportion of these teachers – two-thirds at Waves 2 and 3, in fact – had not had any training for their role as a line manager.

Only half of the teachers who had had training or development to help them with their line management responsibilities rated it as useful. As with training for working with TAs, over half of teachers responding to an open-ended question in the TQ on the matter said that the sum of their line management training had lasted just one day or less. There was clear dissatisfaction with this situation: only one in five at Wave 3 said they were satisfied, compared with one in four at Wave 2; and over a third at Wave 3 said they were dissatisfied. Again, we find that this is an area of professional development that could benefit from attention.

4.2.3 Conclusions on training

Whilst for some new teachers, training on managing TAs was part of their ITT or their NQT year, this was relatively brief, and the overall impression gained from the Strand 2 Wave 2 case study data was that primary school teachers (particularly NQTs) had not really been made aware of the increased significance of working with and managing the additional adults in their classrooms. As was the case with Mark in our vignette, many new teachers were learning about TA deployment on the job and receiving guidance from colleagues who themselves had learned on the job. There is a risk therefore, that without more formalised types of training based on proven good practice, the development and promulgation of ineffective practice will persist.

Where TAs do receive training, schools and teachers must be vigilant in order to avoid what Giangreco (2003) calls 'the training trap'; that is, the tendency for teachers to relinquish instruction of pupils with SEN to TAs who have received more or less any kind of training, no matter how scant. Incidentally, although the DISS project did not collect any formal data on this, our experience is such that we would agree with critics who argue that neither class teachers nor TAs are adequately trained or prepared to support the needs of pupils with SEN (Anderson and Finney 2008; Lamb 2009; and Norwich and Lewis 2001).

It is arguable that with the recent rise in the UK in school-based routes to QTS (e.g. the Graduate and Registered Teacher Training Programmes, and fast-track schemes, such as TeachFirst), new teachers would be in a similar, if not worse, position in terms of their preparation to work with and manage TAs. Many receive a form of induction or training that reflects the culture of the school they work in, and is often underpinned by prevailing attitudes to TAs and their deployment, rather than based on evidence concerning the best ways of working with them. Along with findings on the lack of planning and feedback time – to which we turn shortly – results suggest that much still needs to be done in terms of preparing teachers for working with TAs.

It is also worth pointing out the generational effect that may wash through in the coming years. As a result of the substantial investment in TAs since the late 1990s, pupils who are now reaching the end of compulsory schooling will no doubt view TAs as a natural part of the education landscape – a situation that was not the case for many current practitioners when they were at school. The upper-secondary pupils of today are the trainee teachers of tomorrow, and their attitudes toward TAs, and other support staff they interact with at school, could add another dimension to how TAs are perceived and deployed by the classroom leaders of the future.

4.3 Day-to-day preparedness of TAs

4.3.1 Opportunities for TAs to meet with teachers

The second aspect of preparedness concerns the amount of time to prepare TAs to support pupil learning, and the teachers' responsibility for, and role in, this preparation. A strong and consistent finding across all three TQ survey waves was that most teachers – about 75 per cent – did not have any allocated planning or feedback time with the TA they worked with. By Wave 3, only 27 per cent of teachers said they had allocated time for planning, and only 22 per cent had allocated time for feedback, with TAs.

The situation in secondary schools is particularly troubling: 95 per cent of teachers said that they had no planning or feedback time. Data from the questionnaires and the case studies revealed communication between teachers and TAs to be largely brief and ad hoc. Conversations took place during lesson changeovers, before and after school, and during break and lunch times, and so for the most part, relied on the goodwill of TAs, as we showed in Chapter 3.

The case study visits did much to confirm this picture, revealing the effects of having limited opportunities for TAs and teachers to communicate and plan, prepare for and feedback on lessons and TA-led intervention sessions, and to discuss pupil performance and behaviour. This picture of day-to-day preparedness was also reflected in our vignette. In addition, the case studies captured the experiences of cover supervisors' day-to-day preparation, which are worth reporting because, whilst cover supervision (that is, leading a class in the absence of a teacher) tends to be a discrete role in secondary schools (e.g. cover supervisors do this and nothing else), in primary schools, it was TAs who performed this role.

Many TAs and all of the cover supervisors we interviewed described experiences of – to use their own words – going in to lessons 'blind'.

> The vast majority of the time you just walk in blind ... It's really, really rare we get someone coming down saying, 'You've got my lesson. This is what I want you to do'.
>
> (Secondary cover supervisor)

The lack of planning and feedback time in secondary schools can in part be explained by the fact that teachers typically worked with several TAs each week and so it was difficult for them to find time to meet with them all.

> The problem is always, for teachers, it's time. They haven't got time at the end of the lesson necessarily to spend ten minutes discussing something with the [TA]. And then a lot of our staff are part-time, so finding people can be a difficulty. And as we know, staff are busy at lunchtime and after school.
>
> (Secondary teacher)

Several primary teachers were able to meet with TAs whilst their class was in a school assembly or other large group activity, such as singing. Yet schools in both phases faced the same difficulties in terms of creating more time for liaison.

> First of all when would we do it? [TA] would have to be paid extra money after school or before. When would it happen? ... It would be too time-consuming for me ... You have to remember that time is a constraint. And the more time you take out for planning, then the less time you have for assessment, the less time you have for marking, the less time you have for preparation.
>
> (Primary teacher)

In light of this quote above, it is worth mentioning how some teachers felt that the additional and more demanding responsibilities involved in managing the day-to-day deployment of TAs had, to some extent, offset some of the gains of having a reduced workload in terms of non-teaching tasks (e.g. photocopying and collecting money).

In contrast to teachers' views about the absence of planning and feedback time, some secondary school TAs suggested that there was no need for increasing or improving the opportunities currently available, as they believed that their experience and time spent in the role provided the preparation they needed.

> Because I've been doing the job for so long, and the work rolls over year to year, within five minutes of the lesson I can pick up what's being done.
>
> (Secondary TA)

Some school leaders were open about how the lack of time for communication concerned them: they wanted more time, yet very few provided timetabled slots within the
school day for teachers to meet with TAs or cover supervisors. A few schools, though,
did provide some TAs and cover supervisors with non-contact time of their own, in
which to write up notes on pupils' engagement or behaviour in a lesson, provide written
feedback to the teacher on a lesson they covered, and prepare for intervention sessions
they were going to lead, or lessons they were going to cover in the absence of a teacher.

Given the shortage of available face-to-face meeting time, a few schools tended
towards the use of written forms of communication as a way of imparting instructions
and giving feedback.

4.3.2 The quality of preparation

Analysis of the case study data showed that there were adverse effects in terms of how
well prepared TAs and cover supervisors felt for their roles, particularly those working in secondary schools. In three-quarters of the instances concerning the quality of
preparedness, TAs and cover supervisors described receiving minimal or poor guidance
from teachers; for example, teachers provided little, if any, detail about the specific role
they wanted TAs to take in a lesson, or the task when supporting lower attaining pupils
or those with SEN. Lesson plans and objectives were generally expressed at whole class
level.

Many TAs described working 'on the hoof', and how, in the absence of any specific
explanation from the teacher, they 'tuned in' to the teacher's whole-class delivery in
order to pick up essential content (again, this commonplace situation was reflected in the
vignette). However, this created pressure. In the interview extracts below, we can see
how the level of preparedness TAs feel they require is far in excess of the level assumed
by school leaders. Simply replicating teachers' practice is not sufficient.

> There's usually an objective on the board anyway, so the children know, support
> staff also know what the objective is, you know. And [TA is] very in-tune as well.
> Because she's been here for many years, she knows ... I wouldn't say they need a
> great deal of subject knowledge. They just need to observe what you're doing and
> carry that through.
>
> (Primary deputy headteacher)

> [The teacher] puts up the work on the board, I'm then frantically trying to go
> through it to try and think of different ways to explain it to [pupil with SEN].
>
> (Primary TA)

> If you're going in and you haven't got a clue what's being covered, you're as blind
> as the children or even more so sometimes.
>
> (Secondary TA)

To mitigate the effects of inconsistent or inadequate planning, two primary schools
we visited had established a planning policy to improve the quality of TA preparation.
Teachers were expected to make the role they wanted TAs to take in the lesson explicit.
The teacher and TA who worked in one class described how their system worked.

When you've got someone with you for half the time you should capitalize on that as much as you can really … [So] for us, this [the planning sheet] is a form of communication. I outline to [the TA] briefly what I want her to do so she knows at the start of the week roughly how her week's going to go … Then she fills in for me how that session went, so then I've got notes on how that child did … I can imagine there'd be nothing worse for her than if she walked in the room and I went, 'Oh, I don't know what you're doing'.

(Primary teacher)

My whole week is clear from this, what I'm expected to do … It will be more or less the same: the name or a group of people that I'm working with every week … I'll comment … and that's [teacher's] feedback. If we don't get the chance at the end of the day to feedback, she's got it written … It's beneficial obviously, and the more communication there is between the teacher and their support staff, I think the easier it is for the children … So I benefit from this a lot.

(Primary TA)

Many TAs (like Mandy) were responsible for preparing and delivering literacy and numeracy interventions. Some TAs felt prepared, but only in the sense that they had prescribed materials on which to rely. Preparation for intervention sessions tended to be the sole responsibility of the TA and it was rarely augmented by input from the teacher.

How I plan for it [delivering a literacy intervention] is that there's a scheme of work that's just there for me, and all I have to do is read it. And it has the resources that I need, all of which are able to be photocopied and some put on card or laminated. So everything is there for me and I don't actually have to deviate from the content at all.

(Primary TA)

[The task for literacy intervention] doesn't really go along with the teacher's plans. It's sort of more my own.

(Primary TA)

The consequence of devolving this responsibility to TAs means that an essential component of quality assurance is missing. As the teachers of pupils involved in TA-led interventions became detached from the day-to-day planning, delivery and assessment of interventions, so the quality of TAs' work becomes less and less subject to monitoring by the teacher. The following quote from a primary teacher demonstrates the distance between her and the TA in supporting pupils in her class who were experiencing difficulties with numeracy.

You get advice on how to do it [numeracy intervention] and I imagine [TA] is following that.

(Primary teacher)

In a few primary schools this lack of monitoring extended to lessons planned and delivered by TAs, during periods when the teacher took their PPA time. In the main, however, information and instructions for TAs and cover supervisors leading lessons in the teacher's absence was provided, though it varied in quality and clarity; some departments or teachers within the same school made more effort than others. The implications of poor quality preparation could be significant in terms of managing behaviour and ensuring that pupils produced some work during the lesson. Also, as one headteacher pointed out, it was in the teachers' own interests to provide satisfactory instruction and work for cover lessons: 'because in the end, when they come back, they have to pick up the pieces' – whether this is in the shape of dealing with the behaviour incidents or repeating work.

> There are some [teachers] who don't truly understand the role of a cover supervisor and abuse it ... There's no preparation there with some teachers ... Where the cover supervisor has problems it's because the teacher's planning is poor.
>
> (Secondary headteacher)

4.3.3 The involvement of TAs in the planning and feedback loop

As we have seen, opportunities for TAs to plan, prepare and feedback to teachers are limited, but where teacher–TA communication took place, the case study data revealed the limited extent to which information fed back by TAs was put to use by teachers. Many teachers failed to feed vital information about the pupils TAs supported – their progress, weaknesses, understanding of concepts, engagement with tasks and so on – from interventions and other learning contexts, into their wider curriculum planning and assessment, or use it to inform their interactions with these pupils in classroom situations.

Whilst all the teachers that we interviewed claimed that feedback on pupils' learning, progress and behaviour (both in and away from the class) informed their further lesson planning, TAs and cover supervisors were almost evenly split in the number that agreed with and disputed this. Again, the lack of teacher monitoring of TAs' work was evident in how some teachers did not ask for information on the pupils that took part in the TA-led intervention sessions, nor did they review the work the pupils did in those sessions. The following extract from one interview with a TA reveals this situation at its worst.

> It's [pupil work] all in a folder and probably someone will look at it at the end.
> [Researcher: Where does it go after it's done?]
> In a box in the cupboard ... I've been doing it [intervention programme] last year and a little bit of the year before ... and to be honest with you, I could have anything in them folders sometimes. Because ... sometimes it gets looked at, other times it's taken out of the folder, put in an elastic band and it's put in a box with the books ... I've never really known them to look at it to be truthful ... It is bad, isn't it?
>
> (Primary TA)

A number of TAs found it frustrating that teachers did not tap into their detailed knowledge of the pupils they supported, as they believed they had a lot of useful information to offer. However, it was reassuring to hear experienced TAs say that, where this might once have been attributable to teachers' hostile attitude towards TAs, (what TAs frequently referred to as a 'them and us' situation), such a culture in schools was now largely a thing of the past.

Over the last two or three years, particularly in secondary schools, I think there is more of a general realisation of the fact that [TAs] are around and that they can be rather more useful than some people might have thought three or four years ago.

(Secondary TA)

Feedback from support staff undertaking cover supervision largely concerned the degree to which pupils had completed the work set by the teacher and the behaviour in the lesson. During classroom observations, cover supervisors were seen writing notes on pupils' behaviour and their level of engagement with the set tasks. Some also informed teachers about the quality or quantity of the work they had provided, which only some teachers used to inform further planning.

I'd normally get the lesson plan with a little comment on the bottom as to how it went ... The following day we don't necessarily have time for a catch-up ... But you get feedback on the progress that was made and any kind of behavioural issues that need additional support ... You just adapt it for the next time. I trust [the cover supervisor's judgement] if she says, 'This was too easy for them', or whatever.

(Secondary teacher)

As was the case with information fed back by TAs, the extent to which teachers sought and used this information varied between and within secondary schools. One teacher – although he received notes about cover lessons – did not follow up feedback from cover supervisors, preferring instead to gauge the success of the lesson by the pupils' reactions on his return.

You've got the best people to tell you, in that the next day you've got the kids there and you say to them, 'OK, what did you achieve? What did you do?' Regardless of what someone has told you or what their perception of it is ... you just say, 'What did you actually learn? Did you watch a video or did you do that worksheet? Let me have a look at it'. And then once you've judged what they've actually got from the lesson – from your point of view – [you can decide to] go over it or carry on.

(Secondary teacher)

4.3.4 TAs' subject and pedagogical knowledge

The case study data revealed few instances of TAs gaining subject and pedagogical knowledge through formal or informal training. As we described above, most TAs tend to obtain what they need to know about the subject, and how to present it to pupils, by 'tuning in' to teachers' whole-class delivery and then modelling it. This approach was shared to some degree by some headteachers and teachers who worked with long-serving TAs.

I think it's [pedagogical knowledge] just instinctive to be honest. I think it is [experiential]. Yes, totally. It's not a specifically, 'Go out and learn how to do this'; it's, 'Watch what everybody does and do it our way'.

(Primary headteacher)

The need for subject and pedagogical knowledge had different implications for support staff undertaking cover supervision. Headteachers, following national guidance, said that support staff who led classes in the teacher's absence were not expected to teach; yet many TAs and cover supervisors said that their role inevitably had a pedagogic element. Despite guidance, for the most part, the cover supervision role was not supported by training.

> [Training for cover supervisors] is very much ad hoc … and it is something that we would benefit from nationally. Because, if cover supervisors are here to stay – and I think most schools use them – we need to look and see if there's some way we can support them.
>
> (Secondary headteacher)

In terms of subject knowledge, secondary cover supervisors struggled to support pupil learning in subjects with which they were unfamiliar. But there was evidence that schools were attempting to capitalise on cover supervisors' skills and subject knowledge when assigning cover duties:

> Certain [cover supervisors] … have got specialisms: [X] is very fluent in German; and I'm quite good at art and English; and [Y] is good at performing arts and stuff. I think that is taken into account when assigning the cover.
>
> (Secondary cover supervisor)

4.3.5 Conclusions on day-to-day preparedness

In light of the DISS project findings on the day-to-day preparedness of TAs, we conclude that there is a clear need for teachers to recognise their duty to fully brief the TAs who work in their place. Also, where appropriate, schools should ensure that TAs are given paid non-contact time of their own for preparation, in order to avoid trading on their goodwill. We are currently preparing practical solutions for teachers concerning lesson planning and sharing subject and pedagogical knowledge, in the form of a handbook/ toolkit based on our action research with teachers and TAs. Briefly, we recommend writing lesson plans with TAs in mind: being specific about the nature and purpose of the tasks given to them; providing clear expectations in terms of outcomes for the pupils they support; and being clear about how tasks can be sequenced, and the time available to complete them. In a paper based on the DISS project data, Radford *et al.* (2011) suggest that one relatively straightforward way in which teachers can help TAs to develop their pedagogical knowledge is by sharing their own higher order skills. In addition, subject knowledge could be shared by holding, for example, informal 'mini-tutorials' for TAs, where teachers can brief TAs on topic information or technical processes (e.g. performing complex mathematical calculations). Informal Q&A sessions between teacher and TA could be particularly useful for those supporting pupils away from the classroom, giving both parties the chance to check their understanding of the subject/topic and instructional techniques.

4.4 Conclusions

In this chapter we have drawn on data from the DISS surveys and case studies to describe findings on the training and professional development of TAs and teachers, and the day-to-day aspects of planning and preparation before lessons, and feedback afterwards. As we indicated at the end of the previous chapter, preparedness is the first of the three components of the Wider Pedagogical Role model (along with deployment and practice) that we argue has the greatest bearing on TA effectiveness. We conclude that TAs perform their role with little guidance from teachers because: 1) teachers do not have the time to prepare TAs prior to the lesson; and 2) even where they do, they lack the formal training to know how to make best use of it and to impart information effectively. These key messages can be seen in Figure 4.1.

It is clear, then, that more joint planning and feedback time is needed for teachers and TAs, especially in secondary schools. Further, this is time for which TAs should be paid. The need to prepare teachers to work with and manage TAs through formal initial training and professional development is paramount; there is little use in providing more time for them to liaise with TAs if it results in the same models of deployment and practice that lead to negative learning outcomes.

As TAs themselves described, they operate in the moment, due to a lack of preparation, and many – compared to teachers – work with considerable gaps in their subject and pedagogical knowledge. Also many TAs work in roles that put them in the place of the teacher (e.g. cover supervision and leading interventions away from the class). Those given such responsibilities would no doubt approach their work with greater confidence if given formal training in behaviour and classroom management. In terms of learning and curriculum interventions, TAs need more and better training on the programmes they deliver. A key point to consider in developing such training will be to overcome the intuitive, but mistaken, assumption that less pedagogical skill is required when teaching pupils with SEN; if anything, a higher level of skill is needed.

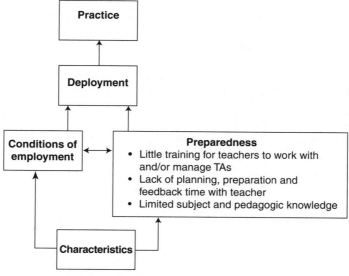

Figure 4.1 The Wider Pedagogical Role model with preparedness

In light of the findings described in this chapter, we have, in Figure 4.1, added the key messages from the preparedness theme to the WPR model. One can begin to see connections between the components; for example, in terms of how TA goodwill makes up for the lack of allocated teacher–TA communication time. The issues concerning the preparedness of teachers and TAs are more deeply connected to those relating to deployment and practice of TAs – the other two important components of the WPR model. It is the findings on deployment to which we now turn, and where we will see more profoundly why TA support can have a negative impact on pupils' academic outcomes.

Key findings

Preparedness

- The majority of TAs experienced training of some kind over the three waves.
- The majority of teachers had not had training to help them work with TAs in classrooms, even though the number of teachers involved in training TAs and other support staff had increased at each wave.
- The majority of teachers did not have allocated planning, feedback or other allocated time with TAs they worked with in the classroom.

Chapter 5

The deployment of TAs

In this chapter we examine the deployment of TAs in schools. We first look at debates about the role of TAs, drawing on the interview material from the case studies. The second section is the heart of the chapter, in which we examine in a systematic way the empirical evidence arising out of the DISS project on the activities of TAs, the contexts within which they work, the kinds of pupils they work with and the pupil's role when interacting with TAs and teachers. Put simply, the aim is to arrive at an answer to the question, 'What do TAs do?' We end with a third section in which we look more closely at the separation of TA-supported pupils from the teacher and the curriculum, revealed by the case studies. Table 5.1 shows the data sources used in this chapter.

5.1 The roles of teachers and TAs

Before we examine the main data on what TAs actually do in classrooms, we start this chapter with a brief discussion of a few of the issues relating to the roles of TAs and teachers, largely drawing on data from the case studies

5.1.1 Role clarity and ambiguity

Despite the often positive view about TAs and the way in which they were seen to provide teachers with indirect help that benefited teaching, it became apparent from the case studies that the role of TAs in classrooms was far more problematic and contentious than might appear at first sight. What is more, a number of difficult issues emerged, as we shall see, when the views of staff are set alongside the results from systematic descriptions of TAs' activities and interactions with pupils in schools. This is in line with a number of

Table 5.1 Data sources for deployment

	Strand 1				Strand 2				
	MSQ	TQ	SSQ	Work pattern diary	Structured observations	Systematic observations	Case studies	Transcripts	MPSS
Deployment	•	•	•	•	•	•	•		

other studies (Bach *et al.* 2004; Beeson *et al.* 2003; Cremin *et al.* 2005; Farrell *et al.* 1999; Mistry *et al.* 2004; Moran and Abbott 2002; Schlapp *et al.* 2003).

We have seen that the difference between teachers and TAs is often portrayed in terms of teachers having a direct teaching input, while TAs just 'support' pupil learning. In the course of many discussions with headteachers, teachers and government representatives, we have heard this distinction expressed as if this is a straightforward and unproblematic difference in roles. On the surface it appears to be a useful and complementary arrangement that is likely to benefit pupils. But a main problem to emerge from the case studies was that once put under the spotlight, distinctions between practices such as 'supervision', 'support', 'monitoring', 'facilitation' of learning, 'teaching' and so on are hard to sustain. Difficulties involved in separating out these different terms are connected to a wider ambiguity over the TA role and how it differs from that of teachers.

5.1.1.1 'Role creep' and professional identity

Despite the common and seemingly sensible way that TAs could be seen to adopt an indirect role, allowing teachers more time to focus on teaching, there was some concern that TAs had taken on too much of a teaching role. The case studies revealed how the issue of 'role creep' was of concern to teachers, not least because of the way it can be seen to threaten the professional identity of teachers.

> They're not qualified teachers and you can't expect them to deliver in the way a qualified teacher would. I'm not knocking them; they're very good … but I don't agree with having teaching assistants covering classes … In Year 6 we're dealing with fairly challenging stuff, actually, for me to get my head round, let alone an unqualified teaching assistant. Or, I should say an unqualified teacher, because that's what they're doing when they're covering a class … the thought that I could just be replaced by somebody unqualified worries me … The government have spent years and years promoting teaching as a graduate profession … get the best of the best in to do this job. And then all of a sudden through the back door: 'It's too expensive now; let's get in cheaper cover'.
>
> (Primary teacher)

Some teachers had professional and personal concerns regarding the way in which the work of TAs had carried over into the teaching and learning functions of teachers. As one primary teacher put it:

> If the TA can now teach without having a teaching qualification it does make me wonder about why I did all the training.
>
> (Primary teacher)

This unease about the line between the roles of teachers and TAs was also expressed by TAs. A senior TA suggested that there was 'a very fine line' between the teacher and TA roles, and that as the TA role had broadened, they were 'getting more to do what the teacher does':

The difference between a TA and a teacher is the TA has not had that qualification to say that you're teacher trained. However, you're quite capable of standing up in front of 30 children and delivering and teaching children, say, a science lesson. Doing it quite well, distributing the work, sitting with a group, and marking that work afterwards. You're quite capable of doing that ... I find myself in the situation where I have done what the teacher has: I've planned this day; I've planned this session; I've delivered a lesson; I've taught these children how to do something that they couldn't do when they came in this morning. So I am teaching these children. I haven't got the qualification; I haven't had the training, but I'm able to do that.

(Primary TA)

A number of TAs were uncertain how their role was different to that of teachers, and on the basis of the case study evidence, much the same could be said for cover supervisors. Describing her job, one cover supervisor's comments were representative of what many school staff had said about this new post and how it blurred notions of 'supervision' and 'teaching':

I think, if anything, that's the issue that caused me most grief when I first started: understanding exactly what my role is, and where I fit in. Because as a supervisor, I'm supervising the lesson; I'm not necessarily teaching, but supervising ... A supervisor, as I see it, would be making sure the pupils understand what's required of them and going through the process of learning and helping them get to the other side, without necessarily actually saying, 'I'm going to teach you.' How can I put it: it's supervising their learning; supervising their behaviour; supervising the dynamics of the classroom. Not necessarily standing in front of the classroom and giving the lesson; talking about that subject.

(Secondary cover supervisor)

5.1.1.2 Ambiguity over responsibilities

It is not only support staff roles that are emerging and changing. Evidence from case studies of secondary schools suggested that the role and professional standing of teachers was subject to development in areas other than those concerning teaching and learning. In some schools there was a redistribution of clerical and routine tasks to an expanded administrative team, but schools had deconstructed the teacher's role still further, separating out teachers' pastoral responsibilities and transferring them to other support staff. This was driven as part of wider reforms including restructuring of teaching and learning responsibilities.

Some TAs had a wider administrative role connected with aspects of pupil development (e.g. social and emotional) that could indirectly affect pupils' classroom performance. This was seen by secondary schools in particular as a way of allowing teachers to give increased focus to the activities that had a direct impact on learning.

The school has dramatically changed in terms of support staff since the teaching and learning responsibilities – TLRs – changed. And with that we took the opportunity to take some work, which had been traditionally done by teachers and employ support staff … [We] did away with heads of year, who were teachers, and the basic reason for that is because their role as the head of year often interfered with their role in the classroom; made them less efficient in the classroom.

(Secondary headteacher)

How pupils perceived the roles of teachers and TAs could reinforce the differences between the two, sometimes to the detriment of TA's status and potential.

The pupils don't show you the respect that they would a real teacher … There is a sort of philosophy within learning support that that [being disciplinarian] is not what we're here for. We want the kids to come in to us willingly … [But] if we're meant to be the nice, friendly face of support, then we can't suddenly change and become the hard-line, 'put you in detention' people … And I feel at times quite powerless because the children will answer you back and you think, 'Well, where can I go now?' And that is difficult.

(Secondary TA)

The comments above reveal that having a less formal relationship with pupils has implications for enforcing discipline. Not only is it difficult to switch from 'friendly face' to 'disciplinarian', but, as some primary TAs suggested, pupils respond differently to TAs depending on which role they are working in. For example, TAs can find it harder to control pupil behaviour in the playground when working as a lunchtime supervisor than when working in the class as a TA. This dual role is quite common among primary school TAs.

The role of TAs in maintaining consistent expectations about behaviour can be important, but, as one TA described, their authority could be challenged:

I sometimes think that my warnings are paid attention to less. Whereas a teacher's warnings − especially a male member of staff − are listened to directly and instantly … Because I'm an assistant and a female, they've got two reasons to think, 'Yeah, whatever. We don't actually listen to you'.

(Secondary TA)

Yet it was also clear, in secondary schools in particular, that teachers did not always fully understand or appreciate the roles and remits of TAs and other support staff, and this could influence their deployment decisions in the classroom.

There isn't that wide vision perhaps, of the teacher realising the support that's there. They don't totally understand what a learning support assistant is about.

(Secondary headteacher)

5.1.2 Positive and negative views about the direct role of TAs

Some measure of the difference in views about the more direct role of TAs was obtained from answers given by headteachers to an open-ended question in the Strand 1 Wave 1 Main School Questionnaire (MSQ). Some respondents gave an evaluative comment on the pedagogical role of TAs. Comments varied from the obviously positive, through to those where reservations were expressed, and then through to comments that were clearly negative or hostile. Each response was coded separately in terms of the degree of support each view had amongst respondents. It should be remembered that there were only 78 such responses, representing only 6 per cent of the schools in the sample, and although the examples are illustrative of the main views, we need to interpret findings with caution.

A positive view was given by 37 respondents (47 per cent of those providing a response). Special school heads were far more likely to express positive views about TAs taking on pedagogical/learning support roles, compared with primary and secondary heads.

> Classroom assistants ... Most of them are more than capable of teaching classes, following lessons planned by teaching colleagues, in the absence of a class teacher. This has not been [the] practice within the school until this academic year when the Workforce Reforms have given SMT [senior management team] a context in which to do this.
>
> (Special school headteacher)

> TAs have had (some, not all) contract modified to enable them to take a class. School relies heavily on ICT to support children so all TAs have had 16 sessions × 2.5 hours of ICT training and some workboards and digital cameras etc. TAs are expected to teach! Albeit groups but these are getting bigger.
>
> (Primary headteacher)

A few views were classified as showing 'reservations.' This view was expressed by 21 per cent of (or 16) respondents and it took the form of 'yes, but ...' type answers, revealing reservations of some kind over this aspect of the National Agreement.

> I do not necessarily agree with TAs covering classes, but in our school, the staff (both TAs and teachers) are keen to give it a go. Without significant additional resources I do not think there is an alternative in meeting this element of workforce reform.
>
> (Primary headteacher)

In contrast there were 25 clearly negative views (32 per cent) where heads expressed their disagreement with, or opposition to, the changes in TA deployment.

> We are having problems organising appropriate LSA [learning support assistant] staff to pupil age/ability. We are not seeing any LSAs applying for HLTA status because they do not want to take whole classes (especially on low pay). We are not happy about the wider tasks and roles expected of LSAs in the Workload Agreement and HLTA status, especially from an Ofsted viewpoint of high expectation in teaching and learning ... This is an initiative on the cheap.
>
> (Primary headteacher)

Nearer the end of the project (at Wave 3), there were signs that this pedagogical role for TAs was less contentious, and that headteachers were more positive about, or perhaps resigned to, TAs having a direct pedagogical role. This was evident in fewer comments in the headteacher responses to the Wave 3 MSQ on the pedagogical role of TAs, and proportionately more of these comments were positive. The positive reactions far out-numbered the negative in special and secondary schools and, in contrast to the first wave, primary headteachers now shared similar views. This was perhaps an indication that the cover and PPA arrangements these schools had put in place – where support staff led classes – had bedded down and were not having an obviously detrimental effect some might have anticipated.

Few schools were found to have their own clear policy on support staff deployment. Many headteachers suggested that a continual state of flux (e.g. in terms of being amid a protracted period of employing and remodelling the support staff workforce) inhibited them from setting down solid guidelines on paper; they spoke of 'organic development' or having to react pragmatically within the dynamic school environment. More so than for TAs, the work of those who had cover supervision responsibilities was under constant review.

5.2 The deployment of TAs

We now turn from the views of school staff to look at, in a sense, more objective sources of data, in order to describe the current role and deployment of TAs in schools. We do this by starting with a relatively broad look at the amount of contact between all catego-ries of support staff and teachers, taken from the Teacher Questionnaires (TQ), and then progressively focus down through a description of the main activities of all categories of support staff, based on 'work pattern diaries' completed by support staff, to a picture of TAs resulting from careful structured observations during five-minute time periods, and finally, an even more fine-grained picture from systematic observations of pupils' moment-by-moment interactions with adults in the classroom.

The topics covered are:

- the amount of contact between teachers and support staff, including TAs (from the TQ)
- identifying the general activities of all support staff, including TAs (from the work pattern diaries)
- the contexts in which pupils are supported by teachers and TAs (from systematic and structured observations)
- which pupils are supported by teachers and TAs (from structured and systematic observations)
- differences in pupil role with teachers and TAs (from systematic observations).

5.2.1 Amount of contact between teachers and support staff

Support for teachers provided by TAs can be examined in a simple way. A basic question in the TQ asked teachers to tick the post titles of support staff who had worked with them, or for them, during the previous week. Looking first at all categories of support staff together, almost every teacher worked with some support staff, and this did not change over the three waves. We also analysed this in terms of the number of different categories of support staff with whom teachers worked. We looked at this in terms of the seven categories of support staff described in Chapter 3 and it was striking that the number of teachers who worked with six or seven categories of support staff increased over the three waves (11 per cent, 29 per cent and 32 per cent for Wave 1, 2 and 3 respectively), while the number who worked with three or fewer categories of support staff decreased over time, especially between Waves 1 and 2 (60 per cent, 34 per cent and 33 per cent for Waves 1, 2 and 3 respectively). This shows, therefore, that over the three waves, teachers came to work with a wider range of support staff.

We also analysed the amount of contact teachers had with support staff, for each of the seven categories. Full results are shown in Table 1 of Appendix 3. Overall, teachers have experienced much more contact with support staff in Wave 3 compared to Wave 1. The biggest increase was between Wave 1 and 2, though this varied between support staff categories. TAs, compared to the other categories of support staff, already had, at Wave 1, by far the most contact with teachers (92 per cent of teachers overall) and so there was little room for increase in subsequent waves (96 per cent at both Wave 2 and 3). Even so, when we looked separately at primary and secondary phases, we saw that there was still a sizeable increase in contact between TAs and teachers in secondary schools; this increased from a relatively low figure of 78 per cent at Wave 1, to 89 per cent by Wave 3.

Contact between teachers and other support staff groups had increased greatly from Wave 1 to Wave 3. There were increases for pupil welfare staff (16 per cent to 33 per cent), technicians (37 per cent to 53 per cent), other pupil support staff (38 per cent to 60 per cent), facilities staff (36 per cent to 57 per cent), administrative staff (55 per cent to 70 per cent) and site staff (34 per cent to 58 per cent) These results give a general but clear indication of the huge increase in day-to-day contact between teachers and all types of support staff, which has accompanied the implementation of the National Agreement and the resulting increase in support staff numbers. Of most relevance to this book is the finding that by Wave 3 virtually all teachers worked with TAs at some point during the last week.

5.2.2 Main activities of all categories of support staff: work pattern diary data

In this section we provide a systematic description of the activities undertaken by support staff over a whole school day. This was based on data from 'work pattern diaries' completed by all categories of support staff, sent out as part of the second Support Staff Questionnaire (SSQ) in 2006. The aim was to build on earlier results (from the first SSQ) used to classify support staff to the seven main categories (see Chapter 3), in which staff simply recorded whether they undertook each activity. In contrast, for the second SSQ, we designed a form divided into 20 minute periods, which listed the 91 most commonly performed tasks, and asked staff to tick which tasks were carried out in each 20 minute period across one school day. In this way we were able to calculate not only the frequency, but also the amount of time spent on different activities. Again, we first present results for all categories of support staff, in order to provide a context within which to better understand TA activities. In order to include all possible hours worked by support staff (e.g. those who arrived early, like cleaners or caretakers, through to those working after school as part of extended services), the 20 minute periods extended from 7am to 7pm. We were able to use 1,670 responses for analysis, which was 62 per cent of the total SSQ responses.

The 91 tasks were grouped into six categories, according to who (or what) was supported and in which way:

1   Support for teachers and/or the curriculum
2   Direct learning support for pupils
3   Direct pastoral support for pupils
4   Indirect support for pupils
5   Support for the school (administrative/communicative)
6   Support for the school (physical environment)

Results for the seven support staff categories and tasks are presented in Table 5.2, in terms of the average time in hours that each of the seven support staff categories spent on the six activity categories. Results relate to the day surveyed, so that, for example, we can see that when all the 20 minute time periods were added up, TAs were found to work 6.1 hours per day on average, and 0.3 hours of this was spent on indirect support for pupils.

Table 5.2 is instructive as a general portrait of activities undertaken by the seven support staff categories overall. The column totals show the average amount of time in each of the six activity types. Most time was spent on support for the school in two ways: administrative/communicative activities took up the most time (1.7 hours), followed by support for the school's physical environment (1.4 hours). Direct learning support for pupils was next in length (1.2 hours), followed by support for teachers/curriculum (0.7 hours). Indirect support for pupils and direct pastoral support for pupils took up relatively less of the day (0.2 and 0.3 hours respectively). Across all categories of support staff, therefore, we see that support for the school outweighed support for pupils: in total, 3.1 hours versus 1.7 hours. This means that over all categories of support staff, about twice

Table 5.2 Time spent on each group of tasks for each of the seven categories of support: data from work pattern diaries

Support staff type	Nature of task Mean hours per day						
	Support for teachers/ curriculum	Direct learning support for pupils	Direct pastoral support for pupils	Indirect support for pupils	Support for school: admin/ communications	Support for school: physical environment	Total hours
TAs and equivalent	1.4	3.8	0.3	0.3	0	0.3	6.1
Pupil welfare	1.4	1.4	2.1	0.9	0.5	0.3	6.6
Other pupil support	0.2	1.5	0.4	0	0	0.3	2.4
Technicians	1.8	1.1	0	0	1.7	1.9	6.5
Administrative	0.1	0	0	0	6.5	0.4	7.0
Facilities staff	0	0	0	0	0.3	3.3	3.6
Site staff	0.1	0	0	0	0.2	5.6	5.9
All categories	0.7	1.2	0.3	0.2	1.7	1.4	5.6

as much time was spent supporting the school, either in terms of administrative or communicative activities, as was spent supporting pupils in terms of direct learning support, direct pastoral support or indirect support.

But support staff groups varied in a number of ways, and this is shown in the rows in Table 5.2. Of particular interest are TAs. In contrast to other categories of support staff, by far the greatest amount of TA time was spent on direct learning support for pupils (3.8 hours per day on average), followed by support for teachers/curriculum (1.4 hours). We captured this finding in the vignette in Chapter 1: Mandy's own calculations revealed how she spent most of her day 'teaching'. Tasks grouped in the work pattern diary category 'direct learning support for pupils' (e.g. delivering lessons/learning activities; helping pupils to understand instructions) are those that have a direct impact on pupil learning. We return to this finding shortly, once we have looked at results from systematic observations.

5.2.3 The contexts in which pupils are supported

5.2.3.1 Systematic observation findings on the activities of TAs

The main aim of the systematic observation analyses, conducted as part of Strand 2 Wave 1, was to give a detailed quantitative description of the behaviours and interactions of pupils with TAs and teachers. These results are reported later in this chapter. But as part of the observation system, we also completed a set of codes that recorded the activities of TAs themselves. These observations were made at the end of each block of ten 10-second observations. A coding frame of ten categories was devised on the basis of pilot observations and is shown in Table 5.3. These categories were classified under two broad headings: 1) those involving contact with pupils; and 2) those when the TA was not directing working with pupils. The results (Table 5.3) give a view of the main activities undertaken by TAs, which complements that from the work pattern diaries.

It can be seen that TAs were twice as likely to be working with pupils as not working with them (64 per cent versus 36 per cent of all observations) (figures rounded). The most common individual activities across both primary and secondary schools were working with one pupil alone (29 per cent of all observations), listening to the teacher teach (20 per cent), working with different pupils by walking or 'roving' around the classroom (16 per cent) and working with a group of pupils (15 per cent), and working with materials (10 per cent). TAs, at least during these observations, very rarely took the whole class or even part of the class.

This is in agreement with the work pattern diary data shown above, and points to one of our main results on the deployment of TAs in schools: while they may once have assisted the teacher, it is now clear that they largely have a direct instructional role, assisting and interacting with pupils. These results are also consistent with information gained from visits to schools in the course of the case studies, the MSQ headteacher comments, and findings from the CSPAR study (Blatchford et al. 2004). These findings therefore make it clear that TAs now have a distinct pedagogical role, supporting and interacting with pupils, and this exceeds time assisting the teacher or the school.

Table 5.3 Deployment of TAs: systematic observations (frequencies and percentages)

	Primary		Secondary		Total	
Not working with pupils	n	%	n	%	n	%
Listening to the teacher teach	406	17.2%	352	23.7%	758	19.7%
Talking to the teacher	109	4.6%	55	3.7%	164	4.3%
Preparing/tidying materials	304	12.9%	62	4.2%	366	9.5%
Marking	16	0.7%	6	0.4%	22	0.6%
Other non-pupil-based activity	65	2.8%	13	0.9%	78	2%
Total not working with pupils	900	38.2%	488	32.9%	1,388	36.1%
Working with pupils						
Working with individual pupil	589	25%	532	35.8%	1,121	29.2%
Working with a group	509	21.6%	71	4.8%	580	15.1%
Walking ('roving') whole class	220	9.3%	375	25.2%	595	15.5%
Teaching part class	4	0.2%	0	0%	4	0.1%
Teaching whole class	52	2.2%	1	0.1%	53	1.4%
Other pupil-based activity	81	3.4%	20	1.3%	101	2.6%
Total working with pupils	1,455	61.8%	999	67.1%	3,842	63.9%
Total	2,355	100.0%	1,487	100.0%	5,230	100.0%

Note: It was possible for more than one activity to be coded in any one observation (because it covered 10 observations and activities could change).

5.2.3.2 The contexts of TA support for pupils: structured observations

In Strand 2 Wave 2 of the DISS study, the systematic observations were replaced with structured observations. To give a systematic account of TAs at work, each observation period of the shadowing day (e.g. one lesson) was divided into five minute blocks. During each interval, the predominant activities of the adults under observation (teacher and TA) were recorded, along with the context (e.g. working with an individual or group; leading whole class, or roving) and the location (in class, withdrawal within class, or out of class). The level of task differentiation was also noted: whether it was the same task, the same task differentiated or a completely different task to that undertaken by the majority of the class (these results are shown later in this chapter). Additional data on pupil attainment was also collected.

In total, there were over 1,500 observations made in 140 lessons and TA-led sessions, both in and away from mainstream classes. Data were collected in eighteen schools (nine primary and nine secondary). TAs were the focus of the observations, but the teacher's behaviour was also coded. We prioritised observations of TAs working with Years 5 and 10, but as expected, some TAs worked across the school with other year groups, and these observations are also included.

Table 5.4 Classroom contexts for support provided by TAs and teachers: structured observations

Context	Primary		Secondary	
	Teacher	*TA*	*Teacher*	*TA*
One-to-one	2%	19%	11%	63%
Small group (2–5 pupils)	6%	41%	7%	17%
Medium group (6–10 pupils)	2%	21%	1%	1%
Large group (11+ pupils)	0%	5%	0%	0%
Roving the classroom	23%	7%	28%	19%
Leading whole class	67%	7%	52%	0%
Total	100% (n=382)	100% (n=308)	100% (n=402)	100% (n=375)

Note: Combines data for TA observations in and out of classroom.

A main set of results concerned the contexts within which pupil support was given. Table 5.4 sets out the six contexts coded and shows data for teachers and TAs separately, in primary and secondary classes. The results show that the contexts in which teachers worked were fairly similar at primary and secondary level. For the most part they were either leading the whole class (67 per cent at primary and 52 per cent at secondary) or 'roving' the class, helping pupils as they went (23 per cent at primary and 28 per cent at secondary). In contrast TAs tended to support pupils in one-to-one, small group or medium group contexts (81 per cent for both primary and secondary). Primary and secondary TAs differed in that primary TAs tended to support small groups (41 per cent), while secondary TAs tended to support individual pupils (63 per cent).

The data in Table 5.4 combine observations of TAs working with pupils both in and out of the classroom (supported pupils spent roughly two-thirds of their time in the classroom, and one-third away from it). When looked at separately, the findings expose an even greater contrast in primary and secondary TA deployment. When away from the classroom, primary TAs worked far more with groups (73 per cent) than with individuals (19 per cent). The reverse was true for secondary TAs: they worked with pupils one-to-one (72 per cent) more than with groups (22 per cent).

These data from the structured observations largely replicated results from the systematic observations (shown in Table 5.3), even though the two forms of data were different in a number of ways. The results, therefore, lead to another key finding: teachers' interactions with pupils are weighted towards the whole class level, whilst the TAs tend to work more often with individuals or groups. Supporting individual pupils is most marked at secondary level, and supporting groups is most marked at primary level. This finding, which we portrayed in the vignette in Chapter 1, provides us with more detail in our description of the TAs' pedagogical role.

Perhaps the most obvious point to emerge is that the deployment of TAs with individuals or small groups, so allowing the teacher to work with the rest of the class, has become the routine 'default' way of using TAs. This is also illustrated in the vignette.

5.2.4 Which pupils are supported by TAs?

As mentioned previously, another and more detailed source of data about TA deployment was through the systematic observations of pupils. These focused on the pupil and were therefore different to the structured observations, which focused on adults, and also different to the results already presented from a different component of the systematic observation results, which also focused on the TA rather than the pupils. These pupil-focused observations were made in English, mathematics and science lessons. A total of 683 pupils were observed in 88 classes, across 4 year groups (Years 1, 3, 7 and 10); 49 schools were involved in the study. As we saw in Chapter 1, the total number of observations, on which our findings are based, was 34,420 – a very sizeable data set. Each individual observation of a pupil took place in a ten-second time interval, and each of the sample of pupils in a class were observed in turn. Eight pupils were selected from three groups: non-SEN; School Action; and School Action Plus/SEN statemented (referred to here as 'SEN').

We provide a full and more technical coverage of the results from the systematic observation results in Blatchford *et al.* (2009). Here we summarise results to show the extent to which the three groups of pupils interacted with teachers and TAs. The figures in Table 5.5 show that teachers tended to concentrate on pupils without SEN (55 per cent of all observations involving the teacher), while pupils with SEN, in comparison to the other groups, had more interactions with TAs (41 per cent of all observations involving TAs). The results in Table 5.5 clearly show that TA interactions with pupils increase, and teacher interactions decrease, with rising levels of pupil need.

We also approached this issue (i.e. which pupils are supported by teachers and TAs) through the structured observations. There was a slightly different way of coding which pupils were supported. For each five minute observation period, the attainment level of the pupils each adult worked with was noted. Information on pupil attainment was provided by either the teacher or the TA, and in line with school records, such as the SEN register. For the purposes of this analysis, information on the type of pupil supported by TAs was broadly divided into three groups: high/middle attainment; low attainment and pupils with SEN; and mixed attainment. These data provide one of the most striking results from the study. The vast majority of in-class TA support was for low attaining pupils and pupils with SEN (74 per cent overall), with this being more common in secondary schools (87 per cent) than in primary schools (61 per cent). TA support was provided for mixed ability groups in 39 per cent of observations at primary, and only 11 per cent at secondary. TA support for high and middle ability pupils was almost non-existent (less than 1 per cent of observations) at both primary and secondary level.

Table 5.5 Which pupils are supported by teachers and TAs?

	Non-SEN	School Action	School Action Plus and SEN statemented	Total (n)
Teachers	55%	24%	21%	100% (15,845)
TAs	27%	32%	41%	100% (2,363)

5.2.5 Differences in pupil role with teachers and TAs: systematic observations

One of the main aims of the systematic observations was to provide a systematic and objective description of the pupil's role and activity when interacting with teachers and TAs.

5.2.5.1 Adult attention: 'audience' versus 'focus' modes

One part of the systematic observation system noted the pupil's role in the interaction; that is, whether the pupil was in 'audience' mode (i.e. listening to the adult address all the pupils or another pupil, whether in a group or whole class context), or in 'focus' mode (i.e. the focus of an adult's attention, whether on a one-to-one basis, or when singled out as part of a larger group or class). 'Focus' mode was further divided into whether the interaction was short (less than, or up to, ten seconds) or 'long' (over ten seconds in length).

We look first at the overall frequencies and percentages of each behaviour (the column to the right of Table 5.6). As seen in Table 5.6, when in interaction with an adult (teacher or TA), pupils were much more likely to be in 'audience' mode (82 per cent) rather than the focus of attention (focus short + focus long = 15 per cent). When they were the focus of attention, this was more likely to be 'long' than 'short'; that is, sustained for the length of the ten second time interval, as opposed to a brief occurrence no longer than ten seconds (focus short 7 per cent, focus long 9 per cent). These results paint a general picture of the degree to which pupils in these schools occupy a generally passive role in classrooms, to a large extent sitting and listening to their teachers.

5.2.5.2 Differences between teachers and TAs

The important results from Table 5.6 concern the marked differences in pupil interactions with teachers and TAs. Pupils were far more likely to be the focus of attention of TAs compared with teachers. In 19 per cent of interactions with TAs, they were coded as 'focus short', compared to 6 per cent for teachers. Moreover, 44 per cent of TA interactions were coded as 'focus long', compared to 5 per cent for teachers. This means that in nearly two-thirds of all interactions with TAs, pupils were the focus of their attention

Table 5.6 Pupil role in interaction with teachers and TAs

Pupil role	Teacher		TAs		Total	
	n	%	n	%	n	%
Focus short	106	5.6%	37	19.4%	143	6.8%
Focus long	95	5.0%	83	43.5%	178	8.5%
Audience	1,647	86.8%	69	36.0%	1,716	82.1%
Other	50	2.6%	2	1.0%	52	2.5%
Total	1,898	100.0%	191	100.0%	2,089	100.0%

(63 per cent), while pupils were the focus of attention in only 11 per cent of teacher-pupil interactions. Put another way, pupils were six times more likely to be the focus of attention of TAs compared to teachers.

Conversely, in the vast majority of pupil interactions with teachers (87 per cent), pupils were in 'audience' mode (i.e. listening to the teacher talk to all pupils in the class or group, or singling out another pupil). In contrast, in only a third of TA interactions with pupils (36 per cent) were pupils in audience mode. In short, with teachers, pupils are one of the crowd, while with TAs they get individual attention.

We then looked at differences between different types of pupils and found that pupils with SEN were more often the focus of attention, and these contacts tended to be sustained rather than short. Only in the case of the group of pupils without SEN did we find equal amounts of focus short and long (5 per cent and 5 per cent). Conversely, the group of pupils with SEN spent less time listening to the teacher talk to others ('audience' mode): 87 per cent for non-SEN; 80 per cent for School Action; and 70 per cent for the SEN (i.e. SEN statemented and School Action Plus) group.

We then brought the two separate sets of analyses together to see if there were any differences in interactions between type of adult and pupils, according to pupil need (i.e. whether the pupil was in the non-SEN, School Action or SEN group). We found that the three pupil groups differed in the extent to which they were the focus of attention from different adults. There were no differences in focus short with TAs, but we found that the amount of extended one-to-one contact (focus long) with TAs increased with level of pupil need, so that the SEN group had by far the most contact of this sort (as a proportion of TA interactions with pupils), and the non-SEN group the least (56 per cent, 34 per cent and 20 per cent for SEN, School Action and non-SEN groups respectively). Conversely, the pupils without SEN spent more time in audience mode with teachers (90 per cent, 86 per cent and 83 per cent for non-SEN, School Action and SEN groups respectively) but also, interestingly, more time in audience mode with TAs (59 per cent, 47 per cent and 27 per cent for non-SEN, School Action and SEN groups respectively). This last result suggests that the non-SEN pupils are more likely to be in groups within which TAs are focusing primarily on children designated as SEN or School Action.

Table 5.7 Pupil-to-teacher and pupil-to-TA interactions

	Teacher		TAs		Total	
	n	%	n	%	n	%
Active interactions						
Begins	47	2.5%	20	10.1%	67	3.2%
Responds	88	4.6%	30	15.2%	118	5.6%
Sustains	66	3.5%	74	37.4%	140	6.7%
Attend	1,425	74.8%	61	30.8%	1,486	70.7%
Not attending	244	12.8%	11	5.6%	255	12.1%
Other	35	1.8%	2	1.0%	37	1.8%
Total	1,905	100.0%	198	100.0%	2,103	100.0%

We then looked at the pupil role in interaction with adults. Our main interest was in the extent to which pupils were simply listening and attending, as opposed to having a more active role. We defined an active role as consisting of three categories of behaviour, shown in Table 5.7: 1) times when a pupil began an interaction by initiating a comment; 2) times when they responded to an adult; and 3) times when interactions were 'sustained' (i.e. they extended beyond a ten second time interval). As can be seen in Table 5.7, pupils' talk to teachers and TAs was very different. They tended to 'attend' far more to teachers (75 per cent versus 31 per cent with TAs). Conversely, they engaged in six times more active interaction with TAs (i.e. the total of 'begins', 'responds' and 'sustains'): 63 per cent, compared with 11 per cent for teachers. Sustained interaction was nine times more likely with TAs compared with teachers (37 per cent versus 4 per cent). Pupil interactions with TAs are therefore more active and longer than those with teachers.

Quite a bit of detail has been presented on TA and teacher interactions with pupils, and so let us summarise the main results. We have found from detailed moment-by-moment observations that pupils have very different types of contact with teachers and TAs. Pupils were six times more likely to be the focus of attention with TAs compared with teachers. Conversely, with teachers, pupils were more often in 'audience' mode; that is, listening to the teacher talk to all pupils in the class or group, or singling out another pupil. The main group of pupils without SEN interacted more with teachers, while the pupils with SEN and those on School Action spent more time interacting with TAs. The amount of individualised attention from TAs increased with the level of pupil need. Pupil interactions with TAs were also more active and more sustained, and it was the pupils with SEN who engaged in most of this kind of behaviour. These differences between TAs and teachers were portrayed in the vignette in Chapter 1.

As we noted earlier, on the face of it, this looks like an educationally sensible arrangement, in that pupils in most need get more individualised attention with an adult and are more active in these interactions. However, the crucial point to make is that we also found in the systematic observation results, shown in Chapter 2, that the amount of contact with teachers tended to decline when TAs were present. At secondary level, teacher interaction with individual pupils is almost halved, and pupil active interaction with the teacher (begins, responds and sustains) is also nearly halved. So pupils tend to miss out on everyday teacher-to-pupil interactions by being supported by TAs. It therefore seems that pupils in most need get more contact with TAs at the expense of interactions with teachers – which is clearly not a good arrangement for these pupils. It is worth repeating our conclusion that interactions between TAs and pupils are an *alternative,* rather than an *additional,* form of pedagogical support to that provided by teachers.

5.3 Separation from teachers and the curriculum

In this section we extend the analysis of the separation of pupils by drawing on data from the case studies. The effect of established models of TA deployment – working in place of teachers and delivering intervention sessions – is that pupils can be cut off from their teachers, the curriculum and their peers. This separation could occur in different ways: from intermittent diversion from teacher talk, when a pupil repeatedly switches between being part of the whole-class audience and having private interaction with the TA; through task or curriculum separation, where a pupil carries out tasks in different subjects altogether; to physical separation, where a pupil can be removed from the classroom and his/her classmates.

5.3.1 Separation in curriculum coverage and planning

Case study visits showed that pupils who receive among the highest levels of TA support can be withdrawn from classes for TA-led literacy or numeracy interventions, 'catch up'/personal study sessions, or pastoral-type support, all of which reduce the amount of teacher-led learning they receive each week. Many pupils classified as having difficulties with learning took part in at least one TA-led intervention strategy per week, and these typically ran more than once a week. Pupils in secondary schools in particular were often withdrawn from non-core subjects to work on their basic literacy and numeracy skills. The structured observations showed that 17 per cent of observations in each phase related to TAs supporting or leading intervention programmes for low attaining pupils and those with SEN. In almost all of these cases, the sessions were held away from the classroom (92 per cent in primary; 90 per cent in secondary), and without a teacher present (99 per cent in primary; 90 per cent in secondary).

The structured observations also showed a high degree of differentiation in the tasks of supported pupils when being supported out of the classroom by TAs. Researchers noted whether the 'physical task' through which TAs were assisting pupils (e.g. a worksheet) was the same as, differentiated from or completely different from the task the majority of the class were undertaking. Almost all the pupils supported out of the classroom were low attainers/had SEN (94 per cent of instances). At primary level, 61 per cent of pupils worked on a different task, and 21 per cent worked on a related but differentiated task. At secondary level, 87 per cent of pupils worked on a different task (there were no instances of pupils working on related but differentiated tasks). As we have argued, although this is an understandable pedagogical strategy, the use of TAs in such ways has the effect of separating supported pupils from coverage of mainstream curriculum topics, as experienced by the rest of the class. The case studies revealed the potential difficulties regarding pupils' withdrawal from, and assimilation back into, lessons and connecting with class work, as might be expected from missing a sizeable part of a lesson. These risks are explained in more detail below.

The case studies also raised questions about the type of activities engaged in when working with a TA. Tasks that attend to pupils' stronger functions, or which are designed to build confidence by practising basic skills, can occur at the expense of tasks that can help pupils make more significant progress. TAs can be put into contexts where repetitive low-level tasks can be a feature of some sessions they lead. It was found that some teachers deliberately planned lower order tasks for cover lessons, and some science teachers postponed practical lessons as TAs or cover supervisors were not qualified or allowed to conduct experiments; so lessons consisted instead of book work or watching videos.

Teachers can rightly say that they have responsibility for curriculum planning for the whole class, but we have seen that in practice the planning and delivery for some pupil tasks can be delegated to TAs. This was seen in the vignette, where Mandy led a speech and language intervention away from the class.

It therefore seems appropriate to query how far teachers take effective responsibility for the curriculum and pedagogical planning for *all* pupils in the class. This would not necessarily mean involvement of teachers in direct face-to-face interactions; it might involve the use of pedagogical ideas separate from teacher input, for example, a consideration of ways in which pupils can be involved in collaborative work in mixed ability groups or peer learning or tutoring. Evidence from the case studies suggests that TA-supported pupils can be excluded from these approaches, especially in the core subjects.

5.3.2 The separation of TA-supported pupils from the teacher and curriculum

The case studies provided more detail on the separation of TA-supported pupils from teachers and the curriculum. Whilst there are clear advantages to localised and, very often, personalised support from TAs – and there is little doubt this has been a main part of inclusion policies in schools – there may be broader consequences in terms of pupil separation.

We have seen from the structured observations that primary and secondary school TAs spent around a third of their time supporting low attaining pupils and those with SEN in contexts away from the classroom and teacher. We have also seen from the structured observations that teachers spent the vast majority of their time working at the whole class level, while TA-pupil interactions took place on an individual or small group basis. It seemed that teachers' responsibility for the whole class, and the need to get through the curriculum, drove deployment decisions, resulting in TAs being in closer contact with pupils with learning and/or behavioural difficulties. As a consequence, there was a risk that the neediest pupils become detached from the teacher. Some teachers were aware of the tension that could result:

> As a teacher you can think, 'OK. You're my problem child; I'm going to focus on you' ... but then you've got 28 other kids who would progress even more if you gave them the attention ... Sometimes she [TA] doesn't work with either of those [pupils] and I will work with them, because they're quite draining, as you can imagine. But I think if she wasn't there, [the pupil] would have been away with the fairies.
>
> (Primary teacher)

One primary school teacher had given her TA the 'main responsibility for moving [SEN] children on'. With a large mixed ability class to manage, she felt that she had neither the 'time to plan as widely' for these children, nor could she 'afford to be going over number bonds when I need to be teaching the rest of them'. These pupils had daily literacy and numeracy sessions, away from the classroom, led by a TA, who had also been given monitoring and assessment duties.

> [TA is] teaching the basics and they come back to me and get the extras ... I just don't have time to go and sit down and analyse and do gap analysis of what they haven't learnt and stuff. I really rely on [the TA] and trust her and know that she'll be doing the right thing with them.
>
> (Primary teacher)

In line with results from the structured and systematic observations, it was noticeable in case study observations how infrequently teachers interacted with pupils supported by

TAs. For example, when roving the class, teachers would not visit the area where pupils and TAs were working and, when they did, the duration of the interactions tended to be equal to or shorter than those they had with other, non TA-supported pupils.

Furthermore, when primary pupils were withdrawn by TAs, they often worked in an area just outside the classroom, yet in almost all such instances, the teacher did not leave the classroom to check on these pupils. One reason for this is understandable: teachers were not willing to leave the class unsupervised. Consequently, the pupils that required the greatest professional input received it the least.

Despite teachers' claims to the contrary, some TAs felt that vital information – for example, regarding progress and engagement in interventions – failed to feed in to teachers' wider curriculum planning and assessment, or be used to inform their interactions with TA-supported pupils in the classroom. As we saw in Chapter 4, many TAs had little opportunity to feed back such information or contribute to lesson planning, and this seems bound to affect teachers' lesson plans.

Observations in one secondary classroom, however, showed that the teacher was responsive to a situation where a pupil was not cooperating with the TA supporting him. The teacher made several timely interventions, giving the TA respite (she was beginning to show frustration) and the pupil necessary and sustained one-to-one attention. During these periods, the TA roved the classroom, making sure other pupils were on task and responding to their queries, in the same manner as the teacher. The result was an effective interchange of roles.

This practice of taking pupils out for TA-led interventions raises the important question concerning how and when these pupils caught up with the work they missed while away from the class. This is in a sense a cost that is not often factored into considerations of the value of interventions. Even on the rare occasions where pupils were given time to complete missed tasks, it was inevitably at the expense of missing something else. In one primary class, a pupil with SEN was absent from a non-core lesson whilst she caught up with work from a core lesson she had missed earlier in the day. One secondary school TA claimed that the onus was on the pupils to catch up.

> That's their responsibility then. [In] a lot of the classes, they don't [catch up].
>
> (Secondary TA)

A number of teachers and SENCos went even further, suggesting that separation in the form of out-of-class interventions should increase. One teacher felt that TAs were undervalued and that schools could get more out of them by deploying them to work with pupils away from the class.

> More independence; give them more independence. So like we have got – if you have got these classes of 30 plus – if you give the TAs the weak ones or the strong ones ... so we've got control of the classroom, and to have a TA taking out whichever end it is – top or bottom.
>
> (Primary teacher)

One result of the large degree of autonomy many TAs were given when working with pupils was that some were taking on greater responsibility for pupil assessment and marking. This was most evident in primary schools. Levels of responsibility ranged from ticking answers to simple maths questions in class, to assessing and reviewing pupil progress in intervention programmes – as we illustrated in the vignette. It is of concern that in some cases, this TA-administered marking and assessment seemed to go unchecked by teachers.

One TA in a primary school was responsible for all aspects of literacy and numeracy interventions for Year 5, which were held away from the classrooms. She worked solely out of class. She planned and delivered tasks, assessed progress and made decisions about how long pupils should spend learning particular concepts and when to move individuals on to the next level of a programme – as well as, she said, marking pupils' work 'just like a teacher would'. The TA was responsible for all recordkeeping and made notes after each session on each pupil's engagement, their success or difficulty with a task, and behaviour. Yet her notes, marking and assessment records, despite being accessible, were rarely viewed or referred to by the Year 5 teachers. As she reflected on this, she remarked that she 'could sit out there teaching French and no one would know!'

In contrast, one primary headteacher acknowledged the implications of allowing TAs with weak literacy skills to mark and assess, and had established a clear marking policy.

> With one assistant we've asked her not to put anything on the bottom … just to tick and to put their initials, but not to make a comment and not to think about the way forward. With one other assistant, we've asked them to make a comment about it. Now that's to do with things like spelling ability … They're not in a position to mark … [It's] about the abilities of different [people] … The roles are quite carefully boundaried … [TAs] are not asked to do anything above what they're able to.
>
> (Primary headteacher)

5.3.3 Other unintended consequences of separation

We finish this chapter by examining three other ways in which data from the case studies showed how the seemingly valuable role of TAs could in fact have unintended consequences.

5.3.3.1 Stereo teaching

One unintended effect of in-class TA-to-pupil interaction extends findings already identified concerning the way in which pupils could be cut off from the teacher even when the supported pupil was in the classroom. TAs often provided additional explanatory information in order to help supported pupils understand the teacher's explanations or instructions given to the whole class during their main teaching input. This was somewhat more the case in primary schools, where the TA often sits next to a pupil during the teacher input; in secondary schools, the TA was often situated at the side of the room during this part of the lesson, possibly in order to minimise the stigmatising effects of TA support (more on this follows).

During the teacher's delivery to the whole class, the intermittent talk from the TA to the pupil effectively separated the pupil from the teacher; in such instances, the pupil was in effect hearing the voices of two adults talking simultaneously, very often about the same thing. Hence we labelled this phenomenon 'stereo teaching'.

You're teaching and the TA needs to be … speaking to the child when you are teaching – sort of re-emphasising or behaviour management – really quietly so it doesn't interfere with the lesson. That's really good; that's skilled.

(Primary teacher)

As the teacher in the comment above suggests – and as our own observations confirmed – this additional talk from TAs to supported pupils does not typically interfere with the lesson flow. However, from the pupil's point of view, it does interrupt their receipt of teacher talk and potentially put them in conflict about which voice to listen to.

Consistent with our observation findings, it is the pupils who may already experience difficulty with concentration who experience stereo teaching most often and are therefore most at risk from its detrimental effects; teacher delivery is broken up with repetition and prompts from TAs, the value of which is questionable.

There are ways in which, for example, prompts from TAs are useful in bringing the pupil's focus back to the teacher when it is clear that their concentration has wandered. However, TAs appeared to be somewhat automatic in their talk to pupils in the whole class delivery context; that is, what they said was not particularly helpful or well timed. Here is one recurring example: when the teacher asks a question to the whole class, she allows a short period of thinking time before inviting answers; yet TA-supported pupils are often denied this time. Once the teacher has finished talking, the TA often turns immediately to the pupil and asks them, 'What do you think?', pressing the pupil to give an instant response. We speculate that one reason why TAs act in this way is perhaps to unconsciously compensate for the protracted periods of inactivity where TAs are passive for the same times (and for the same reasons) as the pupils they support.

5.3.3.2 Dependency versus independence

It was recognised by staff interviewed in the case studies that great skill is needed to get the balance right between skilful support and pupil dependency, so that pupils can begin to work independently. This issue has been covered in previous studies (Moyles and Suschitsky 1997; Ofsted 2004a). The Strand 2 Wave 2 case study data suggest that pupils' dependency on TAs, and the practices that helped them to develop their identity as learners, was a greater issue in secondary schools, though still evident in primary schools.

Sometimes … you have to be careful, because where they need adult support, they get to rely on it. And sometimes they can do a bit by their self.

(Primary TA)

Dependency can lead to pupils taking fewer risks with their work. In observations, it was noticeable that pupils could repeatedly seek validation from the TA. In many instances, they appeared to refer to the TA simply because she was close at hand.

He kind of has to look at me for reassurance: 'Am I right here in what I'm saying?' And I say, 'Yes. Just put your hand up'. You have to do that with him.

(Secondary TA)

Some TAs described the effects of dependency, although it is worth noting that dependency does not necessarily imply learned helplessness or laziness, and may instead reflect genuine need.

> A lot of them can do what they do out there with me fine [intervention work away from the class], and they get into a test and they can't do it.
>
> (Primary TA)

> [X's] reading levels are really, really poor. So by reading the questions I'm also picking out the information that he has to do. But in an exam, I can't do that ... So that makes it difficult for them in an exam ... If it says multiply and [X] says to me, 'What does multiply mean?' I can't tell him that. He should know.
>
> (Secondary TA)

The difficulty in finding the balance between providing the right type and amount of TA support, without nurturing dependence, was recognised by far fewer teachers than TAs. Some teachers recognised the issue of pupil dependency, but were uncertain about how to plan work that prevented this or fostered independence. This meant that TAs were left to arrive at their own judgements about when and how often they should withdraw from the pupil, to let them get on with a task.

> There is a fine line between giving help and actually doing the work for them, which some of the students will try ... [TA's role] is to get them to work by themselves.
>
> (Secondary TA)

> The advantage for the pupil is that the pressure is taken off. They know that if they miss a little bit [of teacher talk]... he can then ask, 'I don't understand any more', and then you can tell him. So the pupil then gets reliant on you ... That's up to you to be able to stop the dependency ... I don't sit with just one ... If they've started work and I know they understand what they're doing, I'll just get myself up and I'll go and sit next to [X], or I'll go and sit next to [Y]. Although they know you're still in the class, or you're still in a safety zone, it still promotes independence.
>
> (Secondary TA)

TAs made what they referred to as 'on the hoof' decisions about when and how to intervene. The need to provide support had to be carefully balanced against practices that took the task away from the pupil or allowed them to disengage. Some TAs were alive to opportunities that let them speak less or to physically withdraw, and therefore allow pupils to work independently.

5.3.3.3 Stigma

TAs described how some of the pupils they supported felt that there was a stigma attached to having TA support. It is therefore worth noting that TAs' decisions to withdraw from these pupils were at times influenced by this factor.

> You try to be as invisible as possible in the class, if the child warrants that. But again, with someone like [X], you can't stick to one particular child because it has

an adverse effect on their behaviour anyway. If you are helping a group it makes it easier for him to interact with the other children as well ... Because he doesn't want to be different from his peers, and if I am sitting there next to him, it's as if he's got a minder and the children don't like that.

(Secondary TA)

This possible negative reaction to being supported by a TA seems to increase as pupils get older. Primary pupils generally liked the TA's support and even preferred it to that of the teacher. The youngest pupils did not distinguish between the roles of the adults in their class: both were perceived as 'teachers'. But secondary pupils began to question the quality of the TA support (e.g. because TAs were not qualified in the particular subject), in addition to the way in which they felt support would be perceived by their peers. We feel that more systematic research is needed on the effects of TA support on the supported pupils' relationships with other pupils.

5.4 Conclusions

We started this chapter by asking the question, 'What do TAs do?' We showed that despite the common view that they support the teacher by taking on routine tasks and supporting the curriculum, there are a number of contentious issues. On the basis of the case studies, we identified issues connected to role clarity and autonomy, distinguishing between terms like 'teaching', 'support' and 'supervision', ambiguity over responsibilities, and problems of role creep and professional identity. We showed the degree to which schools had formal written policies on TA deployment, and how their deployment seemed largely pragmatic.

We found that teachers had experienced much more contact with support staff as a whole in Strand 1 Wave 3, compared to Wave 1. In a sign of the growing presence of support staff in schools, there were noticeable increases in the contact that teachers had with non-classroom support staff (e.g. pupil welfare staff, technicians, other pupil support staff, facilities staff, administrative staff and site staff). Primary school TAs already had, at Strand 1 Wave 1, by far the most contact with teachers, and so there was little room for increase in subsequent waves. However, contact between TAs and teachers in secondary schools increased noticeably between Wave 1 and Wave 3 of Strand 1.

The work pattern diary data showed that, in contrast to other categories of support staff, TAs spent by far the greatest amount of time on direct learning support for pupils, and this exceeded work directly supporting the teacher.

We described the general picture of the TA role that emerged from the case study visits. The most obvious thing to emerge was that the deployment of TAs with individuals or small groups – so allowing the teacher to work with the rest of the class – had become the routine default form of deployment in schools. This has become an essential part of the teaching and learning process in schools, and is seen to have a beneficial role. Many teachers felt that the presence of a TA in the classroom allowed them to meet the needs of pupils with difficulties, and the policy of inclusion, whilst they could focus on the majority of the class.

The most reliable results came from the systematic and structured observations, because they recorded on a moment-by-moment basis how TAs were deployed, and made use of a carefully constructed coding frame. There were two key results: first, primary school

TAs supported small groups, while secondary TAs supported individual pupils; and, second, in the vast majority of cases, TAs supported low attaining pupils and pupils with SEN. This was even more evident when TAs worked with pupils out of the classroom. TAs rarely worked with high and middle attaining pupils.

The systematic observation study allowed a more precise measure of the type of contact between TAs and pupils. Pupils were six times more likely to be the focus of attention with TAs, compared to teachers. Conversely, with teachers, pupils were more often in 'audience' mode, (that is, listening to the teacher talk to all pupils in the class or group, or singling out another pupil). The main group of pupils without SEN interacted more with teachers, while the amount of individualised attention from TAs increased with the level of pupil need. Pupil interactions with TAs were also more active and more sustained, and this also increased for pupils with SEN.

Overall, then, we have found from detailed moment-by-moment observations that pupils have very different types of contact with teachers and TAs. With teachers, they are more likely to be one of a crowd, and this applied particularly to the non-SEN group; while with TAs, they tended to be the main focus of attention, and have more active and sustained interactions with them, and this applied particularly to pupils with higher levels of need.

The results from the observations and the case studies indicated that TA-supported pupils could experience two kinds of separation. The first was from the teacher. The delegation of the harder to teach pupils to TAs is well meaning, but one consequence is that such pupils tend to miss out on everyday mainstream teacher-to-pupil interactions. This can occur in the context of within class support and also occasions when TAs take pupils out of the classroom (e.g. for literacy catch up programmes). This is one reason why we argue that TAs do not so much provide *additional* support, as *alternative* support. This might be one reason why they do less well in terms of academic progress.

In some cases we found teachers deliberately spent less time with these pupils, handing over responsibility to the TA (though teachers would have had responsibility for the overall planning of a lesson). Overall, we query the way in which lower attaining children get less of the teacher's attention. Before teachers had TAs in the classroom, they would have had responsibility for all pupils, and quite likely provided further support for these pupils themselves. It would, therefore, seem appropriate to argue that *all* pupils should get at least the same amount of the teacher's time, and, indeed, that those in most need are most likely to benefit from more of her time, not less.

A second form of separation for TA-supported pupils is in terms of the curriculum. As shown above, TA-supported pupils spend less time in mainstream curriculum coverage, and coverage is interrupted. This may then have a negative effect on academic progress, particularly when couched in terms of tests and ratings of National Curriculum levels achieved, as in the DISS project. Ofsted (2006) have commented on how pupils with learning and behavioural difficulties can be deprived of access to a broad curriculum.

In this book we have queried whether the TA role is most appropriately described as 'indirect' or 'direct'. The evidence suggests that the two types of roles have become combined, in the sense that TAs have a valuable indirect role in supporting the children in most need – thus allowing teachers to spend more time teaching the rest of the class – but they also have a direct role with regard to the individual pupils and small groups that they support, through teaching them directly.

Given what we have revealed in this chapter about TA deployment, and the consequences of the most widespread forms of deployment, we can now add yet more detail
to the 'Wider Pedagogical Role' model. In Figure 5.1 we add the key findings from this
chapter on the deployment of TAs, and these provide more information likely to help
explain the negative impact of TA support, as reported in Chapter 2. For example, we
see can that a TA, such as Mandy, is unlikely to be fully effective if she is inadequately
prepared for tasks (see 'preparedness') and is routinely asked to 'teach' the pupils who
struggle most. In the next chapter, we complete our detailed picture of the TA role by
considering the final component of the WPR model – practice – by examining detailed
data on TA-to-pupil talk.

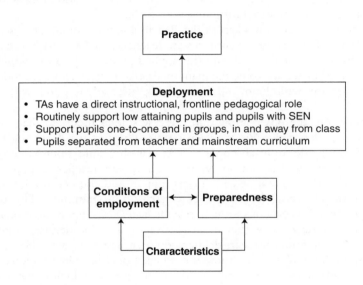

Figure 5.1 The Wider Pedagogical Role model with deployment

Key findings

The deployment of TAs

- Case studies showed that the appropriate type of role for TAs in classrooms was problematic, with issues concerning role clarity and 'role creep', and the appropriateness of TAs taking on teaching activities.
- TAs had a direct pedagogical role, supporting and interacting with pupils, and this exceeded time assisting the teacher or the school.
- TAs in primary schools tended to support children in small groups, while in secondary schools, they supported individual pupils. The vast majority of support provided by TAs, both in and out of the classroom, was for lower attaining pupils and those with SEN.
- With the teacher, pupils are more likely to be one of the crowd (particularly those pupils without SEN). With TAs, pupils are more likely to be the focus of their attention, and they have more active and more sustained interactions (particularly pupils classified as having SEN).
- The more contact pupils had with TAs, the less attention they had from teachers.
- Pupils supported by TAs can become separated from the teacher, and TAs can take on responsibility for tasks (notably learning interventions).
- TA-supported pupils can spend less time in coverage of mainstream curriculum topics, compared with the rest of the class, and coverage can be interrupted.
- Withdrawal from class, typically for TA-led literacy or numeracy interventions, can also reduce teacher-led learning.

Chapter 6

The practice of TAs[1]

In Chapter 5 we explored what TAs do. In this chapter we take this description further and provide a more fine-grained description of the 'practice' of TAs; that is, what TAs say to pupils. We use the generic term 'practice' in a pragmatic way to cover the classroom interactions of both TAs and teachers with pupils. We concentrate specifically on verbal interaction and the data in this chapter are drawn from transcripts of adult-to-pupil interactions. The audio recordings of these interactions were a unique component of the DISS study, in that they extend previous research by capturing the details of TA-to-pupil talk and comparing them with teacher-to-pupil talk.

6.1 Introduction

Study of adult-to-pupil interactions is important, because models of effective teaching, as well as a common-sense view, would see the interactions between educator and pupil as being at the heart of the pupil's educational experience and their learning. The interactions teachers have with their pupils, and the language they use, have long been recognised as playing an important role in pupil learning (Bakhtin 1981; Jones 2007; Nystrand 2006; Wilkinson and Silliman 2000). A key message of this book, however, is that, to date, little is known about the dialogue between TAs and pupils.

In line with Gage (1985), in this chapter we consider classroom interaction in terms of 'lecturing and tutoring [and] all other types of interactions, such as teacher pupil questioning, pupil responding and initiations, as well as pupil work at tables and desks, and the managerial activities that maintain the whole process'.

There have been numerous approaches to the study of teaching interactions, going back many decades (see Creemers 1994; Pellegrini and Blatchford 2000). There have been seminal studies that opened up a window on teaching and classroom interactions, for example, Dunkin and Biddle (1974), Galton *et al.* (1980) and Kounin (1970). These studies had very different conceptual and disciplinary roots, including psychology, sociology, sociolinguistics and ethnography.

There are inevitably different views on what constitutes effective teaching, not least because it will depend on more general views about education, but it is possible to identify a number of features from research. These studies were reviewed by Rubie-Davies *et al.* (2010) and their conclusions can be summed up as follows:

- Effective teachers manage pupil behaviour positively, mostly using statements designed to prevent disruptive behaviour.

- They spend time orientating pupils to lessons and making links to prior learning.
- New concepts are introduced by providing high levels of instructional talk and checking pupil understanding; and effective teachers ask far more questions that require pupils to reason and engage in higher level thinking.
- Effective teachers frequently provide pupils with feedback about their learning and encourage them to participate.
- They also spend time ensuring that pupils are motivated to learn, and that they are not just on-task but are cognitively engaged.
- For adult talk to actively promote pupil learning and conceptual understanding, effective teachers clearly articulate concepts and ideas, make links to prior learning, check to ensure pupils understand new concepts that have been presented, and hence skilfully scaffold pupil learning.

While much is therefore known about the ways in which teachers interact with pupils, and about the characteristics of effective teaching, little is known about the ways in which TAs interact with pupils and the effectiveness of their interactions. Do TAs, for example, interact in similar ways to teachers? This knowledge is vital, because as we have seen in Chapter 5, a major component of the TA role is to support pupils in their learning through interacting with them, often on an individual basis or in small groups. Furthermore, as we saw in Chapter 5, pupils, especially those with SEN and those with low attainment levels, are more likely to have one-to-one, extended interactions with TAs, compared to teachers. This opportunity for extended interaction between individual pupils and an adult might be expected to provide enhanced opportunities to learn, and we might therefore predict enhanced academic progress as a result. Puzzlingly, though, we found in Chapter 2 that TAs do not have a positive effect on pupils' educational progress. One answer to this might be revealed by close study of TA-to-pupil talk and the main aim of this chapter is therefore to better understand the impact of TAs on pupil learning by obtaining such a systematic picture of the nature of this talk, and to contrast it with that between teachers and pupils.

In the last chapter we looked at the deployment of TAs through the lens of structured and systematic observation methods. Though useful, as we have seen, these data are at a relatively general level, being expressed in terms of the frequencies of relatively broad categories of behaviour. In this chapter we explore the talk between TAs and pupils in more fine-grained detail, and in terms of its effectiveness.

We present results from two complementary approaches to the talk between TAs and pupils, and teachers and pupils. First, 'instructional talk analysis' was used to provide a general comparison of the talk of TAs and teachers in terms of everyday, educationally relevant interactions with pupils. The coding scheme was developed on the basis of research on effective teaching, as we describe shortly. Second, 'conversation analysis' – an even more closely textured approach – was used to explore in detail the ways in which teachers and TAs used language, and the effects of various strategies on learners. It was used to provide a sequential analysis of talk, including that of pupils. We present results from each type of approach in turn, and illustrate the results with extracts from the transcripts of teacher-to-pupil and TA-to-pupil talk.

6.2 Instructional talk analysis

We developed a system for coding teacher and TA talk based on research from the effective teaching literature, especially Berliner's model of effective teaching (1987). Berliner proposed that in order for pupils to learn, three components were important: cognitive engagement, sufficient time and success. These components contributed to what Berliner called 'Academic Learning Time'. Hence, effective organisation of materials and pupils and effective classroom management lead to pupils spending more time on learning. Careful explanation of concepts, links to prior knowledge, clearly stated learning objectives and questioning of pupils are teacher practices designed to contribute to pupils' cognitive engagement. Prompting pupils, responding supportively to pupils' answers to questions and providing feedback about learning are all designed to enhance pupil success. Hence, the broad approach of Berliner's theory of effective teaching provided us with a framework for developing categories for coding teacher and TA talk. The unit of interest in this analysis was the teacher and TA 'utterance' (a segment of talk) to pupils.

6.2.1 Method

6.2.1.1 Data collection: audio recordings

Data on TA–pupil interactions were collected in 2007–2008 as part of the Strand 2 Wave 2 case studies. In a sub-sample of 15 schools (8 primary, 7 secondary), a total of 130 lesson length recordings of teacher and TA talk were made, of which 42 were made simultaneously in the same classroom. The main analyses presented in this chapter were conducted on pairs of teacher-to-pupil and TA-to-pupil talk in the same lessons. In order to make the classroom conditions as similar as possible, we also restricted the analysis to lessons in English and mathematics, and to situations where TAs were in the classroom with the teacher (the structured observations showed that TAs spent most of their time in this way). This resulted in a sample of 16 lesson length transcriptions of teacher-to-pupil talk and 16 lesson length transcriptions of TA-to-pupil talk. The results below reflect what we now know from Chapter 5 is the usual classroom context; that is, the teacher working with the whole class and the TA interacting with a small group or an individual.

The audio-recordings were transcribed and then coded. A coding frame was developed to capture all interactions of teachers and TAs with pupils. We wanted to describe talk at the individual utterance level, with a level of categorisation that allowed units meaningful in terms of educational and linguistic form, and frequent enough to be subjected to numerical analysis. We drew on informal and systematic observations from the DISS project and, as described above, Berliner's model of effective teaching. Through an iterative process in which emerging drafts of the coding framework were tried out on the transcripts, and then discussed to sort out differences of interpretation, the final coding framework used here was developed. The coding process was checked for inter-observer agreement, which proved satisfactory (74 per cent).

Each lesson transcript for teachers and TAs was divided into separate utterances and appropriate codes applied. Lengths of utterances varied from single lines to extended sequences of teacher talk to pupils. There were 14 codes altogether, and a summary of these is given in Table 6.1. This covers results for both primary and secondary. They are put together as the number of transcripts in each separately was not large and preliminary analysis did not suggest significant differences between the two phases.

Table 6.1 Comparison of teacher and TA talk level codes

Outcome	Teacher		TA		Teacher and TA significantly different?
	Frequency	Mean%	Frequency	Mean%	
1a. Organisation of pupils	683	16	302	15	
1b. Organisation of materials	75	2	13	1	Close (p=0.06)
2a. Explanation of concept	421	7	116	4	Yes
2b. Statements as prompts	254	4	339	16	Yes
3a. Types of questions	912	16	542	24	Yes
3b. Response to pupil answers	541	9	222	7	
4a. Feedback is about learning/task completion	275	5	84	3	Yes
4b. Use of praise/rewards/criticism	272	5	99	4	
5a. Behaviour management: preventive	53	1.1	10	0.4	
5b. Behaviour management: reactive	347	7	60	5	
6a. Introduction to lesson focus	69	1.5	2	0.1	Yes
6b. Linking to prior learning/future learning/prior knowledge	130	3	23	1	Yes
7a. Motivation/engagement: cognitive focus	409	8	63	3	Yes
7b. Motivation/engagement: task focus	785	15	420	15	
Total	5,226		2,295		

There were a large number of utterances coded: teachers had 5,226 and TAs 2,295 (it was possible for more than one code to be applied to an utterance, so frequencies exceed the number of utterances). Comparisons of frequencies of each code for teachers and TAs are, to a degree, misleading, because differences might simply reflect the fact that teachers speak more than twice as much as TAs overall. To address this, the frequency of each type of talk, relative to the total number of codes, for each lesson and for each adult, was also calculated and these average percentage scores as well as basic frequencies of occurrence are presented in Table 6.1.

6.2.2 Results

The results indicated a statistically significant difference between teachers and TAs for seven of the codes in Table 6.1. Teachers tended to engage in proportionately more explanation of concepts (2a), feedback about learning/task completion (4a), introduction to lesson objective/focus (6a), links to previous/future lesson/prior knowledge (6b), and promoting engagement/motivation: cognitive focus (7a). Conversely, TAs engaged in proportionately more statements as prompts (2b), and types of questions (3a). We now look in more detail at differences between teachers' and TAs' talk to pupils in the seven categories where there were differences between teachers and TAs.

Within each talk level category, there were a number of qualitatively different kinds of behaviours; for example, different types of explanation, statements and questions. These were often as revealing as the overall frequency of occurrence, and we refer to these below, along with numerical information and illustrative extracts from the transcripts. All pupil names are fictitious.

6.2.2.1 Language use: concepts

6.2.2.1.1 EXPLAINING CONCEPTS (2A)

Teachers spent proportionately more time explaining concepts than did TAs (7 per cent versus 4 per cent). Overall, teachers were able to adjust explanations to the pupil level, and explain and re-explain concepts so they were at a suitable level for pupils. Generally, explanations were clear and designed to assist and develop pupil thinking.

> Seven times three is 21, 0.2 times three is 0.6. 0.01, because that 1 is one hundredth times three, is 0.03 – giving an answer of 21.63.
>
> (Teacher)

On the other hand, explanations by TAs were less common. They generally appeared more concerned with completing tasks than with developing understanding. There were several instances in which there was no concept development, or explanation throughout the lesson. Sometimes the explanations were incorrect. Of the 16 lessons involving TAs analysed in this study, there were nine in which the TAs explained concepts to pupils; of these nine lessons there were five in which at least some of the concept explanations were inaccurate (as we will see in more detail in the section on conversation analysis) or confusing for pupils. We used an actual example from the transcript dataset in the vignette in Chapter 1: Mandy's misunderstanding of the difference between a whole number and a rounded number.

6.2.2.1.2 STATEMENTS AS PROMPTS (2B)

TAs were significantly more likely than teachers to provide pupils with prompts (16 per cent versus 4 per cent). The structure of teacher and TA prompts differed. Prompts from teachers were mostly designed to enhance pupil thinking; for example:

> When you're deciding on the genre quite often they are mixed. But you've got to think which one is the main one.
>
> (Teacher)

In contrast, prompts from TAs frequently supplied pupils with the answer. This meant that the TAs were, in a sense, doing the work for the pupils, and pupils did not therefore need to engage in thinking. At times, TAs asked pupils to engage in thinking, but would then supply pupils with an answer; for example:

You need to explain what that phrase is telling you, Veronica. Does it make you feel that she's angry for him, or she's upset for him, or …? Use whatever word you feel. You need to say that Grace Nichols feels upset … because she's upset because he's now living in London.

(TA)

Overall, of 254 prompts by teachers, there were 29 (11 per cent) in which the teacher supplied the pupils with the answer, whereas for TAs, of 339 prompts, 208 (61 per cent) provided pupils with the answer; only 131 encouraged pupil independence and thinking. Where pupil thinking was not encouraged as part of the prompt, the TAs supplied pupils with answers, told them what to write for answers, provided them with ideas, wrote answers for them, read out questions and/or spelled words out for pupils, without encouraging independence. On the other hand, teachers tended to supply answers having previously provided prompts that had not led to a suitable pupil response.

6.2.2.2 Language use: questions

6.2.2.2.1 TYPES OF QUESTIONS (3A)

This was the single most frequent type of talk for teachers and TAs, though there were proportionately more of these from TAs compared to teachers (24 per cent versus 16 per cent). Closed questions were the most common form of questions used by both groups. However, whereas teachers used both open and closed questions, TAs almost exclusively asked closed questions of their pupils. Of the 542 questions asked by TAs, only 37 were open questions (7 per cent), whereas of the 912 questions asked by teachers, 194 were open (21 per cent). It was rare for teachers to supply pupils with answers to questions. Generally teachers would re-phrase questions, or provide additional information, so that pupils did the thinking and could answer the questions; for example:

> Why is it a square? … why do we say that's a square and that's not a square? That's a rectangle – OK? It's got four sides – but it's not a square, it's called a rectangle. Now – can you tell me why that's called a square and that's called a rectangle? What's different? What do you see different?

(Teacher)

In contrast, TAs often asked pupils a question and then answered it for them:

> OK – what are we up to? This one – 111 – a hundred and eleven. So the nearest ten would be …? No, no – that's hundreds. A hundred and eleven. Just take off the hundred and look at the eleven – so what number are you going to take it to? … Ten, isn't it? … If you've got to take it to the nearest ten – you've got ten or twenty. Eleven is closer to ten, isn't it? … So it's a hundred and ten. Yes?

(TA)

Teachers often used questions to check a pupil's understanding of a concept or an idea, whereas when TAs checked pupil understanding, they tended to simply ask pupils directly whether they understood without probing further. In the next extract, for example, when checking pupil understanding of facts, the teacher asks the question at the end of the sequence to confirm pupil knowledge. Questions such as this were common with teachers when checking pupil understanding.

> So some people think it has to be just a single digit because it stands on its own, and you think it can't be a single digit. So why do you think that? What's your reasoning behind that?
>
> (Teacher)

Conversely, the example below shows a TA providing an explanation for rounding off numbers; she then simply asks if the pupil understands, and when the pupil indicates she does, the TA moves on to something else. In the case of the TA below, this happened repeatedly during the lesson until the TA expressed frustration at the child saying they understood when they clearly did not.

> It's four hundred – because that's below five, isn't it – the thirty-two? Like three is below five – so it would be one thousand, four hundred, wouldn't it? Do you understand that?
>
> (TA)

6.2.2.3 Feedback

6.2.2.3.1 FEEDBACK ABOUT LEARNING OR TASK COMPLETION (4A)

Teachers tended to provide more of this kind of talk than TAs (5 per cent versus 3 per cent). All teachers provided pupils with feedback, whereas only 11 TAs did so. Moreover, teachers provided pupils with feedback about their learning more frequently than they did about the task or pupil behaviour and, with the exception of one teacher, all provided several instances of feedback about learning in each lesson. For example:

> When marking your stories, your genres, I was really pleased. I looked at them and I think probably just about everybody had views on the genre they were writing. Some of you need to be really careful because the comedy genres – some of them were getting a bit on the nonsense, silly side; so you've got to think about how you can use comedy without being silly and writing nonsense.
>
> (Teacher)

However, fewer instances of feedback related to learning could be found for TAs (four TAs provided at least one instance). More frequently, feedback from TAs related to task completion, for example:

> Try not to do it so fast and you might do it a bit neater. [And later] Oh, that's looking super now.
>
> (TA)

The balance of feedback related to learning and feedback related to task completion was similar for teachers and TAs, but larger for teachers. Overall, of the total 275 instances of feedback by teachers, 192 (70 per cent) statements were feedback related to pupil learning, and 83 (30 per cent) were in connection with either task completion or task-related pupil behaviour. In contrast, of the total 84 feedback statements by TAs, 54 (64 per cent) concerned pupil learning, while 30 (36 per cent) were related to task completion or task-related behaviour.

6.2.2.4 Orientation

6.2.2.4.1 INTRODUCTION TO THE LESSON OBJECTIVE/FOCUS (6A)

Introducing the lesson or ensuring pupils were aware of the lesson objective or focus did not make up a major proportion of any lesson. However, there were clear differences between teachers and TAs. Whereas 13 teachers at some stage during the lesson informed pupils of the focus, no TA did this.

There was one example of a response by a TA who was asked by a pupil what they would be learning. Her reply shows she was unsure of the lesson objective; instead she focused on a task the pupils would complete. This was the only instance of TA talk referring to lesson focus.

> I don't know what we're doing today. I know we're going to start with a game on the board. So that will be quite good.
>
> (TA)

6.2.2.4.2 LINKS TO PRIOR KNOWLEDGE/PREVIOUS LESSONS/FUTURE LEARNING (6B)

Although relatively infrequent, teachers engaged in proportionately more of this type of talk than TAs (3 per cent versus 1 per cent). Without exception, all 16 teachers linked the current lesson to knowledge they knew pupils already possessed, to previous lessons (usually the previous day or week), or to future learning, (i.e. teachers explained why the pupils were going to learn about a particular concept or topic). Some TAs (9) did make similar links, but their statements were in relation to prior learning (at times within-lesson links) or on completing work for a forthcoming examination. Typical teacher and TA statements are below:

> Remember last lesson. What did we make last lesson? We were building, weren't we? Well we need to be able to do these (two-dimensional shapes) so we can construct accurately.
>
> (Teacher)

> What did we say 25 per cent was yesterday? When we was doing fractions?
>
> (TA)

6.2.2.5 Promoting engagement and/or motivation

6.2.2.5.1 PROMOTING COGNITIVE ENGAGEMENT (7A)

Teachers also engaged in more of this type of talk than TAs (8 per cent versus 3 per cent). Teachers frequently attempted to promote pupil thinking and cognitive engagement. While ten TAs did try to foster pupil thinking, this was a much less common practice than it was for teachers. Many teachers made reference to encouraging pupil thinking, for example:

> You need to go back and you need to think about the words that you can use in your story. They need to be creative words; they need to be fairly important, significant words. Words like when we discussed symbolism – that make up layers of meaning.
>
> (Teacher)

Here is an example of a TA enhancing pupil learning:

> When the problem arises, how are you going to solve the problem? You've got to think about how the problem will be solved and then what happens at the end. A good ending to your story, OK?
>
> (TA)

6.2.3 Discussion of instructional talk analysis

A major finding, which we prefigured in our vignette in Chapter 1, was that the interactions of teachers and TAs with pupils were both quantitatively and qualitatively different in several areas. At a general level, we found that teachers had a formal style of delivery, while TAs were more informal, chatty and more likely to use colloquial language with pupils. Both teachers and TAs were usually relaxed and positive with pupils, but some TAs were very informal and familiar with pupils, and TAs often provided pupils with answers and completed work for them. In terms of talk more obviously directed at pupil learning, teachers spent more time explaining concepts than TAs, and TAs' explanations were sometimes inaccurate or confusing. Teachers used prompts and questions to encourage thinking and check understanding, while TAs more frequently supplied pupils with answers. Teachers tended to use feedback to encourage learning, while TAs were more often concerned with task completion. There were differences as well in dealing with the purpose of lesson talk: teachers, but not TAs, informed pupils about the focus of the lesson. Teachers, more than TAs, linked the current lesson to pupil prior knowledge, and attempted to promote pupil thinking and cognitive engagement in a task, while more TA talk was about task and non-task matters.

Evidence from the transcripts, therefore, suggests that teachers were more likely than TAs to show aspects of effective teaching in their talk, as described above (that is, talk requiring pupils to reason and engage in higher level thinking, and providing pupils with feedback about their learning and encouraging them to participate). In terms of Berliner's model of effective teaching (1987), teachers were more likely to encourage pupils' cognitive engagement. Teachers more often used talk to cognitively challenge pupils (Alexander 2006) through the questions they asked and the prompts they used.

The instructional talk analysis, therefore, identified two overarching differences between teachers and TAs in their interactions with pupils: first, teachers were more focused on learning and understanding, while TAs focused on completing tasks; and, second, teachers appeared proactive and in control of lessons, while TAs were in a more reactive role – probably, as we saw in Chapter 4, because they had little time to prepare for, or input into, the lesson. Again, we demonstrated this in our vignette.

6.2.3.1 Contextual factors

One obvious factor to be considered when comparing teacher and TA talk to pupils is the extent to which the contexts within which the talk takes place are equivalent. As we have seen, for the most part, teacher talk to pupils was in whole class or large group contexts, whilst talk between TAs and pupils was often in a small group or an individual basis. There is a dilemma here in that it might be seen to be more valid to compare teacher and TAs when in exactly the same classroom contexts. However, the DISS study was set up to examine the nature of classroom talk under normal classroom conditions, and teachers – as we have shown – almost exclusively work with the whole or vast majority of the class, and TAs almost always work with small groups and individuals. The recordings analysed in this chapter therefore reflect the reality of talk from teachers and TAs as experienced by pupils. It is true that comparison will reflect the social situation within which talk takes place, but this is still the talk experienced by the pupils on an everyday basis. The same issue applies to the attainment level of the pupils. As we have seen, for the most part, TAs support lower attaining pupils or pupils with SEN, whereas the teacher often teaches the rest of the class. The attainment levels of the pupils with whom teachers and TAs interact are therefore likely to differ. Nevertheless, this again reflects the reality of the way in which TAs are deployed; as we saw in Chapter 5, TAs almost never support middle or high attaining pupils. Teacher-to-pupil and TA-to-pupil talk may therefore to some extent reflect the teaching contexts within which they both operate, and the attainment levels of the pupils with whom they interact, and so strict comparisons between teacher and TAs need to be treated cautiously. Nonetheless this reflects the kinds of talk pupils experience on a daily basis with teachers and TAs.

These differences between TAs and teachers were based, for the most part, on data collected on the interactions of TAs and pupils when working in the classroom at the same time as teachers. Although the structured observations showed that this constitutes the most prevalent form of deployment of TAs, it might be thought that the differences would not be so marked when interactions between TAs and pupils are examined out of the classroom (e.g. in targeted curriculum interventions). In the classroom, the TA often has to respond to lessons planned by the teacher and this may explain why they appeared to be in a more 'reactive' rather than 'proactive' mode. Situations out of the classroom may be different, with TAs in more direct control of the material covered. In this regard, studies of the effectiveness of specific curriculum interventions given by TAs with appropriate training (e.g. Savage and Carless 2008) appear to show more positive effects on pupil learning.

We examined this possibility with the instructional talk analysis. We compared differences between in and out of class transcripts. The results need to be treated cautiously because of the smaller number of out of class sessions we obtained, but the results showed that differences between teachers and TAs were *more* marked out of the classroom; that is, they involved even more prompting and little explaining or focus on understanding by TAs. This appeared to owe much to situational factors, with the work out of class involving TAs supporting individuals by practising work already done in class and prompting them to keep on-task and complete the work. Moreover, in contrast to the curriculum interventions mentioned above, which report positive results on pupil attainment, the majority of the out of classroom sessions we observed were often not part of a coherent curriculum intervention, nor were they carefully set up and monitored by teachers.

6.3 Conversation analysis

The main purpose of this second approach to the talk of teachers and TAs to pupils was to explore more fully how they used language and the effects of various strategies on pupils. Conversation analysis (CA) has its origins in Garfinkel's ethnomethodology and Goffman's studies of order in interaction, and is proving a valuable tool for gaining detailed insights into pedagogical discourse (Koshik 2002; McHoul 1990). The approach is inductive, as it involves rejecting assumptions about the data and paying open-minded attention to detail. Using CA thus offers the potential for fresh understanding of the key differences between the TA-to-pupil and teacher-to-pupil interactions. Instead of coding single utterances, as in the instructional talk analysis, it offers a sequential analysis and takes account of the talk of the pupils. In order to further standardise the contexts within which talk takes place, we concentrate on mathematics lessons. This ensures that the oral contributions of the teacher and the TA occur within the same lesson, and concern the same mathematical concepts and procedures. Furthermore, as classroom talk in mathematics has been subjected to recent analysis, comparisons can be made with research into effective teaching in such lessons (Myhill 2006; Smith *et al.* 2004).

This section will examine selected features of teacher and TA talk with pupils by focusing on three aspects: 1) turn allocation; 2) topic organisation; and 3) how repairs are accomplished. As we shall now discuss, these are central to classroom learning.

6.3.1 Features of teacher and TA talk

6.3.1.1 Turn allocation

In whole class interactions, teachers typically allocate turns and pupils have few opportunities to select a turn themselves. Teachers therefore exercise tight control over who has the right to participate. How turns are allocated in mathematics lessons is important because of the way that discourse promotes conceptual understanding. The notion of 'inclusive teaching' is a key characteristic; it involves creating a classroom culture where each contribution is valued equally and teachers adopt deliberate strategies to ensure that the less able can participate (Kyriacou and Issitt 2008).

6.3.1.2 Topic

In everyday terms, 'topic' means 'what is being talked about' but in CA 'topic' is used as a technical term referring to the negotiation of discourse in real time (Svennevig 1999). The way in which topic is generated has a significant bearing on the degree of pupil participation. In a typical classroom, teachers solicit topic through initiations (I) that generate pupil responses (R), which are subsequently given evaluative feedback (F). This three part IRF sequence is widely known and well documented in mathematics lessons (Myhill 2006; Smith *et al.* 2004). As teachers have more subject knowledge, initiations usually involve asking questions to which they already have the answer. Consequently, pupil answers tend to be brief. One concern is that extensive use of IRF limits pupil engagement and participation. In terms of pedagogy in mathematics, 'going beyond IRF' is likely to bring about more effective teaching (Kyriacou and Issitt 2008). This can be accomplished by initiations such as open questions, devices like 'tell us what you think …' and authentic questions to which the adult does not know the answer (Radford *et al.* 2006).

6.3.1.3 Repair

A third area of interest is 'repair' sequences. Classroom talk is abundant with errors and misunderstanding, because pupils, especially those with SEN, or those with low attainment levels, are continually pushed to the limits of their understanding. Precisely how adults respond has important implications for pupil involvement in learning. CA studies of repair have shown how adults deal with children's incorrect responses and lack of clarity (Schegloff 2007; Schegloff *et al.* 1977). In the classroom, teachers correct children's talk more readily than in everyday conversation (Macbeth 2006). Yet, to foster pupil independence, teachers should avoid direct correction and, instead, employ strategies such as clueing (McHoul 1990), prompting, hinting and supplying a model (Radford 2010a). These studies demonstrate that withholding correction, through the use of devices like prompts and hints, affords pupils the maximum opportunity to self-repair and find the answer themselves. Indeed, asking for clarification and fostering reasoning through the use of 'why' questions, instead of correction, are considered as indicators of effective teaching in mathematics (Back 2005; Kyriacou and Issitt 2008; Smith and Higgins 2006).

6.3.2 Data collection: audio recordings

Four of the 16 pairs of transcripts used for the instructional talk analysis were examined in more detail using CA. In order to make the classroom conditions similar, lessons were chosen that focused on mathematics, and involved two primary (Year 5) and two secondary classes (Year 8). The selection of teacher and TA participants was random. Information on the lesson focus and the role of the TA is presented in Table 6.2.

The analysis entailed repeated examination of the recordings and transcripts by one of the team, who has worked extensively with CA. The initial selection of extracts was motivated by a search for sequences of adult–pupil talk that had a pedagogical focus, yet, in line with CA, the analysis was open ended in that the discourse patterns and themes emerged from the data itself. Using the method of constant comparison the emergent themes were re-worked according to new examples. Each turn was analysed to uncover the detail and establish the perspective of the participants. Questions used to interrogate the data included: 'How is that turn/phrase designed?'; 'Why does X use that turn/phrase now (in relation to the prior turn(s))?'; and 'What work does that turn/phrase accomplish (in terms of what happens next)?'

Table 6.2 Conversation analysis: lesson focus and role of TA

School	Role of TA	Mathematical focus of lesson
TA 1	Support two children with statements[a] (Sam, Tom)[b]	Difference between fractions and whole numbers Rounding up/down to the nearest 10, 100, 1,000
TA 2	Support child with SEN in small group (Kim)	Long division with remainders
TA 3	General SEN support (Liam, Fiona, James)[c]	Converting decimals to whole numbers and fractions
TA 4	Support boy with statement (Matthew)[d]	Geometry: properties of triangles and making box-like nets

Notes:
a A 'statement of SEN' is issued in the UK when a child requires significant additional resources, often in the form of a TA.
b Sam has Aspergers, an autistic spectrum disorder; Tom has learning difficulties.
c Liam has a literacy difficulty, Fiona has Attention Deficit Hyperactivity Disorder, James has additional support for behaviour.
d Matthew has Aspergers.

6.3.3 Results

A longer analysis of the data can be found in Radford *et al.* (2011). Several themes emerged from interrogating the data and the results are set out in terms of the three areas just described.

6.3.3.1 Turn allocation

6.3.3.1.1 INCREASING PARTICIPATION BY GIVING ALL PUPILS A VOICE

In this section we analyse an extract (Extract 1) in which a teacher interacted with a class of pupils. This extract illustrates effective use of verbal strategies for inclusive turn taking. The teacher is skilful in eliciting a variety of ideas from pupils following group discussion.

The pupils have been discussing the concept of a 'whole number' and the teacher is pleased with their 'good/fantastic teamwork'. She gives them a clear message that working together and collaborating is expected. There is an established turn-taking system for gaining feedback from each discussion group. First, she invites ideas with an 'open invitation' (line 4). Use of the word 'might' suggests that several answers are possible, as opposed to a single correct answer. Indeed, she does accept ideas from each group enthusiastically, praising their 'good idea(s)' (lines 6, 10), even when the initial ideas display an inaccurate or partial grasp of the concept (lines 5, 8, 11, 12). Using the word 'idea' leaves the floor open for other suggestions, rather than closing down on the right answer. The teacher finally targets the correct answer (line 16) and pushes for elaboration (line 20). She provides particular encouragement, 'well done', when the correct answer (line 24) is given. Her final turn (lines 24–26) offers a very clear explanation of the concept, based on Ruri's answer.

(1)* Giving all pupils a voice (Teacher 1)[2]

1	T	I'm really excited because you've had good teamwork. You've used
2		your skills, your numeracy skills and your teamwork was fantastic.
3		So I'm going to come back to this table. I'll start off with this table.
4		**What do you think a whole number might be?**
5	P	It might be something that hasn't got any left, hasn't got like halves in it.
6	T	It hasn't got any halves in it. Ok, that's a good idea. What about Ross's
7		group? **What do you think?**
8	P	We think it might be a fraction that goes into (.)
9	T	So you think it's a number that can be multiplied by itself? Fantastic.
10		Ok Amy, **you had a good idea.**
11	P	We thought that one two three (.) that could (.)
12	P	If it had a zero at the end, so like a thousand
13	T	Aah fantastic (.) Oh I see you're thinking whole number without the W, so
14		that sort of hole. So you think it's a number that looks like it might have a
15		hole in it, like a zero, like an eight, like a six. Yes? Very interesting. Well
16		Ruka was the first person who got it right. So **you can tell me what you**
17		**think it might be.**
18	P	It hasn't got a half in it.
19	T	It hasn't got a half in it. And you did say that, this table.
20		But is it just a half?
21	P	No
22	T	**What else could it be Ruri?**
23	P	A fraction.
24	T	Any sort of fraction. Well done. Apart from six sixths would mean that it is
25		a whole number. So a whole number is a number that stands on its own.
26		A number without a little bit more. Ok?

★ The first column includes line numbers that are referred to in the analysis. Bold type denotes an important element in the analysis. (.) is a short pause of less than a second.

The teacher consistently treats the pupils' answers as important. All of their ideas are given a public forum and provide models for others in the class. Also, since the pupils made decisions about their ideas in a group, they have authority. '*We* think' (line 8) suggests that the group has been in discussion and arrived at agreement over their ideas. This teacher is skilful in the way she gives everyone a voice, running the risk of displaying inaccurate models, whilst ultimately pursuing the right answer, in order to display a good example.

6.3.3.2 Topic

6.3.3.2.1 INITIATING TOPIC THROUGH OPEN INVITATIONS

Extract 1 also illustrates the use of strategies to initiate topic (bold print). These turns are treated by the children as opportunities to supply their own ideas and understandings. The format is an open invitation, designed as 'What do you think?' in lines 4, 7 and 17. As a 'mental' verb, 'think' focuses on pupils' thoughts and ideas and use of 'you' is suited to hearing their voices. Furthermore, there is frequent use of words like 'might' (lines 4, 17) and 'could' (line 22) in these open invitations which suggest to pupils that a range of responses are possible, rather than a single correct answer.

6.3.3.2.2 OPEN AND CLOSED APPROACHES TO TOPICAL PURSUIT

How topic is pursued in order to explore concepts was handled in very different ways by TAs and teachers. Teachers used open feedback which served to elaborate pupil explanations whereas closed questions by the TA had a different effect. In Extract 2 the teacher uses questions (lines 1, 111) but she opens up the talk when she asks Jim/Ruka to justify their reasoning. Use of the expression, 'Tell me why/how', allows for a range of possible responses. In response, Jim and Ruka explain their earlier, very brief answers. Indeed, their explanations, especially when further elaborated, provide useful examples for others in the class of possible working-out strategies. Such open feedback is valuable in the follow-up turn after the pupil's answer. As mentioned above, in relation to the instructional talk discussion, the different teaching contexts within which teachers and TAs operate might be significant here; the teacher has an advantage because she can select any member of the class to demonstrate their reasoning. By contrast, the TA is working with a single child or small group and therefore can only draw on the restricted resources available to them.

In the same lesson, the TA uses a closed question (Extract 3, line 2). The only response after this type of yes/no question is agreement or disagreement and although Tom's response (line 5) is unclear, it is brief, so the pupil has limited opportunity to expand or explain. Furthermore, 'do you understand' does not come after a pupil response (in a follow-up turn) but in the middle of the TA's own turn whilst she is explaining the working-out strategy, and at a point when the pupil may be minimally engaged and responsive.

In a secondary school lesson on geometry, both the teacher and the TA (Extracts 4 and 5) use closed questions but there were different effects. The teacher calls on pupils' prior knowledge of technical terms and properties ('did you know'; 'do you remember?'). She flags up key concepts for pupils to notice by referring to the 'special name' and contrasts the properties of the 'isosceles' triangle (Extract 4, line 11) with the better known right-angled one (lines 29–31).

The TA is silent throughout most of the lesson (Extract 5). Her main involvement, orally, is to support on-task behaviour (lines 1, 4); she uses three closed questions (lines 2–3) concerned with task completion. She refers to conceptual knowledge when she asks Matthew to write down the term 'isosceles', which is useful because repetition of technical vocabulary supports the child's learning. On the other hand, the TA does not explore the pupils' understanding of the properties of shapes here, or elsewhere, in this lesson. She could have, for example, prompted Matthew to recall both the name and the properties of an isosceles triangle.

(2)* Pupil-oriented open feedback (Teacher 1)[2]

1	T	So a whole number one. Do you think one is a whole number Jim?
2	J	Yes (quiet)
→ 3	T	You do. **Tell me why you think that.**
4	J	Because it doesn't have any
5	T	Sorry darling? Sam was interrupting us.
6	J	Because it doesn't have any over.
7	T	Because it's standing on its own. Yes. It doesn't have a decimal or
8		a fraction or anything. Ok…
		((several lines of talk))
111	T	What do you think it could be Gina?
112	G	Ten
113	T	Well done. Is she right Ruka?
114	R	Yes
→ 115	T	**How do you know? Tell me how you know she's right.** So if
116		you're rounding 12 to the nearest 10.
117	R	Because if it's, it's because if it's more than five to nine it goes up
118	T	Ok fine. So, if your number is between which, if we want to go
119		back down?
120	R	Uhh. It's between one and four.

*   The first column includes line numbers that are referred to in the analysis. Bold type and → denote an important element in the analysis.

(3) Closed question (TA1)[2]

1	TA	So if you've got a 150 here it's going to go upward isn't it.
→ 2		Because it's five or more. So two hundred. **Do you understand?**
3	Tom	**** (unclear)
4	TA	Because if you've got a hundred and fifty
5		***
→ 6		**Do you understand me darling?**
7	P	***
8	T	Back to their desks I think.

(4) Pupil orientation to explore terms and concepts (Teacher 4)[2]

	1	T	Ok what's the name of that shape?
	2	M	Triangle
→	3	T	It's a triangle. **Did you know the special name it has?** Special
	4		name. Let's have a look over here. Look. Ok. Let's see. Thank
	5		you. Just have a look over there Matthew, the blue folder over there
	6		and see if you can find the names of the
	7	M	Shape
	8	T	This shape
	9	M	Shape it's called shape on the board
→	10	T	See if **you can find the actual name** of it. It's got a **special name**
→	11		Those two sides are the same. Good. What measurements are...
			(Several lines of talk about measurement and shape names)
→	28	T	Elaine what's the special name of this triangle? **Do you**
→	29		**remember the names of the triangles?** We know what a right-
	30		angled triangle looks like. Do we know what the name?
→	31		**Do we know what the special name** of this triangle is?
	32		(1.0)
→	33	T	No? A something triangle
	34	C	Isosceles triangle
	35	T	Say it again Costa
	36	C	Isosceles
	37	T	An isosceles triangle. Well done.

(5) Closed questions and task completion (TA 4)[2]

	1	TA	When you're working I'll explain.
→	2		Matthew are you writing the names down? Have you put
→	3		isosceles on there? Right. Can you write there isosceles triangle.
	4		Ok boys. Right Sian. Sit up, sit up.

6.3.3.3 Repair

Given that TAs usually work with children who have learning difficulties, it is perhaps understandable that many of the pupils' turns are either inaccurate or phrased minimally. As a consequence, how TAs phrase their feedback is therefore crucial, not only because this kind of talk will be frequent, but also because it provides the opportunity for enhancing thinking and fostering independence.

(6) High quality feedback (Teacher 1)[2]

	1	T	Now if I was rounding to the nearest 100 (.) say if I had 172.
	2		What would that be if I rounded to the nearest 100? Not to the
	3		nearest ten, to the nearest 100? Ruka?
	4	R	A hundred and seventy. ERROR[3]
→	5	T	That would be to the nearest ten. I want it to the nearest 100.
→	6		Seventy I know you've got 170, but you're still rounding to the
→	7		nearest ten. I want it to the nearest 100 which means I have to
→	8		have two zeros. Yes Gianni?
	9	G	Uhhm is it one hundred?
	10	T	Will it be one hundred?
	11	Tom	Is it seven hundred?
	12	T	No. Oh isn't it interesting? Tom?
	13	Tom	Two hundred
	14	T	Good boy well done Tom. Now, if you have a look, imagine we
→	15		have 72 you'd know that that would go to a 100. So all we need
→	16		to do if we're putting a 100 on the front is think. Ok 172 I know
→	17		that if this part is past, is five or more. I need to round it up. And
	18		you just think about..

6.3.3.3.1 QUALITY FEEDBACK TO ENHANCE UNDERSTANDING

In Extract 6 the teacher provides very clear feedback (lines 5–8) concerning why Ruka's response is incorrect and also extends her understanding. She draws on her own conceptual grasp of place value to give the explanation and then re-focuses Ruka on the problem by repeating what is needed. The hint about needing 'two zeros' is taken up by the three pupils who answer in the following turns. When the correct answer is given (line 13), the teacher takes another opportunity to enhance their understanding by reminding them of how to decide when to 'round up'.

6.3.3.3.2 TA GIVING THE ANSWER (FEEDBACK AS DIRECT CORRECTION)

All of the TAs used different strategies from the teacher. As in Extract 7, instead of initiating Sam to make the repair, the TA uses feedback (the F turn) to supply the correct answer (lines 3, 8). Furthermore, the turns are formed to seek agreement since they are either a yes/no question (line 3) or a final 'Yes?' (line 8). The only subsequent response for Sam is either 'yes' or 'no', a minimal contribution. The TA did take an opportunity at lines 5–6 to explain how to work out the answer. This feedback would have been more powerful at line 3 since it would have prompted him to think of the answer independently.

(7) Giving the answer (TA 1)[2]

	1	TA	((Discussing how to round 111 to the nearest 10)) So what number are you going to take it to?
	2	S	Dunno. NO RESPONSE
→	3	TA	Ten isn't it?
	4	S	Yes.
	5	TA	If you've got to take it to the nearest ten, you've got ten or twenty.
	6		Eleven is closer to ten isn't it?
	7	S	So is it two hundred then? ERROR
→	8	TA	So it's a hundred and ten. Yes?
	9	S	Yes.

(8) Correction withheld (Teacher 3)[2]

	1	T	How many numbers are after the decimal point?
	2	J	One.
	3	T	So how many zeros are you going to have?
	4	J	One.
	5	T	One. So it's going to be over what.
	6	J	Nine over one. ERROR
→	7	T	No what's it going to be.
→	8		**What's the number without the decimal point.**
	9		(1.0)
→	10	T	**Nineteen over ten, which can be shortened to, without the**
→	11		**decimal point, to make it easier? How many tens in nineteen?**
	12	J	One.
→	13	T	**Remainder?**
	14	J	Nine.
→	15	T	Nine. **So you have one whole one and nine what?**
	16	J	One point nine er (3.0)
	17	T	Nineteen over ten.
→	18		So you have one whole one and what would you have in there?
	19	J	Nine?
→	20	T	Over?
	21	J	Ten.
	22	T	One and nine over ten. One whole one and nine over ten. Right…

6.3.3.3.3 WITHHOLDING THE ANSWER THROUGH OTHER INITIATION (PROMPTS AND HINTS)

In a Year 8 lesson, pupils are converting a decimal (1.9) into a whole number and a fraction. In Extracts (8) and (9) the pupils display their lack of understanding (error at line 6, Extract 8). The teacher example shows how she employs a series of moves in the F turns that enable the pupil to work towards finding the answer independently. First, she gives a clear message that there is an error (line 7) and then she uses hints (lines 8, 11) and prompts (lines 13, 15) that foster self-regulation. Overall, she offers a number of strategies that could help the pupil work out the problem alone.

In contrast, when children made errors, the TAs rarely used any scaffolding techniques. Instead, as in Extract (9), the TA uses questions that call for Liam to think (lines 1 and 3) but when he encounters difficulty (line 4) her feedback moves are either phrased minimally or may even be misleading (line 9). Generally, the F turns either supply the answer or involve a high level of prompting to ensure that the youngster achieves success. Given that the TA works in close proximity to this pupil on a daily basis, she may well be sensitive to the pupil's difficulties in learning mathematics and therefore be making use of strategies to ensure that he achieves success. Yet, over use of prompts can increase dependency on the adult so techniques are needed that maximise pupils' opportunities to think and work out a solution on their own.

6.3.3.3.4 ABSENCE OF REPAIR

As we noted earlier, with regard to the instructional talk analysis, TAs rarely explain or develop concepts compared to teachers and when they do, inaccurate and contradictory information can be given. When working in small groups, TAs give pupils problems to practise so it is essential that they have good understanding of the basic concepts and working-out strategies. In Extract (10), the explanations that are used to assist the pupil are incorrect at both lines 6 and 18–19 and the TA does not self-correct these errors. She

(9) Lack of prompts and hints (TA 3)[2]

	1	TA	How many times does ten go into nineteen?
	2	L	One
	3	TA	One so put a one here (.) right. How many have we got left over?
	4	L	Eighteen? ERROR
→	5	TA	No.
	6	L	Ten?
→	7	TA	No (.) if you've got=
	8	L	=a hundred
→	9	TA	Take ten from nineteen.
	10	L	Nine.
→	11	TA	Nine (.) so you've got nine tenths. One and nine tenths. Yes,
	12		Right. Violet put the chair down.

appears to lack understanding of place value, notably hundreds, tens and units. In saying '75 is above 50' and 'thirty four' she is mixing up 'hundreds' with 'tens' and 'units'. There are also contradictory instructions: 'round it up' is repeated twice at line 10, giving Sue the message to go up (not down) to the next thousand and, at line 15, she does supply an answer that is higher. In (16) the TA shows that what she wanted was 'rounding down', not 'up'. Inaccurate information clearly poses challenges for learners.

6.3.4 Discussion of conversation analysis

In summary, the key finding from the second method of analysing TA and teacher talk to pupils (i.e. conversation analysis) is that teachers generally 'open up', whereas TAs 'close down' talk with pupils. We saw this in all three aspects of talk analysed in this section. In terms of turn-taking, inclusive teaching is evident when teachers use strategies to ensure the participation of a range of pupils and convey messages that all contributions are valued. In relation to topic initiation, teachers use open invitations that children interpret as opportunities to offer their ideas. When pursuing topic, teachers employ open feedback strategies to get pupils to justify their reasoning. They also prompt learners to think of technical terms, explain working-out strategies and reinforce the properties of mathematical concepts. When responding to incorrect answers (repair), teachers hold back on direct correction to avoid giving the correct answer outright. As found in other studies,

(10) Inaccuracies and contradiction (TA 1)[2]

	1	TA	One thousand seven hundred and fifty one. But then it's to go to
	2		the nearest thousand. What would I do?
	3	S	Go to the nearest thousand.
	4	TA	Right. So the nearest thousand is::
	5	S	Two
→	6	TA	Two hmm. Good girl. Because **seventy five is above fifty.**
	7		Do you understand?
	8	S	Yes
	9	TA	Promise? Let's give you another one then.
→	10		Ok **round that up** to the nearest thousand. Right? **Round that up**
	11		to the nearest thousand. Remember what I said. Two
	12		thousand three hundred and forty. That will be what?
	13	S	Two thousand (.) three (.) two thousand three hundred and forty
	14	TA	Yes. To the nearest thousand is::?
	15	S	Three thousand
→	16	TA	You didn't **round it down** did you? If you tell me you understand if
→	17		you don't I won't be able to help you sweetheart. All right. Now
→	18		look **thirty four**. Look let me show you (.) you've got nought to
	19		fifty and then you've got fifty to ninety-nine

they have a repertoire of scaffolding techniques such as hints and prompts (Radford 2010a; 2010b). Overall, within each lesson, teachers use at least some strategies that foster pupil independence and encourage pupils to think for themselves.

By contrast, rather than using these opening up strategies TAs *close down* pupils in several ways, which results in pupils having less active involvement in learning talk. In terms of topic generation, TAs have fewer opportunities owing to their individual support role, to open up the topic. Closed questions are used to support and encourage pupils to complete written tasks. This emphasis on task completion might arise from a belief that teachers value completed written work over oral discussion. In terms of pursuit of topic to explore concepts, TAs are well placed to deliver such one-to-one support, given guidance and training. In relation to repair, when pupils make errors or fail to find the answer, TAs readily supply it or correct immediately. The absence of scaffolding strategies, such as prompts, hints and withholding the answer means that pupils have fewer opportunities to think for themselves. On the other hand, by supplying answers TAs ensure that learners succeed and avoid the emotional consequences of failure. However, inaccurate explanations and contradictory information as well as unhelpful hinting, owing to limited grasp of mathematical concepts, does need addressing. Overall, it seems clear that help is required to ensure that TAs can use strategies that foster active pupil participation in learning.

6.4 Conclusions on practice

We have found that teachers value TAs, as they have a better personal understanding of pupils (in part, because they are more likely to live locally) and because they work so closely with them. Interactions between TAs and pupils were viewed positively in terms of the increase in individual attention, differentiation, help with inclusion and pupil engagement. The systematic observation results, reported in the previous chapter, showed that pupils were more likely to passively 'attend' to teachers, while they (especially pupils with SEN) engaged in far more active longer interactions with TAs. On the face of it, these results suggest the educational benefits of talk with TAs. This would be supported by the view that too much classroom talk is brief, and learning would benefit from more extended dialogue with pupils (e.g. Alexander 2006). Pedagogically, it looks like TA-to-pupil talk is more helpful than that between teachers and pupils, where the individual pupil tends to be one of a crowd and passive.

However, in this chapter we reported results from close analyses of transcripts of teacher and TA talk to pupils, and these showed a number of qualitative differences between the talk of TAs and teachers in the same classroom. Overall, putting together findings from the instructional talk analysis and the CA analysis suggests that teachers and TAs differed on three main dimensions:

- an emphasis on learning versus completing tasks/procedures
- a proactive versus a reactive role in classroom interactions
- 'opening up' versus 'closing down' the discourse.

It is now possible to complete the last component of the Wider Pedagogical Role model, which we do in Figure 6.1.

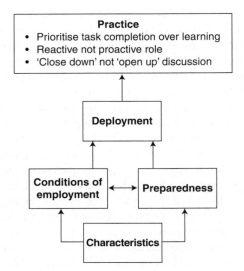

Figure 6.1 The Wider Pedagogical Role model with practice

The finding that TAs at times did not understand the concepts they were supposed to be helping pupils acquire (as with Mandy in our vignette) was particularly troubling, especially given that they often support the pupils in most need. A further point is that TAs did not appear to have received sufficient training to understand how to develop pupil thinking. They frequently provided pupils with answers to questions or tasks, with the result that pupils did not need to think for themselves. TAs appeared to be stifling pupil independence. Such qualitative differences in teacher versus TA talk may provide one explanation for the provocative finding that pupils who received more support from TAs actually made less progress than similar pupils who had less TA support.

As described in Chapter 1, historically, there has been a lot of interest and research on educational effectiveness. In the final chapter, we discuss the implications of the results from the DISS study for models of educational effectiveness. However, in light of the findings on classroom talk analysed here, it is worth ending this chapter by prefiguring the two main points we will discuss later: 1) the need to adapt existing models to take account of the management of TAs by teachers and schools; and 2) how models of effectiveness, when applied to teachers, will also need to be applied to TAs. This is unavoidable given that we have seen that TAs are engaged in a direct pedagogical, instructional relationship with pupils. The overriding question, starkly highlighted by the results presented here on TA practice, concerns what we consider to be the appropriate role of TAs. Again, we pick up on this in the last chapter.

Key findings

The practice of TAs

TAs' interactions with pupils, compared to teachers' interactions with pupils, tended to:

- be more concerned with the completion of tasks rather than learning and understanding
- be reactive rather than proactive
- 'close down' rather than 'open up' talk and conceptual understanding.

Chapter 7

Conclusions

7.1 Introduction

In this book we have described and then discussed results from the largest study yet conducted on support staff in schools. Over the last decade, in the UK and other countries, there has been a huge increase in the numbers of support staff, particularly those in classroom- or pupil-based roles, whom we have called teaching assistants (TAs). We saw in Chapter 1 that this increase was due to several developments: national curriculum initiatives; the introduction, in 2003, of the National Agreement, which aimed to address teacher workloads and raise educational standards; and the increase in the numbers of pupils with SEN in mainstream schools.

At the beginning of the book we presented a vignette of the interactions between one TA and a pupil she supported. We showed how Mandy interacted with Reece, and several other pupils with learning difficulties, and, as Mark (the class teacher) thought, this appeared to be a sensible arrangement, because it allowed these few pupils to get more individual attention, while he could devote more time to the rest of the class. But in the course of this book we have seen that there are some inadvertent but important problems with this form of TA deployment, in terms of the reduction in contact with the teacher and the quality of instruction from the TA. Of particular concern has been the impact of TAs on teachers and pupils. We saw in the vignette, and the results in Chapter 2, that there have been benefits in terms of teachers' job satisfaction and workloads, but we have also seen troubling findings on the relationship between the amount of support given by TAs and pupils' academic progress: children with most support from TAs make significantly less progress than similar pupils with less or no TA support. The bulk of this book has been devoted to an attempt to explain these findings by use of our Wider Pedagogical Role (WPR) model. In Chapters 4, 5 and 6, we built up a picture of preparedness, deployment and practice respectively, which we argue goes a long way in both describing the current situation regarding TAs in UK schools, and also offering explanations for why TAs have a negative effect on pupils' academic outcomes. At the end of each chapter, we added to the WPR model, and we are now able to present the full model in Figure 7.1.

We stress, as we did at the start of this book, that to hold TAs personally responsible for the impact of the support they provide would be too simplistic. This is demonstrated in the WPR model, which presents a contextualised picture of how TAs work, and shows how the effects of TAs need to be seen in terms of the decisions about their deployment and preparedness, made by school leaders and teachers, which are outside the control of TAs.

In this last chapter of the book, we identify key implications for policy and practice arising from the WPR dimensions. We identify what we feel is a main task for education policy at present: addressing whether TAs should have a pedagogical/instructional role. A concern with paraprofessionals in education touches on a number of fundamental issues in education more broadly and we end the book by addressing implications for several of these: teacher and school effectiveness; the education of pupils with SEN; and also the role of paraprofessionals in public services more generally.

Before we proceed with this chapter, it might be helpful to clarify a point that may well have struck some readers. It might be pointed out that, contrary to our findings, there are examples of effective and innovative practice, where TAs can be seen to have a positive effect on pupils' progress. This would be consistent with the reviews of Alborz *et al.* (2009) and Slavin *et al.* (2009). Some authors have argued that, in contrast to the picture identified by the DISS project, they have found a positive picture, and that positive learning outcomes are likely to flow from high levels of preparedness, creative deployment and effective practice by teachers and TAs (e.g. Balshaw 2010).

How do we reconcile the two points of view? We do not disagree that a more positive picture can be found in some schools, in line with Balshaw (2010) and the reviews just cited, but we need to point out we did not encounter a lot of the good practice they identify in our extensive visits to schools and our intensive classroom observations. The DISS project surveys were the most comprehensive yet, and so should be taken seriously as a broadly representative picture of the situation in schools at the time of writing. We have no doubt, however, that with the appropriate training, preparation

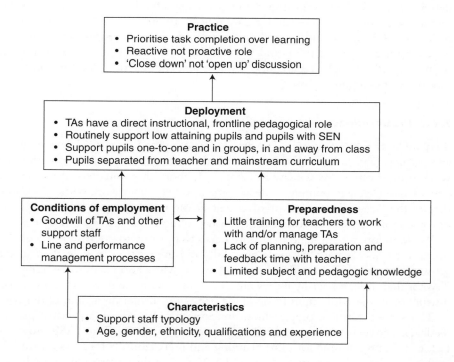

Figure 7.1 The Wider Pedagogical Role model

and collaborative working arrangements in schools, TAs can have a positive effect; it is just that this is not at present typical, and there is still a lot of work needed in order to specify forms of TA preparedness, deployment and practice that work well. In this book, we have reported what was evident under normal circumstances, not what is possible in some schools with training and resources. One main task of this last chapter is to identify ways in which all schools can make the most effective use of TAs.

7.2 What can be done? Implications and recommendations for policy and practice

In order to address the implications and recommendations for policy and practice, arising out of the DISS study findings, we organised a set of small working groups comprising headteachers, local authority (LA) advisors, teacher/TA trainers and SENCos to work with the research team on the key components of the WPR model and the develop-ment of on-going professional development work. (We did not include TAs in these groups because our purpose was to develop a dialogue built around the findings from the DISS project, with staff with decision-making responsibilities at the classroom and school level.) We have also had extensive discussions with headteachers, teachers and local authority staff (e.g. with responsibilities for TAs and for pupils with SEN) during INSET and consultancy work we have undertaken since the project's findings were published. We have also, at the time of writing, embarked on a project funded by the Esmée Fairbairn Foundation that is developing with schools alternative solutions to TA deployment, and then evaluating change over the school year. This chapter is informed by these activities and the research teams' reflections on them. We also draw on the work of Michael Giangreco and his colleagues, and other commentators and researchers. We have organised our discussion and recommendations under the three main dimensions from the WPR model: preparedness, deployment and practice. We conclude with a sec-tion on rethinking policy on TAs.

7.2.1 Preparedness

'Preparedness' took two forms. The first was training and professional development of TAs and teachers (e.g. to know how to direct and organise the work of TAs with whom they worked most often). As we saw in Chapter 4, about three-quarters of teachers reported never having had any training or development to help them work with TAs, and this was despite the fact that teachers' involvement in the training or development of TAs and other support staff had increased at each wave to more than half by Strand 1 Wave 3.

We therefore recommend that more needs to be done to prepare newly qualified and in-service teachers with the necessary skills and preparation to help them manage the growing number of TAs with whom they work. More also needs to be done to prepare TAs for their role, especially if they are to continue with the now common, pedagogical, instructional role with pupils (though see below for further discussion of this role).

The second form of preparedness concerns the day-to-day aspects of planning and feedback between teachers and TAs. A consistent finding of the DISS project was the lack of meaningful time for joint planning and preparation before lessons, and for feed-back and reflection afterwards. At Strand 1 Wave 3, only a quarter of all teachers had any such time with TAs. Teachers in secondary schools were particularly unlikely to have such time, with only 1 in 20 having any timetabled time with a TA. Perhaps unsurprisingly, TAs and cover supervisors felt underprepared for their roles, and reported picking up subject and pedagogical knowledge by 'tuning in' to the teachers' whole class delivery. This is another basis for saying that TAs (as we saw in the previous chapter) often operate in a reactive rather than proactive way, responding to the immediate demands of the lesson and the pupils and not building on prearranged instructional aims. On the basis of these findings, we argue that more time should be available for joint planning and feedback, especially in secondary schools.

Results on TAs' 'conditions of employment', concerning their goodwill and working additional unpaid hours, are also relevant here. Chapter 3 showed that TAs gained a great deal of satisfaction from their work, but many worked extra hours, and there was a significant decrease over the three waves in the number of TAs being paid for extra work. As a result of these findings, we recommend that there is a need for careful consideration of the extra hours worked by TAs, and that they are appropriately rewarded. More could also be done to address the supervision and line management of TAs.

What is common to our recommendations concerning preparedness and conditions of employment is the view that we need to move beyond the present situation, which has developed informally, to a more formal approach to the preparation of TAs and of teachers as the managers of TAs. Indeed, in the course of the discussions with practitioners in our working groups, a strong call was made for training for teachers in how to work with and manage TAs to be mandatory, rather than optional, as is widely the case now. Those participating in the groups who were experienced in providing courses for TAs (typically at the local authority level) said that training was or could be provided, but was not always taken up by schools. If it is not acceptable for teachers to teach without evidence of appropriate training, why should it be acceptable for lesser standards to apply to TAs? If they are to have a pedagogical role (see below), there needs to be a much firmer view about their preparation.

Another suggestion was that there should be a similar induction year for TAs, just as there is an induction year for teachers (what might be called an 'NQTA' year), followed by similar attention to continuing professional development. In Finland, for example, TAs undergo a year of full-time study at a vocational institute, the equivalent of 1,600 hours; plus, they undertake a total of 12 weeks of school-based practice in the field, and qualify via a final examination (Takala 2007).

Some secondary school leaders who contributed to the working groups had dedicated department-based TAs who had a degree in the departmental subject (e.g. maths). However, evidence suggests that these are rare cases. Moor et al. (2006) suggested that only about 8 per cent of mathematics departments in English secondary schools had TAs or other support staff, such as administrative assistants, attached to subject departments. In only a third of these instances (about 2.5 per cent of secondary schools in England) were these maths-dedicated support staff regarded as specialists in the subject itself, either through background or training.

Working group participants echoed another of Moor et al.'s (2006) findings regarding teachers' high level of satisfaction with the amount and quality of in-class support that they received from department-based TAs. But while this might be considered a more effective kind of deployment – and would certainly lead to more confidence about the TAs' subject knowledge – it would still be important to monitor their practice and their pedagogical understanding.

On the issue of planning and feedback time, we believe – and this was supported by the working group participants – that this did not mean there should be *joint* planning, in the sense that teachers and TAs have an equal role in the construction of lesson plans and tasks; the TAs' role is not to plan or design classroom instruction, but rather to make an important contribution by effectively implementing delegated tasks for which they are (or should be) specifically trained. The exact boundaries around TA responsibilities for the design of curricular activities will need to be flexible, but we need to avoid a situation in which an over concern with partnerships or collaborations between teachers and TAs has obscured very real differences in roles. We also need to avoid the situation found in a number of classrooms where TAs had effectively taken over curricular arrangements for pupils they supported – as in the case of Mandy in the vignette. The participants in the groups were equally unified about the need for allocated time for monitoring, feedback and discussion between teachers and TAs. The DISS project case studies found that the limited opportunities for feedback meant that TAs were unable to pass often valuable information on pupils' participation, engagement, successes and struggles on to teachers.

Messages emerging from our present current collaborative research with schools suggest that, at the school level, schools should plan and deliver a full formal induction for new TAs and allow them to shadow an experienced and effective TA. School leaders should also implement an annual audit of TAs' skills and knowledge, teachers' skills relating to working with/managing TAs, and teachers' knowledge relating to SEN.

Another key message to emerge has been the use of audio/visual equipment to deliver in-house training. Schools we have been working with have trialled the use of recordings of experienced and effective TAs in action (e.g. doing group work) as the basis for training and discussion.

There is a clear need for teachers to routinely share detailed information with TAs prior to lessons, supplemented with discussion. The DISS project revealed the limited extent to which teachers made the role and tasks of the TA explicit for each lesson, and this must change. Similarly, mechanisms must exist for TAs to feed back to teachers.

In terms of day-to-day preparedness, there must be a wholesale tightening-up of existing practice. Teachers must be clear and specific about what is to be taught during each session and how it must be taught. Teachers must ensure that plans for TAs are realistic in terms of expectation and expertise; TAs should not be asked to work outside of their zone of comfort or competence. Teachers must also empower TAs to question or seek clarification on any aspect of their lesson plan that is unclear. Schools could consider holding after-school sessions where TAs can be taught the particular pedagogical techniques the teacher wants them to adopt; or Q&As where TAs can ask teachers about curriculum matters to improve their subject knowledge. Again, there is evidence from our on-going collaborative work with schools that they are adopting more effective models of TA preparation (e.g. by using teachers' PPA sessions to deliver such training).

In order to avoid Giangreco's 'training trap' (2003), it is essential that TAs are provided with on-going supervision and feedback on how they carry out teachers' instructions, particularly when deployed in overtly pedagogical contexts. In their study of tutoring for young struggling readers, Jenkins *et al.* (2000) highlighted the importance of consistent feedback and supervision from teachers:

> You can't just train [TAs] and expect them to carry on. They need help trouble-shooting when problems come up or when new lesson activities are introduced.

They need help keeping on track, adhering to the lesson activities, and they need encouragement.

(Jenkins *et al.* 2000)

Teachers must closely monitor the outputs from TA-led sessions. After all, they are legally responsible for the progress of *all* pupils in their class; this is not a duty that can be delegated to TAs. Teachers must regularly mark pupils' work and discuss any issues with TAs, particularly if a child is not making the expected progress, or whose behaviour is cause for concern. It is essential to ensuring long-term impact that teachers make greater efforts to link what is covered in intervention sessions to whole class teaching and broader assessment of pupil progress; pupils must see a clear connection between what is taught and learnt in the two contexts. Performed effectively, we believe that this will validate the value and impact of TA-led interventions in the minds of teachers, pupils, parents and TAs themselves.

7.2.2 TA deployment

Gunter and Rayner (2007) and Hammersley-Fletcher (2008) argue that the remodelling agenda was designed to address school processes and affect cultural change, and was nothing to do with learning processes and pedagogy. However, it is quite clear from the DISS findings on the deployment of TAs that there are profound implications for pedagogy: TAs mainly have a direct pedagogical role in the classroom, and they are routinely deployed to work with lower attaining pupils and those with SEN, especially in mathematics and English.

Much as it has in the UK, the evolution of paraprofessional support in the USA has led to a similar situation: paraprofessionals have become the default 'primary person responsible for the implementation of behaviour strategies, instructional interventions, and providing one-on-one support' (Hughes and Valle-Riestra 2008). As we described in Chapter 1, this also appears to be the case in many other countries as well, and there are still others giving serious consideration to the more widespread use of TAs.

Giangreco (2009) has drawn attention to the absence of any 'theoretically grounded, field-tested, decision-making models [that] exist in the professional literature for determining the need for ... paraprofessional supports for pupils with disabilities in [mainstream] classrooms'. He argues that the over-reliance on paraprofessionals (particularly in one-to-one contexts) is a critical issue of conceptual and practical importance, and is an issue in urgent need of attention.

Our findings support Giangreco's (2009) conclusions that TA support, as currently organised in the UK, is 'conceptually questionable', often 'unduly restrictive', and has 'inadvertent detrimental effects'. But we also echo his caveat to these conclusions: whilst the findings from research paint a troubling picture in terms of the effect of TAs on pupil outcomes, it would be inappropriate to use this as a rationale to unilaterally or abruptly cut or reduce the number of TAs in classrooms. We are mindful of a number of interviewees in our case studies who commented that without TAs – and indeed other support staff – their schools would have struggled to maintain current levels and quality of provision. This was put succinctly by the headteacher in the vignette at the beginning of this book: 'Without the TAs, this school would fall apart'. Moreover, the DISS study has led to a number of recommendations that, if carried through, could lead to forms of deployment likely to fulfil the huge potential of TAs in schools.

Whilst there may be advantages of personalised support – and there is little doubt this has been a main part of inclusion policies in schools – it tends to mean that TA-supported pupils are cut off from their teachers and the curriculum. As we saw in Chapters 2 and 5, the systematic observation component of the DISS study showed that pupils with more TA support have less interaction with the teacher, and as a consequence miss out on everyday mainstream teacher-to-pupil interactions. This situation seems likely to be the main reason for the negative effect on academic progress, particularly when progress is couched in terms of measures based on National Curriculum levels achieved, as in the DISS project. This is why we argued in Chapter 5 that schools should examine the deployment of TAs to ensure that they do not routinely support lower attaining pupils and pupils with SEN, and why we suggest that pupils in most need should if anything get more, not less, of a teacher's time.

Separation from the curriculum is as marked and serious as separation from the teacher. Teachers can rightly say they have responsibility for curriculum planning for the whole class, but as we saw in Chapter 5, in practice the lesson-by-lesson curriculum planning and implementation for some pupils can be delegated to TAs. In many classrooms, TAs have inadvertently become the primary educators of pupils they support.

To avoid this situation it is essential that TAs are not given responsibility for planning tasks for interventions; this should remain with the teacher – it is their legal duty after all. Teachers must take full responsibility for planning interventions and sharing and imparting their detailed plans with TAs. School leaders must recognise the importance of this and could assist by establishing a clear school policy on lesson preparation.

These recommendations were broadly supported by the practitioners involved in our working groups. In considering appropriate ways of deploying TAs in classrooms, one of the key themes to emerge was the distinction between *intervention versus routine allocation*; that is, the need to move from a situation where TAs are routinely allocated to a classroom role, in which they support the pupils in most need, (often without monitoring or follow up), to a role in which they are involved, preferably as part of a team, in targeted interventions.

The overarching point to emerge is that the TA's contribution should be carefully positioned alongside that of teachers, and TAs should be clearly informed about, and monitored in, their role. This will impact on the debate about the pedagogical role of TAs, which we come to later, because the role will need to be informed by clearly articulated curricular aims and associated practice, and monitoring and feedback. The deployment of TAs is best seen as operating for periods of time (e.g. a term), which are then reviewed, rather than the kind of routine and open-ended form of deployment that is often the case at present.

Situations within which the TA withdraws pupils from the classroom, no matter how well informed and skilful the intervention, will still give rise to concerns about the possible separation from the curriculum and the teacher, and steps will need to be taken to ensure that pupils' experience of the curriculum is not fragmented. This point also applies to the successful literacy interventions reviewed by Alborz *et al.* (2009); though pupils may show gains in areas connected to the intervention, this may not necessarily transfer to curriculum experiences and achievements in the rest of the mainstream curriculum. Moreover, time spent out of the classroom will mean missing on-going coverage of the curriculum in the classroom, as experienced by the rest of the class. Schools, therefore, need to ensure that TA-led interventions are integrated into pupils' overall learning experiences. Some participants in the working groups, mindful of this problem, said that pupils should *not* be withdrawn from core subjects to take part in TA-led literacy and numeracy interventions. As our emerging work with practitioners suggests, one recommendation connected to preparedness (shown previously) relates to teachers becoming better informed of pupils' performances in the TA-led interventions. This seems sensible given that teachers need to give pupils on these programmes the opportunity to apply their learning from interventions (usually delivered outside the classroom) in the context of whole class learning.

In line with the recommendations on deployment given here, participants in our working groups suggested that more needy pupils should receive more of the teacher's attention. A relatively straightforward approach adopted in some schools would be to ensure that the teacher takes pupils in most need for periods of time, while the TA takes middle or higher attaining pupils. Where classes are taught in attainment groups, teachers should spend at least as much time with the lower attaining group as she does with other groups. Simple as this sounds, it should be noted that in the DISS study this arrangement was rarely found.

7.2.3 TA practice

Perhaps the central dilemma to emerge from the DISS project results concerns the appropriate role of TAs when interacting with pupils. There is common agreement that face-to-face interactions are at the heart of the learning process for pupils. For too long there has been a collective denial that TAs are actually 'teaching', and that they are instead, in some rather unclear way, just 'supporting' pupils. The DISS project makes it quite clear that this convenient view is misplaced: TAs are in effect 'teaching' pupils, in the sense of engaging in interactions with an instructional purpose; and, furthermore, this is often instead of teaching by the teacher. We have, therefore, to take very seriously the quality of the interaction between TA and pupil, because it will often be the main form of educational interaction a pupil will have with an adult in school.

Results from the DISS project showed that teachers sometimes valued TAs, because they understood pupils better (many TAs live in the same neighbourhoods as the pupils) and because they worked so closely with them. Across the case studies it was widely noted that interactions between TAs and pupils were often less formal and more intimate than those between teachers and pupils. Fraser and Meadows (2008) found that pupils characterised the best TAs as demonstrating care, kindliness, friendliness, helpfulness, warmth and attentiveness. Dunne *et al.* (2008) referred to what they call 'a discourse of care', which shows TA's functional priorities as a predominantly nurturing role, in contrast to the educative one adopted foremost by teachers. Barkham (2008) argues that this is somewhat inevitable given the general profile of TAs as mothers and carers, though our experiences in schools suggest that the 'Mums' Army' label by which TAs were once collectively known, is now largely redundant.

We saw in Chapter 2 that there can be advantages to this type of talk, in terms of pupil behaviour, engagement and participation. Findings from the systematic observation component reported in Chapter 5 made it clear that pupils' interactions with TAs are longer, more sustained and more interactive compared with their interactions with teachers, and on the face of it therefore, more pedagogically helpful. But close analysis of transcripts of teacher and TA talk to pupils, presented in Chapter 6, showed that TA interactions with pupils are different in *quality*. We concluded on the basis of the instructional talk analysis that there were two key dimensions on which teachers and TAs differed. TAs tended to be more concerned with the completion of tasks rather than learning and understanding and they tended to be reactive rather than proactive. In addition, a third key difference between teacher-to-pupil talk and TA-to-pupil talk, revealed by the conversation analysis, is that teachers generally 'open up' pupil talk, whereas the TAs 'close down' pupil contributions, both linguistically and cognitively. TAs, therefore, do not always know how to make the best use of the extended, more frequent interactions they have with pupils, compared with teachers.

7.2.3.1 Should TAs have a pedagogical role in schools?

So here lies the dilemma. As discussed in Chapters 1 and 6, although there are different views about what constitutes effective teaching – and there are all manner of ways in which what counts as 'effective teaching' will vary depending on pupil age and social background, school subject and so on – there would probably be general agreement that effective teaching should stress understanding and conceptual development, rather than purely performance and task completion. Good teaching shows sophistication, sensitivity and sound subject and pedagogical knowledge.

Put like this, one can see that teaching is a difficult and challenging task with huge consequences for pupil learning. The transcripts shown in Chapter 6 made it clear that features of language that promoted pupil learning were present far more consistently in teachers' talk to pupils than they were in TAs' talk to pupils.

This leads to a fundamental question: should TAs have a pedagogical role at all? If the answer is yes, we need to work out what this pedagogical role should look like. If, on the other hand, we take the view that they should not have a pedagogical role, then we must again decide what this non-pedagogical role should look like. It is our view that this issue has been given far too little attention, even though it is at the heart of many other issues connected to TA deployment. Both views are defendable, but both require careful and public consideration of the consequences for preparedness, deployment and practice. In the following sections, we look at the two views in more detail.

7.2.3.1.1 TAs SHOULD NOT HAVE A PEDAGOGICAL ROLE

The DISS findings on the effects of TA support on pupil progress, as well as the findings on TA deployment and practice, might well suggest that TAs should *not* have a direct instructional role with pupils. This is supported by other studies which have found no effect or question the value of TA-to-pupil interactions (Gray *et al.* 2007; Klassen 2001; Reynolds and Muijs 2003).

One obvious and extreme version of a non-pedagogical role, in line with the discussion in the first chapter of this book, and the National Agreement, would be if the TA helped the school or the teacher, but did not have a role in which they interacted directly with the pupils. This could involve helping with routine clerical tasks, like photocopying, which we know from Chapter 2 have contributed to reducing teacher workloads and positively affected their job satisfaction. But it also needs to be pointed out, as we saw in the description of the results from the work pattern diaries completed by TAs in Chapter 5, that TAs did not operate in this indirect role as frequently as they did in a direct role, supporting pupils. So, in order to bring about this model of a non-pedagog-ical role, a major change in current forms of deployment will be needed.

Another form of non-instructional role would be helping the teacher with classroom management. Ofsted (2005) pointed out that the main behaviour problem in schools is the 'persistent, low-level disruption of lessons that wears down staff and disrupts learn-ing'. Results from the systematic observations suggest that the presence of TAs limits the need for talk to manage this kind of problem. TAs might therefore be more effective in terms of having an indirect effect on pupil learning by helping with classroom organ-isation, limiting negative and off-task behaviour, and ensuring lessons run smoothly. However, Giangreco and Broer (2005) found that although TAs spent one-fifth of their time providing behavioural support to pupils, they were relatively untrained and underprepared, and often lacking in confidence when it came to managing pupils with challenging behaviours. As is the case for teachers, the less time TAs spend dealing with off-task behaviour in their interactions with pupils, the more time they have to make a potentially positive contribution to schools. Many TAs work in schools with challenging conditions. It has recently been calculated that TAs in the UK tend to be employed more by schools with higher numbers of pupils from low income families (Cook 2011), and this makes it even more important that greater efforts are made to build on TAs' existing capacity to manage behaviour through training, and offer formal training to new TAs.

Another version of a non-pedagogical role, but with scope for interacting with pupils, would be to build on the DISS findings on positive approaches to learning (PAL). TAs might be better deployed to support the development of pupils' 'soft' skills (e.g. confi-dence, motivation, dispositions toward learning, and facilitating collaborating between pupils) that many now see as important for work in school, but also beyond in the world of work. We saw in Chapter 2 that for six of the seven age groups studied, there was no consistent picture. The clearest results were for a positive effect of TA support for pupils in Year 9 (13–14-year-olds). Research on TAs' and pupils' perceptions of suitable TA attributes has suggested that TAs have the requisite dispositions one associates with nurturing soft skills: adaptability; patience; sensitivity; empathy; approachability; support-iveness; responsiveness; attentiveness; and a sense of humour (Dunne et al. 2008; Fraser and Meadows 2008). Further research is required to describe the practice that produced these outcomes, which can in turn inform models of TA development.

Results from small-scale studies support the DISS Year 9 PAL findings. Headteachers and teachers in a study by Gray et al. (2007) were also asked to indicate, from a ten item list, the areas of the pupils' learning experience most affected by TA support. Areas where TAs were deemed to be 'highly effective' were confidence in and enjoyment of read-ing, self-esteem and independent writing, rather than overall reading performance and fluency (which were the areas where TAs were deemed to be least effective). Downer's (2007) study of TAs, who were trained to deliver short daily bursts of word recognition teaching to 53 pupils in Years 1 to 8, found that the majority of pupils improved in self-esteem and confidence, and some boys with behaviour difficulties were reported to have improved in terms of their social behaviour.

This non-instructional role could be seen as a valued contribution to the overall edu-cational programme. However, we need to be very clear what we mean by 'soft' skills and the interactions used by educators to facilitate them. A couple of participants in our working groups suggested that TA practice can be seen in a positive way as more aligned to current trends in education, such as the 'learning to learn' and 'wider skills' movement.

But we argue that these are not lower forms of educational aim, and can demand high-order pedagogical skills of educators. Reconfiguring the TA's role with these initiatives in mind may not be consistent with a high quality education.

Similar problems are also likely to stem from attempts to 'personalise' learning: the more learning is individualised to meet a pupil's needs, the more important pedagogy is likely to be. Knowing how to teach concepts and scaffold learning in myriad ways, and to recognise and change a teaching strategy when it is not working, are a part of effective teaching, as we saw in Chapter 6. The evidence from the DISS study shows that TAs do not possess such skills to the same extent as teachers.

7.2.3.1.2 TAs SHOULD HAVE A PEDAGOGICAL ROLE

If, on the other hand, we take the view that TAs *do* have a potentially valuable contribution to make to pupils' academic development, and that they can be deployed in face-to-face pedagogical interactions, then the DISS findings make it clear that we need more clarity over just what it is we expect of them.

As described above, the most convincing evidence of the potential of TAs to directly impact pupil learning positively comes from studies of learning interventions involving TAs. Reviews by Alborz *et al.* (2009) and Slavin *et al.* (2009) of studies that examined the effect of TAs who have a pedagogical role delivering specific curricular interventions (mostly for literacy), tend to have a direct positive impact on pupil progress when TAs are prepared and trained, and have support and guidance from the teacher and school about practice.

Savage and Carless (2005) have also shown that trained TAs can deliver effective early preventive programmes for literacy difficulties for children in Key Stage 1 (5- to 7-year-olds). Immediate post-tests showed that all pupils in an intervention group outperformed those in a control group. Savage and Carless (2008) followed up half of the sample of 100 or so children involved in one study to evaluate the effects of a reading intervention delivered by TAs 16 months later. Although this was a modest sample, children who showed signs of responding to the original intervention were significantly more likely to achieve average results in national Key Stage 1 literacy tests and teacher ratings of attainment, than those who did not respond. Gains in reading following early phonic reading interventions delivered by TAs appear to 'stick' for many children.

However, we need to be careful before assuming that TAs can substitute for teachers in learning interventions. Slavin *et al.*'s (2009) synthesis of evidence shows the effect size for TA-led one-to-one reading tuition is far less than the effect size for teacher-led one-to-one reading tuition. This suggests that qualified teachers should work with pupils whose needs demand a higher set of pedagogical skills. At the very least, on-going regular (e.g. half termly) monitoring of TA-led interventions is essential, not least so that such pupils can be identified early in order to assess whether they should receive teacher-led interventions.

Moreover, although evidence for the effects of TA-led interventions on pupil learning may be positive, data from the structured observations in the DISS project show that leading interventions accounted for only around 40 minutes of a TA's day. This is echoed in findings from Farrell *et al.* (2010). For the majority of the time a TA's pedagogical role is less structured, less precise, largely unmonitored and it exposed weaknesses in their subject and pedagogical knowledge. Therefore, if TAs are to have a pedagogical role, we argue that it should be limited to delivering structured and well-planned interventions, for which they must be properly trained and prepared. Interventions should ideally be on a one-to-one basis, but if delivered in groups, the number of pupils per group should be limited. As we saw previously, we also need to be sure that there is consideration given to the continuity of pupils' experience of the mainstream curriculum coverage, when they are withdrawn from the class for interventions.

The establishment of clear roles for TAs should inform training and preparedness. TAs need specific formal training to teach intervention sessions – possibly alongside teachers. One key consideration will be the need to upgrade TAs' pedagogical expertise in order to overcome the instinctive, but mistaken assumption that less pedagogical skill is required when teaching pupils with SEN or low attaining pupils; as we have said, if anything, a higher level of skill is needed. We can see here how the decision to place TAs in pedagogical roles has implications for teachers' professional jurisdiction and legitimacy (Wilkinson 2005).

7.2.3.1.3 A SUPPLEMENTAL ROLE

Giangreco (2009) has provided a valuable commentary on the appropriate role of TAs, and argues that any instruction delivered by paraprofessionals should be 'supplemental, rather than primary or exclusive', so that they are not required to make overarching pedagogical decisions. This is to a degree represented in earlier views about TAs just 'supporting' pupils, while teachers engaged in actual 'teaching'; though we have seen that in practice this is not what occurs.

Causton-Theoharis *et al.* (2007) have taken this idea further and used the interesting analogy of TAs as sous-chefs:

> [their] role is not to plan or design classroom instruction, but rather to make important contributions to classroom instruction by effectively implementing important delegated tasks for which they are specifically trained. Like sous-chefs, [TAs] provide useful supports that help keep things running efficiently and effectively.
>
> (Causton-Theoharis *et al.* 2007)

They list the type of supplementary instructional, rather than primary instructional activities, that they argue are appropriate for TAs to perform in literacy lessons: re-reading stories with pupils; reinforcing skills by leading a game or activity; listening to pupils read; practising letter names and sounds; leading phonics/sound-categorisation activities; and performing alphabetising and rhyming exercises.

On the basis of the DISS results, we strongly suggest that more work is needed on conceptualising the pedagogical role of TAs in their everyday interactions with pupils. This needs to be done publically, based on research evidence, such as that from the DISS project, and this should then inform decisions about TA deployment and practice. We also suggest that this needs to be built into professional development, school deployment decisions and the management, support and monitoring of TAs. This might begin with developing a view of teachers' overall responsibilities to the curriculum, assessment, classroom management, etc, and then working through where TAs' responsibilities might fit. One possible scheme is Arends' model of teaching (1994), in terms of three core functions: first, executive (providing leadership to pupils); second, interactive (face-to-face instructions with pupils); and third, organisational (working with colleagues, parents and others). One way to position the role of TAs might be to argue that there could be overlap between teachers and TAs in the interactive function, but perhaps not the executive or organisational functions, which would remain the preserve of teachers. But there then needs to be work on the effective interactive strategies adopted by teachers and TAs with pupils (these may be seen as different or complementary). In our view, we need more imaginative and informed ways of positioning the pedagogical role of TAs relative to teachers. This important work can then inform everyday interactions with pupils, and be built into professional development, school deployment decisions, and the management, support and monitoring of TAs.

7.2.4 Rethinking policy on TAs

An extreme take on the findings on pupil progress, as described in this book, could be used to drastically cut the number of TAs in schools. However, as we have argued, schools have much to gain from TAs, and few, if any, would wish to lose them. Reframing their purpose and role in schools is therefore essential to fending off any accusations of wasteful expenditure, with the added advantage of giving TAs their own identity and value, which is demonstrable through a measurable impact on pupils.

We believe it is important to move forward in order to establish clear and uncontested roles for teachers and TAs, and produce the systems to support and maintain the demarcation, so that each role – though different and complementary – is valued and respected on its own terms.

One key way in which we can argue for developing TAs' unique identity and status within both the school and wider workforce is therefore to distinguish it, *on its own merits*, from the role and function of teachers. In other words, the challenge is to build on what has just been said about the appropriate role of TAs – pedagogical or non-pedagogical – in order to define the role of the TA and show how it adds value to a pupil's educational and/or personal development in a way distinctive in the school workforce.

It might be helpful, when conceiving the TAs' role, to take the idea of 'added value' a step further. We suggest the value in first envisaging the classroom as it would be with the teacher but without the TA and then making decisions about how the teacher would need to organise things to provide the best educational experience for all pupils in the class. Following this, the TA could then be introduced back into the classroom, so to speak, in such a way that they then provide an additional resource. This would help identify ways in which the TA adds value to what the teacher provides, rather than replacing the teacher.

A connected point is to say that school leaders will want to make employment and deployment decisions regarding TAs in terms of providing value for money. Responses to the question concerning whether TAs should have a pedagogical role can be couched in terms of identifying the nature of the 'value' that is sought. Is it in terms of measurable learning outcomes, or is it to be expressed in other terms? This kind of calculation will also need to be made in relation to whether limited funds are spent on TAs, or whether, given the concerns raised in this book, some of it should be spent on specialist teaching.

As well as value for money, it is important for schools to work toward a good, professional working context for TAs. Thankfully stories we heard of TAs being treated in a non-collegiate way – for example, being exiled from the staff room – seem largely to be a thing of the past. Headteachers we interviewed in the case studies, as well as those participating in our working groups, referred to establishing and upholding a 'school ethos' that strongly influences perceptions of TAs (and other support staff), teachers' relationships with them and pupils' attitudes towards them. Many of the headteachers spoke in terms of engendering a culture of respect; all adults working in the school, teacher or support staff, were equal, in the sense that pupils and other members of staff were expected to show TAs the same level of respect and courtesy as shown to teachers.

However, as we hope has been made clear in this book, when it comes to effective leadership for learning, something far more fundamental is required. There needs to be a strong commitment or capacity to review models of TA preparedness and deployment, and TA practice. As a way of summing up the chapters on preparedness, deployment and practice of TAs, and the discussion on these facets in this chapter, we present some of our key recommendations in Box 7.1.

7.2.4.1 The teacher's role

The recommendations in Box 7.1 are largely about changes to the way TAs are prepared and deployed. But one of the things to emerge from the DISS project, and worth stressing here, is the way that change is also required in the teacher's role. In particular, teachers will have to work through a more inclusive pedagogical strategy, in which they deal with the learning of *all* pupils, and not effectively delegate to TAs the day-to-day responsibility for the learning and care of pupils with SEN and lower attaining pupils. Accordingly, we conclude that teachers should take responsibility for lesson-by-lesson curriculum planning and pedagogical planning for *all* pupils in the class, including those supported by TAs.

7.2.4.2 Schools need to change

The key driver for change is the school itself. Our view, based on extensive visits to schools and discussions about this topic, is that a fundamental change is required. Senior staff need to fundamentally review how their school deploys TAs and what expectations they have of them, and, crucially, they need to then lead change. We have often found that headteachers – and many others in education – see the truth in our findings, and are willing to consider implications for their schools. But too often we have found that action is delegated to relatively junior members of staff or middle leaders, not necessarily connected to, or reporting directly to, the senior management team. This can mean change is piecemeal and sometimes puts staff delegated the responsibility for change in a difficult position, particularly if change requires amending employment contracts (e.g. in terms of hours of work). So change needs to be sanctioned and led from the top. We hope that we have been able to show that this is not an option, but a necessity. Retaining the status quo, in terms of current methods of deploying TAs, is letting the most vulnerable children down.

The level of inconsistency and lack of depth with which some schools had engaged with the issues represented by the components of the Wider Pedagogical Role model lead us to recommend that schools need to explicitly and rigorously set out the quality of provision and support in relation to anticipated academic outcomes for all pupils. The working group participants were again in broad agreement with the urgent need to tackle

---

Box 7.1 Key recommendations

Conditions of employment

- Careful consideration of extra unpaid hours worked by TAs
- Ensure TAs are appropriately rewarded

Preparedness

- Training in how to work with and manage TAs to be a mandatory part of initial teacher training
- Full formal induction for TAs (e.g. on school policies), plus opportunity for shadowing an experienced TA
- More joint planning and feedback time, especially in secondary schools
- Teachers' plans need to be shared with TAs and supplemented with daily discussion
- The role and tasks of the TA for each lesson should be explicit
- TA feedback is useful for further planning, therefore mechanisms must exist for TAs to feed back to teachers
- Regular and thorough monitoring systems in place to limit the negative effects of TA support (e.g. pupils not making the expected progress in TA-led interventions are given extra support from the teacher)
- Teachers given training and guidance in school systems for monitoring and evaluating TA interactions with pupils, and how to handle sensitive situations (e.g. correcting ineffective practice)
- Including TAs (and other support staff) in the performance management cycle, and ensuring that teachers who carry out reviews are properly trained and supported

Deployment

- TAs should not routinely support lower attaining pupils and pupils with SEN
- Address separation of pupil from the teacher and the curriculum

Practice

- Establishing the extent of the pedagogical role of TAs
- Work through ways in which TA roles relate to those of teachers in order to ensure that the TA role is distinct, but complementary to that of the teacher

---

this issue, particularly in the wake of what the DISS findings imply for school test results, league table standings and inspection.

This may seem straightforward, but there are problems, some of which are technical. The consensus view of respondents to the DISS surveys, echoed by interviewees in case studies, was that TAs led to improved outcomes for pupils; yet we have seen that the more objective results on the association between TA support and pupil progress showed a quite different picture. A concern about evidence for a positive effect might also be applied to Ofsted's evaluations of the impact of support staff on pupil standards. Ofsted's 2008 report on the effectiveness of the school workforce reforms, for example, judged that 7 out of its sample of 23 schools had 'made good use of the wider workforce to help narrow the gap between the highest and lowest performing pupils'. The report cited how the impact of the deployment of HLTAs and TAs in one secondary school was 'reflected in' the progress made by 'pupils with learning difficulties and/or disabilities' who had gone from 'underachieving in comparison to their contemporaries' in 2005, to 'progressing as well as other pupils' by 2007 (Ofsted 2008). Yet Ofsted do not give the technical methods by which they arrived at these judgements, and the evidence base for these claims is not clear. If there are difficulties in establishing sound data on academic progress for Ofsted, the problems are even harder for schools, who may not have the expertise to collect, analyse and interpret such data.

Our recommendations deliberately address the fact that schools – especially given the impact of the recent global economic downturn – are very unlikely to receive any additional funds from government in the immediate future with which to implement deployment decisions. It is within the context of schools working within already stretched budgets that, at the time of writing, we are undertaking research on TA deployment: working in collaboration with schools to develop, and then evaluate, creative strategies to TA deployment and preparation.

7.3 Implications for the education of lower attaining pupils and pupils with SEN (in mainstream schools)

In Chapter 1 we briefly set out the background to the deployment of TAs in mainstream schools in relation to the education of pupils with SEN, and policies of inclusion in mainstream schools. We saw that one of the main reasons for the growth in TAs was to help with the inclusion of pupils with SEN. In some respects, the situation looks positive: TAs have a positive effect on pupil attention in class, individual attention, classroom control and positive approaches to learning (at least, in Year 9). Many school staff reported to us, via survey responses and case study interviews, that without TAs, it would be very difficult for them to integrate pupils with SEN. TAs help the teacher by looking after the pupils with difficulties, as well as pupils who are not attaining at the level expected.

Historically, the Education Act 1981 gave legal weight to the recommendations of Baroness Warnock's inquiry into SEN (1978) and was the catalyst to the substantial increase in the number of children with SEN being educated in mainstream schools. The Act introduced the system of statementing, whereby a statutory assessment of a pupil's SEN was set out in a legal document alongside the provision required to meet those needs; in effect, creating a bespoke package of care.

The evolution of debates over the last thirty years concerning the rights of pupils with SEN to be educated in mainstream schools can be seen in the move from 'integration' to 'inclusion' (Moran and Abbott 2002; Lindsay 1997; Thomas 1997). Recent developments (e.g. the New Labour government's ten-year Children's Plan, 2007) suggest that a trend towards 'personalisation of learning' might supplant 'inclusion' as the way education for pupils with SEN is described and thought about in the future (Alexander 2009).

However, whether we call it 'inclusion', 'personalisation', or something else, there are clearly problems; even if it is not formally recognised in policy, TAs, as we have seen in this book, have become integral to inclusive practice and the delivery of provisions for children with SEN.

For parents of pupils with SEN, winning the battle for a statement is too often seen as the conclusion of the process rather than just one phase in providing what is needed for the child (Hartas 2008; Jones and Swain 2001; O'Connor 2008; Penfold et al. 2009). In the interests of maximising scarce resources, some schools subsume all the funding for SEN provision into one pot for redistribution among a large number of pupils with SEN – not all of whom will have a statement – which has the effect of pupils with a statement subsidising the support of those without (Dyson et al. 2004; Jones and Swain 2001; Penfold et al. 2009). Furthermore, as the needs of pupils with SEN can vary greatly, this practice of bundling funding and pupils with SEN together often leads to generic types of support provided by TAs.

The problem, as will now be clear, is that this arrangement appears to have led to unintended consequences. We have seen that there is a negative relationship between the amount of TA support and the academic progress of pupils. Although the relationship applies to groups of pupils who differ in terms of the severity of SEN, there is evidence that it is more marked at Wave 2 of the DISS study for pupils with the most severe forms of SEN in mainstream schools (see Webster et al. 2010). In a similar way, Klassen (2001) found that pupils who had a statement of SEN for a specific literacy difficulty or dyslexia, and who were assigned TA support for literacy, made less progress than their unsupported peers.

We have also seen that other results show that TAs tend to spend most of their time supporting pupils with SEN, broadly defined. It is something of a scandal that stronger questions have not been asked about the effects of this arrangement on the academic progress and learning of the pupils in most need. It looks as if the use of TAs in this way has helped inclusion at the expense of pupils' learning.

As we have seen, this situation has come about through the conflation of two developments: the move to inclusion and the growth in support staff in schools. These have, to a degree occurred, in parallel, but in an implicit and largely unremarked way, the two have come to be connected in practice.

This situation raises significant concerns about the support given to pupils with SEN and raises questions about social justice, civil rights and discrimination as they apply to such pupils. Moreover, recent statistics have shown that there is a growing interconnection between SEN and deprivation. Government data from 2009 shows that pupils with a statement of SEN in primary and secondary schools are twice as likely to be eligible for free school meals as pupils without SEN (DCSF 2009). The highly regarded Cambridge Primary Review, published in 2009, put the needs of vulnerable children at its heart. The review concluded that 'there is an urgency about providing educational and social support for particular children in difficulty which cannot wait for primary education – or society as a whole – to become more equitable and inclusive' (Alexander 2009). In addition, school failure – in terms of leaving compulsory education without qualifications, or having inadequate literacy and numeracy skills – is known to have long-term damaging effects on society, as well as for the individuals concerned (Feinstein et al. 2008). Educational failure feeds into social problems, and the additional financial expenditure required to ameliorate these problems – through the involvement of social welfare, health and judicial systems – is, to a considerable degree, avoidable.

The routine default form of TA deployment can be seen as counter to aims of inclusion. In the USA, the system by which children are placed in special education refers to choosing the most appropriate setting with the 'least restrictive environment'. Yet Giangreco (2009) considers one-to-one paraprofessional support to be 'among the most restrictive support options' in a mainstream classroom; therefore, it should be 'a last resort rather than a first or only option'.

In line with many others, we argue that the education of pupils with SEN in mainstream schools is in need of serious attention. The Lamb Inquiry addressed many of the criticisms of the statementing process, and the then New Labour government accepted the recommendations in Brian Lamb's final report in December 2009. We argue that the point at which the statement is translated into provision is a cause for serious concern, and an area we know little about in any detail. The majority (85 per cent) of parents of children with SEN who contributed to the Lamb Inquiry were satisfied with their child's current placement (Lamb 2009). Yet Ofsted (2006) concluded that there is a misconception that support from TAs can ensure good quality intervention or adequate progress by pupils, and evidence from the DISS project supports this view. Put simply, we do not yet know what the provision set out in an SEN statement looks like to the pupils on the receiving end. Without being clear and rational about what pupils with SEN experience, we cannot make effective judgements about which provisions work best. More research is needed which documents examples of practice and policy, as reflected in everyday educational experiences, which work well, which work less well, and which can inform future policy and practice. We are pleased to say the Nuffield Foundation has agreed to fund research on this topic and, at the time of writing, work on this study is now underway.

Elsewhere, the outcomes of the DISS project have resonated with senior officials and policymakers. Ofsted's national SEN adviser and a senior DCSF official with responsibility for SEN claimed, in 2009, that the £5 billion spent annually on SEN – most of which represents spending on 'unskilled TAs rather than specialist training for staff' – 'fails to make any significant difference' to pupil outcomes (Maddern 2009). These officials challenged headteachers to reconsider ineffective TA deployment practices, and referred to impending public sector spending cuts as an expedient to change.

It is an interesting fact that while we now have much more profound understanding of a number of types of SEN (e.g. ADHD and autism), we have not seen an accompanying increase in effective ways of supporting such pupils in mainstream schools.

It therefore follows from the DISS results that there is a need for a fundamental review of the education of pupils with SEN, from the point of view of the supported pupils themselves and what best helps them, but also teachers and TAs and what strategies work well. At the time of writing the government has published a Green Paper on the education of pupils with SEN and disabilities (DfE 2011). Whilst we welcome the fact that this addresses the contribution of school support staff to the education of pupils with SEN and disabilities, and cites the DISS project, we are concerned that the key messages arising from the DISS project have been overlooked. We are pleased that the need to address ways in which support from TAs leads to pupil separation from the teacher and curriculum is acknowledged, but the proposed guidance on how schools should address this problem is, in our view, too open-ended. The Green Paper does not offer any challenge to the status quo in terms of how TAs are deployed by schools to support the needs of pupils with SEN and disabilites. We are deeply concerned that the failure to fully engage with the fundamental questions raised by the DISS project will reinforce current models of practice, which continue to let down disadvantaged children.

We are aware that there are a number of academics working in the field of SEN who will have some difficulties with the approach adopted to SEN in this book. Balshaw (2010) and Fletcher-Campbell (2010) have offered interesting commentaries on a previously published paper of ours on the implications of the DISS project for pupils with SEN (Webster *et al.* 2010), and have argued that we adopt an outmoded model of SEN, which 'focus[es] on perceived weaknesses in individual pupils and the 'supportive' interventions supposedly needed' (Balshaw 2010), and which offers 'no challenge to the curriculum or pedagogy to which the pupil is exposed', nor accounts for 'the possibility of the social construction of special educational needs' (Fletcher-Campbell 2010). We do not disagree that we used a simple classification of SEN in the study; this was unavoidable for the purposes of statistical analysis. On the other hand, such an approach did allow us to arrive at clear systematic results on the way pupils with SEN tended to get more support from TAs, at the expense of interactions with the teacher.

Fletcher-Campbell (2010) suggests that we have overlooked the significance of a number of sociological constructs including 'exclusionary processes, status and power'. Whilst we recognise that these are important, these constructs do not address the essential point of our work: to explain the unexpected and troubling negative relationship between the amount of TA support and academic progress. The essential point we would make about the commentaries of Balshaw and Fletcher-Campbell is that, whatever their merits in terms of a general commentary on support staff in education, we are not sure they engage with what we argue is at the heart of the problem: the negative effect of TAs on pupil attainment and whether TAs should have a pedagogical role. We are pleased that Ofsted's 2010 review of SEN provision is very consistent with key messages arising out of the DISS project, as this extract from their report makes clear:

> Barriers to learning which were observed by inspectors included lack of careful preparation and poor deployment of adults to support children and young people. Where additional adult support was provided in the classroom for individuals, this was sometimes a barrier to including them successfully and enabling them to participate. In too many examples seen during the review, when a child or young person was supported closely by an adult, the adult focused on the completion of the task rather than on the actual learning. Adults intervened too quickly, so preventing children and young people from having time to think or to learn from their mistakes.
>
> (Ofsted 2010)

What is more, Ofsted's guidance for inspectors with the responsibility for assessing SEN (2011) has also been influenced by the DISS findings. The inspectorate recommends that, when arriving at judgments, inspectors should find out:

- Whether TAs always work with the lowest attaining group
- At what stages of learning the teacher becomes involved with pupils with SEN who are frequently supported by TAs
- What interaction the teacher has with pupils with SEN
- Whether working with TAs prevents social interaction with other pupils
- Whether TAs have sufficient subject knowledge to ensure their input (e.g. questioning) promotes thinking and learning as opposed to task completion

- Whether teachers are clear about what they want pupils to learn, as this may not always simply be the subject content
- How interventions link into other lessons in school – pupils should not be 'missing out' or be expected to 'catch up'.

(adapted from Ofsted 2011)

The Ofsted review and guidance on SEN provision, however, does not go as far as raising the question that we have, concerning the appropriate pedagogical role of TAs.

There is a wider educational consideration here. In practice, as we have seen, pupils with a statement of SEN and pupils on School Action or School Action Plus now tend to be supported by TAs alongside lower attaining pupils (though it is recognised that these broad categories of SEN and lower attaining often overlap; this issue of over-identification has been highlighted by Ofsted (2010)). TAs tend to support these pupils – in groups at primary, and individually at secondary. This means that lower attaining pupils and those with SEN can be supported by TAs rather than teachers. As Giangreco *et al.* (2005) in the USA has argued, an implicit form of discrimination has developed with the least able and most disadvantaged pupils receiving less educational input from teachers than other pupils. If there are grounds for saying that pupils with SEN are not appropriately served by this arrangement, there are also grounds for saying that lower attaining pupils are equally poorly served.

If we are serious about being concerned with the well known 'tail' in educational (under)performance, and the way in which it is has persisted over many years despite concerted efforts to deal with it, then we should take very seriously the educational experiences of supported pupils, and the way that current methods of deploying TAs may not be helping their educational progress as much as we may have thought. Of course there will be other factors at work here, including support from home, parental aspirations, and material factors affecting educational achievement, but the way they are supported in schools – and by whom – will also play a part.

Michael Giangreco suggests it is appropriate to ask what parents would think of current arrangements if it applied to their own children. How many parents of children not classified as having SEN would be comfortable with an arrangement in which their son or daughter was supported for much of their time, at least in the core subjects, by TAs and not – as they might have expected – by teachers? One might also ask what teachers would think of current arrangements if applied to *their own* children.

One invidious process that we also mention here is the interconnection between pupil learning difficulties, low expectations of staff, and the pedagogical and subject knowledge deemed to be appropriate for supporting them. We have seen, and questioned, the way in which it can in practice be seen as appropriate for those with the least subject and pedagogical knowledge to support pupils who are struggling, and therefore seen to be operating at lower levels. In one sense, this seems natural: as the pupils are not so advanced, then staff with lower levels of subject knowledge can work with them, while the teacher moves the rest of the class on. Such work with the rest of the class may go well beyond the capabilities and understanding of TAs, but looked at from a different point, this is an unacceptable arrangement, driven by the way lower expectations are affecting a limited view of how it is possible to help such pupils progress. We have seen that the quality of talk and preparation is limited, especially in relation to the complex learning needs of pupils. We have also seen that this arrangement can lead to the separation of TA-supported pupils from the teacher, the curriculum and peers. We need to move from an arrangement where pupils with the most complex and difficult learning difficulties are taught by staff with the least subject and pedagogical knowledge to one where such pupils routinely receive the most highly qualified and specialist teaching.

7.4 The role of government: the National Agreement and school workforce remodelling

In the previous sections, we have given our recommendations on the preparedness, deployment and practice of TAs, and we have argued that schools are the key drivers for change. We have also argued that in order to use TAs effectively, we need to rethink the teacher's role as well. These developments are at the school level, and in a sense bottom-up. Interestingly, however, the key reason for change in the past decade in the UK, as we saw in Chapter 1, was centrally led, via the National Agreement and workforce remodelling plans implemented by the last New Labour Government. In this sense, the key driver in the recent past has been top-down, and we have seen a number of ways in which this has led to good, but also problematic outcomes.

The DISS project was carried out immediately after the signing of the National Agreement in 2003, and amid a five-year process of school workforce remodelling. Although the study did not specifically cover the implementation of the National Agreement per se (although a study by Hutchings *et al.* (2009) did; see below), the DISS project has observations and comments that are relevant to how the vast majority of schools went about remodelling their workforces in order to tackle teacher workload and raise standards. So what do the DISS findings tell us in terms of how successful schools in England and Wales have been in meeting these two aims?

Excessive teacher workload was seen as a key contributor to the teacher recruitment and retention crisis of the early 2000s, and to which the National Agreement was a three-step approach in response to reducing the burden on teachers. As we saw in Chapter 1, the three steps were: 1) reducing their administrative tasks; 2) reducing, and eventually removing, the obligation for teachers to cover lessons for absent colleagues; and 3) providing the equivalent of a half-day per week, guaranteed non-contact PPA time. Though the government gave schools the freedom to arrive at their own solutions to operationalise these elements of the National Agreement (e.g. using qualified supply teachers to cover classes), schools tended to manage the process by extending and developing support staff roles. Decisions to go down this route were almost always financially driven.

The DISS results have shown that, in the case of teacher workloads, there has been a lot of success. We found significant improvements in terms of teacher workloads, job satisfaction and levels of stress, largely as a result of TAs and other support staff taking on routine clerical tasks. This was an anticipated outcome of the National Agreement, and, as expected, helped free up teachers' time so that they could concentrate on teaching and related activities. Another government-funded research project (conducted by Hutchings *et al.* 2009), which looked at the success of remodelling strategies, suggested that headteachers, and, to a lesser extent, teachers reported that workforce remodelling had made it more possible for them to focus on teaching and learning, and had reduced stress. The same study reported no overall reduction in teachers' workloads, but this can be explained by the broader view the research took of efforts to reduce workload over and above those involving support staff, as the DISS project was restricted to. In this sense, the contribution of support staff to meeting the first aim of the National Agreement can be seen as successful.

The second aim of the National Agreement – raising pupil standards – is, as we have seen, problematic. There has been an assumption, echoed in government papers and policy documents (see Chapter 1), that the deployment of TAs in school will raise standards. But we have seen too that the objective data on pupil progress shows the amount of TA support has a negative effect on pupil standards. It therefore seems that the National Agreement has had mixed results, with the successful elements of the National Agreement existing side-by-side with some worrying aspects of broader TA deployment.

The political context and the role of government in driving reform in workforce arrangements in schools now – at the time of writing – looks very different. The present coalition government in the UK has already signalled that the recent concerted initiatives on support staff, sponsored by the last government, are to be abandoned. It has scrapped the 'social partnership' involving teacher associations, unions and employers, which provided guidance and policy on the use of TAs, and the body set up to consider much sought after national arrangements on pay and conditions for TAs (the School Support Staff Negotiating Body). It has also wound up the Training and Development Agency for Schools, which had responsibility for TA training, and its responsibilities have been taken over by the Department for Education. It also appears that there will be no further funding for HLTA accreditation. There are other uncertainties concerning funding for TAs, and also for pupils with SEN. These developments mean there is a lot of uncertainty about the future position of TAs in the school workforce. What is more, local authorities – which had a role to play in the funding and guidance given to schools – are facing an even more uncertain future, as more and more of their responsibilities and functions are devolved to schools, other bodies (e.g. charities and third sector organisations), or taken on by central government.

Whether one agrees or not with these developments, it means that there is change in the role of central government in the employment and deployment of paraprofessionals in education, and uncertainties over leadership at this level. Practically, decisions about TAs in the future are likely to be more and more in the hands of individual schools, and this may well be what the present government would like to see.

7.5 The WPR model and school and teacher effectiveness

As described in Chapter 1, historically, there has been a lot of interest and research on teacher and school effectiveness. The results from the DISS study have two main implications for models of educational effectiveness in UK schools.

First, models of teacher and school effectiveness need to be updated so they now include the changed reality of schools today (at least in the UK), which involves large numbers of TAs and other support staff. Existing models of teacher effectiveness (e.g. those by Creemers (1993) and Dunkin and Biddle (1974)), map important teacher influences on pupil attainment and learning. Moreover, other models, such as that proposed by Berliner (1987), provide guidance in terms of promoting and enhancing pupils' cognitive engagement and learning. The assumption underpinning these models is that educationally effective input is provided by teachers. These models must now recognise and reflect the fact that input is also now provided by TAs. Moreover, we need to include teachers' management responsibilities for TAs, which will affect the situation. School effectiveness research has stressed the important school-level factors likely to be a sign of effective schools. The key factors associated with successful schools (e.g. Creemers 1993) will need to be augmented to include the school-level management and decision-making regarding TAs. These additional factors have changed the landscape of debate about effective teaching and schooling.

Whether we conceive of TAs as having a pedagogical role that directly impacts on learning, or a non-pedagogical role that indirectly impacts on learning, models of educational effectiveness must be amended. The Wider Pedagogical Role model offers a way of doing this, which can be absorbed into existing models. With reference to Creemers and Kyriakides' (2008) dynamic model of educational effectiveness, the classroom-level factor 'learning environment' could be modified to include TA-to-pupil interactions. Again, one of the classroom-level factors Creemers and Kyriakides include in their model concerns the 'management of time': the ways in which teachers maximise teaching time and pupil engagement. The ways in which opportunities to learn and time on-task are measured could be enhanced by considering 'management of people', and how teachers use TAs in service of these aims.

The second implication of the findings for teacher and school effectiveness is that models of effectiveness, when applied to teachers, will also need to be applied to TAs. This is unavoidable if TAs continue to have a direct pedagogical, instructional relationship with pupils – in which case they are to all intents and purposes 'teaching'. To pick up on the earlier discussion about the appropriate pedagogical role of TAs, if they are to retain a pedagogical role, then ideas about effective teaching need to be applied to TAs, as well as teachers. We need, therefore, to consider the use of questioning, explanations, prompts and feedback by TAs, as well as by teachers. Drawing on the DISS data on adult-to-pupil interaction, Radford *et al.* (2011) suggest that one relatively straightforward way in which teachers can help to improve TAs' practice is by 'sharing their own higher order skills and knowledge and helping TAs to develop questioning techniques that open up interactions with pupils and to know how to provide quality feedback'.

7.6 The wider context of paraprofessional roles across public services

In the introduction we showed that there is a general trend across different professions (e.g. police, health care, legal services and social work) toward the use of paraprofessional roles. In the light of the results from the DISS project, we now return briefly to consider the similarities and differences between the different roles in different sectors.

In some respects, the use of paraprofessionals in education is similar to those in other professions. Support staff have, as we have seen, and in line with the National Agreement, picked up routine, lower level activities, and in this way freed up time for teachers to engage in important professional activities, such as lesson planning, assessment and teaching. This contribution of paraprofessionals is therefore similar to that in other professions, and on the face of it seems a positive working arrangement.

But in other ways the situation with regard to paraprofessionals in education is very different, and this is where some difficult issues have emerged. We have seen that TAs have moved beyond an indirect role, through which they help the teacher or the school, to a largely pedagogical, interactive and direct role with pupils. In this respect they are engaged in similar, frontline activities to teachers. We have seen that in the case of pupils in most need, TAs have, in practice, taken over from teachers; they are not augmenting but substituting for the teacher.

Separation of roles in other professions may not be entirely straightforward, but there is not likely to be such a strong transference of professional responsibility from professional to paraprofessional roles. To take an obvious example, this would not be seen as acceptable in, say, medicine, in relation to diagnosing and treating illness.

One reason why the transfer of central professional responsibilities from professional to paraprofessional roles may have happened in education and not other areas is because it might not appear that the stakes are as obviously high as in other professions, like medicine or the police, because the effects are not so visible. The academic progress of a pupil may not be immediately clear, and is not usually, as we have seen, formally assessed on a regular basis; the inadvertent consequences of paraprofessional support are, therefore, not so evident.

This connects with the issue of 'role clarity', which was a consistent theme in the DISS project case studies as seen in Chapter 5. It is evident that recent policies and workforce remodelling have enlarged the role and responsibilities of TAs and have made the demarcation between teachers and TAs sometimes unclear and sometimes controversial (see Chapters 1 and 5). As we saw in Chapter 1, they also called into question the professional status of teachers (e.g. Thompson 2006). Wilkinson (2005) argues that as teaching does not have the codified body of formal knowledge, which typically defines 'a profession', it is unable to mount a convincing defence against the expansion of TAs. Davison (2008) is one of a number of critics who believe that central control and standardisation has reduced teachers to 'deliverers' of the curriculum, and reduced 'teacher education to the production of skilled technicians'. What is more, some teachers have deemed these relatively straightforward 'teaching' tasks suitable for non-professionals to perform, thereby in a sense providing an unintended and unfortunate commentary on their own profession.

However, there are quite obvious ways in which teachers and TAs differ. The DISS findings show that they have very different rates of pay and types of contract (e.g. term-time only contracts are still the norm for many TAs, whereas teachers are salaried). Teachers' conditions of service are also different from TAs (e.g. teachers must hold a legal status (QTS) in order to practise and there are mandatory procedures for performance review). Entry-level training is also very different: teachers must undertake a period of university-based initial teacher training, or pursue a school-based route to QTS; whereas there is no equivalent expectation or entry-level qualification for TAs. In terms of subject knowledge, teachers are graduates; whereas – as the DISS Strand 1 surveys revealed – the highest qualification among the majority of TAs (59 per cent) was at GCSE level. Teachers tend to define themselves as having much greater specialist knowledge than TAs; teachers interviewed by Wilson and Bedford (2008) believed that TAs required only 'a certain level of education'. The training of teachers means that they have a different level, not only of subject knowledge, but also pedagogical knowledge – something revealed in the transcripts of talk between teachers and pupils and TAs and pupils in Chapter 6.

There is another way in which the differences between professional and paraprofessional roles in education might be further apart than may at first appear. In contrast to the delegation of tasks, which characterises the use of paraprofessionals in some professions and contexts, supporting pupils in education often involves an educational relationship and teaching process, and this makes the use of paraprofessionals for this role problematic – especially when there is a separation of pupil from the teacher and the curriculum in the ways we have seen. Education is perhaps inherently different to other sectors in which paraprofessionals are becoming established because it involves an ongoing pedagogical relationship, and not just delegation of skills (e.g. nursing/medical procedures) to paraprofessionals. The teaching/learning process is in interpersonal, long-term and developmental in nature – not a one-off professional encounter more typical of lawyers and the police.

7.7 Future research

Enough is known from the DISS project to help explain the troubling results concerning effects of the amount of TA support on academic outcomes, and enough is known to be able to develop recommendations on preparedness, deployment and practice, and other dimensions. Recommendations follow from main findings concerning the routine deployment of TAs to lower attaining pupils and pupils with SEN, and the separation of such pupils from teachers and the mainstream curriculum. As stated near the beginning of this chapter, we are presently working on a collaborative research project with schools in two local authorities in order to develop policy and practice, which could then be used by other schools. This work (funded by the Esmée Fairbairn Foundation) will benefit from a careful evaluation in order to inform further policy regarding TAs.

The DISS research has shown that support for pupils with SEN in mainstream schools is often provided by TAs, not teachers, and this might explain the negative impact of TA support on pupil progress. However, we have found that there is surprisingly little systematic information on the overall support experienced by pupils with the highest level of need, or how these experiences compare with the provision set out in SEN statements, which detail how these needs are to be supported. As we stated above, we are embarking on a study (funded by the Nuffield Foundation) which will address factors that influence the effectiveness of this 'additional support' in mainstream settings and provide what we believe is a much-needed perspective on inclusive practice vital for informing policy-making and classroom practice.

Our work suggests to us the value in at least four areas of future research and these are described in Box 7.2.

To conclude this book, we restate the two key interrelated messages that have emerged from the DISS project, and of which policymakers and practitioners alike should take careful note. First, that it is erroneous to personalise the negative findings on pupils' academic progress to TAs; it is, as we have described using the Wider Pedagogical Role model, the decisions made *about* – not *by* – TAs (e.g. on their role and purpose) which provide the most compelling account for these results. And second, that it is by systematically addressing *all* the factors that comprise the WPR model – chiefly TAs' conditions of employment, preparedness, deployment and practice – that schools can begin to put into place the systems and models of deployment that we believe can lead to a demonstrable positive impact on outcomes for all pupils.

Box 7.2 Suggestions for future research

1   We propose that there is a strong case for research that seeks to examine effects not just of the amount of TA support (as in the DISS project) but particular facets of the Wider Pedagogical Role of TAs on pupil learning, behaviour and attitudes to learning. This study could also attend to alternative forms of assessment, that provide more detail and which address smaller periods of learning in comparison to beginning and end of year attainment measures. As in the DISS study, one would need to control for a range of factors, including level of pupil need, which might be expected to affect the relationship between WPR and pupil outcomes.

2   As in the UK, there has also been an increase in TA numbers in many other countries. We think there is much to be gained from an international perspective on the use of paraprofessionals in education. We hope the DISS findings will act as a stimulus for such an interest. A systematic comparison of approaches to the professional development, preparedness, deployment and practice of education paraprofessionals would do much to aid policy and general practice in different countries.

3   The DISS project and this book have been primarily concerned with TAs' effect on pupils' learning and attainment. There have been a number of suggestions in the study that TAs may also have effects on the relationships supported pupils have with their peers. This might be positive, in terms of encouraging social interaction, but also negative (e.g. in terms of separating pupils from their peers and not allowing them so much time to engage in collaborative group work with peers). The effect of TAs on pupils' peer relations needs more attention from research.

4   As we demonstrated in Chapter 1, TAs represent just one way in which a range of public sector services, in the UK at least, have developed a paraprofessional tier (e.g. the health service, police force and social work). We feel that there may be some value to furthering our understanding of the extent to which the roles of professionals and paraprofessionals are clear, distinct, legislated, protected and reinforced in these different areas. The WPR model may provide a useful framework for exploring other paraprofessional roles, and arriving at judgements about their perceived effectiveness in sectors outside of education.

Appendices

Appendix 1

Table 1 Description of methods of DISS project data collection and response rates

Strand 1	
Surveys	• Three biennial waves of a large-scale, national questionnaire survey sent to mainstream primary, secondary and special schools • Responses from 6,079 schools, 4,091 teachers and 7,667 support staff, including 1,864 (24%) TAs

Strand 2	
Work pattern diaries	• Support staff recorded which of 91 tasks they did every 20 minutes for one working day in the academic year 2005–2006 • Respondents recorded duration of each task per 20 minute slot • 91 tasks were grouped into six categories for analysis • 1,670 responses from individual support staff, including 310 (19%) from TAs
Structured observations	• 27 TAs across 18 schools (9 primary; 9 secondary) were shadowed for one day each • Activities of teachers and TAs recorded every five minutes, plus information on contexts and tasks carried out by TAs with supported pupils • 1,500+ observations of teachers, TAs and pupils took place in 140 lessons, both in and away from the classroom
Systematic observations	• 686 pupils in Years 1, 3, 7 & 10 observed for two days, across 49 schools (27 primary; 22 secondary) in English, mathematics and science lessons • 34,400+ observations made in ten second intervals
Case studies	• Observations carried out in 65 mainstream and special schools (30 primary; 21 secondary; 14 special) • 591 interviews conducted with 65 school leaders, 105 teachers, 233 support staff (including 114 TAs) and 188 pupils
Adult-to-pupil interaction	• 42 simultaneous digital voice recordings made of teacher-to-pupil and TA-to-pupil talk in lessons • 32 lesson-length transcripts made in English and maths lessons used for analysis (16 teacher-to-pupil; 16 TA-to-pupil) • Utterances: 5,226 teacher; 2,295 TA

Main pupil support survey (MPSS)	• Survey of effects of TA support over a school year on pupils' positive approaches to learning (PAL) (e.g. motivation, confidence) and academic progress
	• 8,200 pupils across 153 schools: 2,528 pupils and 76 schools in Wave 1; 5,672 pupils and 77 schools in Wave 2
	• Seven year groups covered: Years 1, 3, 7 & 10 (in Wave 1) and Years 2, 6 & 9 (in Wave 2)
	• PAL outcomes: teacher ratings of whether pupils' PAL had improved, remained unchanged or decreased
	• Academic progress outcomes: attainment at start and end of school year, based on key stage assessments, National Curriculum levels and teacher assessments
	• Amount of TA support for each pupil measured by teacher estimates of amount of TA support and four measures from systematic observations

Appendix 2

Table 1 Associations between combined staff ratings of total TA support and pupil attainment (controlling for pupil characteristics: baseline attainment, SEN status, gender, eligibility for FSM, ethnic group). Wave 1

Year	Amount of support	English Estimate (95% CI)	Maths Estimate (95% CI)	Science Estimate (95% CI)
1	0%–10%	0	0	0
	11%–50%	−1.8 (−3.0, −0.7)	−0.3 (−1.5, 0.8)	−1.7 (−3.6, 0.2)
	51% +	−2.8 (−4.6, −1.0)	−2.3 (−4.0, −0.6)	−2.1 (−4.6, 0.4)
	p-value	0.002	0.02	0.13
3	0%–10%	0	0	0
	11%–50%	−2.6 (−3.9, −1.4)	−2.1 (−3.2, −1.1)	−1.1 (−2.4, 0.2)
	51% +	−3.8 (−5.9, −1.7)	−3.5 (−5.1, −1.8)	−1.4 (−3.7, 0.8)
	p-value	0.002	<0.001	0.20
7	0%–10%	0	0	0
	11%–50%	−1.6 (−3.4, 0.2)	−0.4 (−2.2, 1.3)	−0.7 (−3.0, 1.6)
	51% +	−4.2 (−6.2, −2.2)	−3.0 (−4.9, −1.1)	−2.6 (−5.4, 0.2)
	p-value	<0.001	0.007	0.19
10	0%–10%	0	0	0
	11%–50%	−1.6 (−3.4, 0.2)	0.0 (−0.5, 0.6)	0.4 (−0.4, 1.1)
	51% +	−4.2 (−6.2, −2.2)	−0.4 (−1.0, 0.1)	−0.3 (−1.0, 0.5)
	p-value	<0.001	0.19	0.35

Note: Estimates represent the difference in attainment between each support group and those receiving the lowest amount of TA support.

Table 2 Associations between combined staff ratings of total TA support and pupil attainment (controlling for pupil characteristics: baseline attainment, SEN status, gender, eligibility for FSM, ethnic group, income deprivation, EAL, pupil age). Wave 2 – Years 2, 6 and 9

Year/ Subject	Amount of support	All pupils Estimate (95% CI)	Non-SEN Estimate (95% CI)	School Action Estimate (95% CI)	SA+/Statement Estimate (95% CI)
Year 2	0%	0			
English	1%–10%	−0.9 (−1.3, −0.4)			
	11%–25%	−1.3 (−1.7, −0.8)			
	26%–50%	−1.4 (−2.0, −0.9)			
	51% +	−2.9 (−3.5, −2.3)			
	p-value	<0.001			
Year 2	0%	0	0	0	0
Maths	1%–10%	−0.1 (−0.7, 0.5)	−0.5 (−1.0, 0.0)	1.3 (−0.3, 2.9)	0.2 (−2.0, 2.4)
	11%–25%	−0.4 (−1.0, 0.2)	−0.4 (−0.9, 0.2)	−1.7 (−3.2, −0.2)	−0.4 (−2.5, 1.8)
	26%–50%	−1.5 (−2.2, −0.8)	−1.9 (−2.7, −1.2)	−0.4 (−1.7, 1.0)	−1.7 (−3.8, 0.4)
	51% +	−2.0 (−2.9, −1.2)	−1.9 (−2.9, −0.9)	−1.2 (−2.6, 0.2)	−4.3 (−6.0, −2.5)
	p-value	<0.001	<0.001	0.001	<0.001
Year 2	0%	0			
Science	1%–10%	−0.0 (−0.8, 0.8)			
	11%–25%	−0.2 (−1.0, 0.6)			
	26%–50%	−0.5 (−1.4, 0.4)			
	51% +	−1.6 (−2.7, -0.5)			
	p-value	0.01			
Year 6	0%	0	0	0	0
English	1%–10%	−0.5 (−0.9, −0.2)	−0.5 (−.0, −0.1)	−0.1 (−1.1, 1.0)	−1.7 (−3.1, −0.5)
	11%–25%	−1.1 (−1.5, −0.6)	−0.9 (−1.4, −0.3)	−0.6 (−1.7, 0.5)	−3.1 (−4.4, −1.8)
	26%–50%	−1.5 (−2.0, −1.0)	−1.6 (−2.4, −0.8)	−1.0 (−2.0, 0.0)	−3.6 (−4.9, −2.2)
	51% +	−1.7 (−2.3, −1.1)	−1.1 (−2.1, −0.1)	−2.6 (−3.9, −1.3)	−2.9 (−4.3, −1.5)
	p-value	<0.001	<0.001	0.002	<0.001
Year 6	0%	0	0	0	0
Maths	1%–10%	0.0 (−0.5, 0.4)	−0.3 (−0.8, 0.3)	−0.3 (−1.5, 0.8)	2.1 (0.4, 3.7)
	11%–25%	−0.9 (−1.5, −0.4)	−0.9 (−1.5, −0.2)	−0.7 (−1.9, 0.5)	−1.2 (−2.8, 0.4)
	26%–50%	−1.4 (−2.1, −0.7)	−1.1 (−2.1, −0.2)	−1.1 (−2.3, 0.1)	−2.3 (−4.0, −0.7)
	51% +	−1.3 (−2.2, −0.4)	−0.6 (−1.7, 0.5)	−1.7 (−3.2, −0.1)	−1.8 (−3.5, 0.0)
	p-value	<0.001	0.03	0.21	<0.001

Year/ Subject	Amount of support	All pupils Estimate (95% CI)	Non-SEN Estimate (95% CI)	School Action Estimate (95% CI)	SA+/Statement Estimate (95% CI)
Year 6	0%	0	0	0	0
Science	1%–10%	−0.2 (−0.9, 0.6)	−0.1 (−0.9, 0.6)	−0.5 (−2.6, 1.7)	−0.8 (−3.2, 1.6)
	11%–25%	−0.5 (−1.2, 0.2)	0.0 (−0.7, 0.8)	−1.2 (−2.9, 0.5)	−3.3 (−5.5, −1.1)
	26%–50%	−1.3 (−2.2, −0.4)	−1.3 (−2.5, −0.1)	−2.5 (−4.1, −0.8)	−0.3 (−2.6, 2.0)
	51% +	−1.9 (−3.4, −0.4)	−9.6 (−14.2, −4.9)	−0.2 (−2.4, 2.1)	−3.6 (−5.9, −1.2)
	p-value	0.03	<0.001	0.04	0.003
Year 9	0%	0	0	0	0
English	1%–10%	−2.4 (−3.3, −1.5)	−2.4 (−3.5, −1.3)	−4.3 (−6.4, −2.2)	−1.0 (−3.1, 1.1)
	11%–50%	−1.7 (−2.8, −0.7)	−4.0 (−5.4, −2.6)	0.0 (−1.7, 1.7)	0.8 (−1.5, 3.2)
	51% +	−1.7 (−2.8, −0.6)	−1.5 (−3.2, 0.2)	−1.1 (−2.9, 0.7)	−1.6 (−3.5, 0.3)
	p-value	<0.001	<0.001	0.008	0.16
Year 9	0%	0			
Maths	1%–10%	−1.3 (−2.2, −0.4)			
	11%–50%	−0.5 (−1.7, 0.5)			
	51% +	−1.5 (−2.6, −0.5)			
	p-value	0.003			
Year 9	0%	0			
Science	1%–10%	−1.6 (−2.5, −0.7)			
	11%–50%	−1.2 (−2.2, −0.3)			
	51% +	−2.3 (−3.2, −1.3)			
	p-value	<0.001			

Notes: Estimates represent the difference in attainment between each support group and those receiving the lowest amount of TA support.
Results only presented for each SEN group where a significant interaction with level of TA support was found.

Table 3 Associations between systematic observation TA support measures and pupil attainment (controlling for pupil characteristics, baseline attainment, SEN status, gender, eligibility for FSM, ethnic group) Wave I

Year	Support measure	Subject	Pupil group	Estimate (95% CI)	P-value
I	Presence[a]	English	SEN	−3.6 (−6.2, −0.9)	0.008
	Presence[a]	Science	All	6.6 (2.7, 10.6)	0.002
3	Presence[b]	Science	Non-SEN	0.31 (0.01, 0.61)	0.04
	Proximity[c]	English	All	−2.7 (−4.2, −1.2)	<0.001
	Proximity[c]	Maths	All	−2.3 (−3.5, −1.0)	<0.001
	Proximity[c]	Science	All	−2.1 (−3.6, −0.6)	0.006
	Interaction[c]	English	Non-SEN	−5.1 (−7.3, −3.0)	<0.001
	Interaction[c]	Maths	All	−2.4 (−3.8, −1.1)	<0.001
	Interaction[c]	Science	All	−2.2 (−3.8, −0.6)	0.006
	Attention[d]	English	Non-SEN	−3.0 (−4.7, −1.3)	0.001
7	Presence[c]	English	All	−0.32 (−0.57, −0.08)	0.01
	Interaction[d]	English	Non-SEN	−4.1 (−7.2, −1.0)	0.009
10	Proximity[c]	English	All	−1.2 (−2.0, −0.4)	0.005

a   Estimate is difference between pupils supported >80% of time compared to <80% of time
b   Estimate is effect of increasing percentage of TA presence by 10%
c   Estimate is difference between pupils supported >10% of time compared to <10% of time
d   Estimate is difference between pupils supported some of time compared to not at all

Notes:
CI = confidence interval
TA presence = when a TA was present in the classroom during observations
TA proximity = when pupil supervision by a TA was either one-to-one or as part of a group
TA interaction = when the pupil was interacting with a TA
TA attention = when the pupil interacted with a TA, and in addition, the pupil was the focus of the TA's attention

Appendix 3

Table 1 Members of support staff who have worked with teachers or for teachers during the last week (result for the Teacher Questionnaires (TQ))

	Wave	Primary Number (%)	Secondary Number (%)	Special Number (%)	All schools Number (%)
TAs	1	1122 (97%)	339 (78%)	204 (96%)	1681 (92%)
	2	810 (99%)	238 (86%)	196 (99%)	1247 (96%)
	3	598 (97%)	184 (89%)	147 (98%)	929 (96%)
Pupil welfare	1	108 (9%)	110 (25%)	75 (35%)	296 (16%)
	2	144 (18%)	97 (35%)	110 (56%)	351 (27%)
	3	132 (22%)	83 (40%)	105 (70%)	320 (33%)
Technicians	1	320 (28%)	263 (61%)	91 (43%)	680 (37%)
	2	289 (35%)	208 (75%)	115 (58%)	615 (47%)
	3	255 (42%)	165 (80%)	93 (62%)	513 (53%)
Other pupil support	1	445 (38%)	142 (33%)	95 (45%)	693 (38%)
	2	504 (62%)	149 (54%)	119 (60%)	774 (60%)
	3	372 (61%)	111 (54%)	103 (69%)	586 (60%)
Facilities	1	409 (35%)	154 (35%)	87 (41%)	657 (36%)
	2	462 (56%)	117 (42%)	129 (66%)	710 (55%)
	3	344 (56%)	108 (52%)	105 (70%)	557 (57%)
Administrative	1	577 (50%)	300 (69%)	124 (58%)	1013 (55%)
	2	555 (68%)	210 (76%)	150 (76%)	917 (71%)
	3	393 (64%)	167 (81%)	117 (78%)	677 (70%)
Site	1	361 (31%)	152 (35%)	94 (44%)	613 (34%)
	2	520 (63%)	144 (52%)	139 (71%)	804 (62%)
	3	351 (57%)	116 (56%)	99 (66%)	566 (58%)

Notes: Responses from individual post titles were combined. Figures represent the number (and percentage) of teachers working with one or more members of each support staff category.
Total responses from each TQ wave: Wave 1 = 1,827; Wave 2 = 1,297; Wave 3 = 950.

Notes

1 Introduction

1 All full-time equivalent teachers and support staff in nursery, primary and secondary schools, city technology colleges and academies in England.
2 All full-time equivalent teachers and support staff in local authority nursery, primary and secondary schools in Wales.
3 Includes staff defined as: classroom assistants; additional support needs auxiliary or care assistant; nursery nurse; behaviour support; and foreign language assistant.
4 All full-time equivalent teachers and support staff in local authority maintained and grant-aided primary and secondary schools in Scotland.
5 Local authority maintained primary and secondary schools, city technology colleges and academies.
6 WAMG defined 'cover supervision' as 'occur[ing] when there is no active teaching taking place. Pupils would continue their learning by carrying out a pre-prepared exercise under supervision ... [and] ... should only be used for short-term absences' (WAMG 2004).
7 We are currently preparing a handbook/toolkit based on effective TA preparation, deployment and practice developed through an action research project, funded by the Esmée Fairbairn Foundation. The book contains practical strategies developed by teachers in order to address the problems associated with the widespread models of TA deployment outlined in this book.

2 The impact of TAs

1 The reason for the change in year groups was because of lengthy delays in Wave 1 in getting information back from schools; this was speeded up by collecting end of key stage test data from government agencies.
2 Numbers in separate ethnic group categories were not large and so were combined into two groups. The 'white' group included white British, Irish, traveller of Irish heritage, gypsy/Roma and any other white background. The white British group made up the vast majority of this group. The 'other than white' group comprised white and black Caribbean, white and black African, white and Asian, any other mixed background, Indian, Pakistani, Bangladeshi, any other Asian background, black Caribbean, black African, any other black background, Chinese and any other ethnic group. All categories and data were supplied by the Deptartment for Children, School sand Families (now the Department for Education).
3 Two level multilevel statistical models were used, with pupils nested within schools. For the PAL analyses, the outcome was a two-point scale, so multilevel logistic regression was used. For the attainment analyses, the attainment scores were continuous, so multilevel linear regression was used.

3 Characteristics of TAs and their conditions of employment

1 WAMG defined 'cover supervision' as 'occur[ing] when there is no active teaching taking place. Pupils would continue their learning by carrying out a pre-prepared exercise under supervision ... [and] ... should only be used for short-term absences' (WAMG 2004).

4 Preparedness

1 According to Best Practice Network (BPN), the organisation responsible for HLTA assessment, there was a significant change to HLTA funding following the change in government in England, in May 2010. From this date, the TDA no longer provided local authorities with funding for 'HLTA preparation'; the process henceforth was to be funded instead by schools or individuals. At the time of writing this book (2011), BPN themselves were awaiting further news from the coalition government on the precise future for HLTAs and those wishing to gain HLTA accreditation.

6 The practice of TAs

1 This chapter was co-written with Julie Radford and Christine Rubin-Davies, and should be cited as Radford, J., Rubie-Davies, C., Blatchford, P., Russell, A. and Webster, R. (2012) 'The practice of TAs', in Blatchford, P., Russell, A. and Webster, R. *Reassessing the impact of teaching assistants: how research challenges practice and policy*, 94–117, Oxon: Routledge.
2 In all extracts, T = teacher, TA = teaching assistant and P = pupil. All other names and initials refer to pupils.
3 ERROR refers to a pupil turn that is treated as problematic by the adult.

References

Alborz, A., Pearson, D., Farrell, P. and Howes, A. (2009) *The impact of adult support staff on pupils and mainstream schools*, London: Department for Children, Schools and Families and Institute of Education.

Alexander, R.J. (2006) *Towards dialogic teaching* (3rd edn), Cambridge: Cambridge University Press/ Dialogos.

Alexander, R. (ed.) (2009) *Children, their world, their education: final report and recommendations of the Cambridge Primary Review*, London: Routledge.

Anderson, V. and Finney, M. (2008) '"I'm a TA not a PA!": teaching assistants working with teachers', in G. Richards and F. Armstrong (eds) *Key issues for teaching assistants: working in diverse and inclusive classrooms*, pp.73–83, Oxon: Routledge.

Angelides, P., Constantinou, C. and Leigh, J. (2009) 'The role of paraprofessionals in developing inclusive education in Cyprus', *European Journal of Special Needs Education*, 24(1): 75–89.

Arends, R. (1994) *Learning to teach* (3rd edn), New York: McGraw-Hill, Inc.

Bach, S., Kessler, I. and Heron, P. (2004) 'Support roles and changing job boundaries in the public services: the case of teaching assistants in British primary schools', paper presented at International Labour Process Conference, Amsterdam, April.

Back, J. (2005) 'Talking to each other: pupils and teachers in primary mathematics classrooms', paper presented at Fourth Congress of the European Society for Research in Mathematics Education, Sant Feliu de Guixols, Spain, February.

Bakhtin, M. (1981) *The dialogic imagination*, Austin, TX: University of Texas Press.

Ball, S. (2003) 'The teacher's soul and the terrors of performativity', *Journal of Education Policy*, 18(2): 215–228.

Balshaw, M. (2010) 'Looking for some different answers about teaching assistants', *European Journal of Special Needs Education*, 25(4): 337–338.

Barber, M. (1997) *The learning game*, London: Indigo.

Barber, M. and Brighouse, T. (1992) *Partners in Change: Enhancing the Teaching Profession*, London: Institute for Public Policy Research (IPPR).

Barkham, J. (2008) 'Suitable work for women? Roles, relationships and changing identities of "other adults" in the early years classroom', *British Educational Research Journal*, 34 (6): 839–853.

Bassett, D., Haldenby, A., Tanner, W. and Trewhitt, K. (2010) *Every teacher matters*, London: Reform.

Beeson, C., Kerry, C. and Kerry, T. (2003) *The role of classroom assistants*, Birmingham: National Primary Trust.

Berliner, D. (1987) 'Simple views of effective teaching and a simple theory of classroom instruction', in D. Berliner and B. Rosenshine (eds.) *Talks to teachers* (pp. 93–110), New York: Random House.

Blatchford, P., Bassett, P., and Brown, P. (2005) 'Teachers' and pupils' behaviour in large and small classes: a systematic observation study of pupils aged 10/11 years', *Journal of Educational Psychology*, 97(3): 454–467.

Blatchford, P., Edmonds, S. and Martin, C. (2003) 'Class size, pupil attentiveness and peer relations', *British Journal of Educational Psychology*, 73(1): 15–36.

Blatchford, P., Russell, A., Bassett, P., Brown, P. and Martin, C. (2004) *The effects and role of Teaching Assistants in English primary schools (Years 4 to 6) 2000–2003: results from the Class size and Pupil-Adult Ratios (CSPAR) Project. Final Report. (Research Report 605)*, London: DfES.

Blatchford. P., Russell, A., Bassett, P., Brown, P., and Martin, C. (2006) 'Effects of class size on the teaching of pupils aged 7 to 11 years: implications for classroom management', paper presented at AERA Annual Meeting, San Francisco.

Blatchford, P., Russell, A., Bassett, P., Brown, P., and Martin, C. (2007) 'The role and effects of teaching assistants in English primary schools (Years 4 to 6) 2000–2003', *British Educational Research Journal*, 33(1): 5–26.

Blatchford, P., Bassett, P., Brown, P., Koutsoubou, M., Martin, C., Russell, A. and Webster, R., with Rubie-Davies, C. (2009) *The impact of support staff in schools. Results from the Deployment and Impact of Support Staff project. (Strand 2 Wave 2)* (DCSF-RR148). London: DfES.

Brophy, J.E. (1989) 'Research on teacher effects; uses and abuses', *The Elementary School Journal*, 9(1): 3–21.

Burgess, H. (2008) *Primary workforce management and reform (Primary Review Research Survey 6/4)*, Cambridge: University of Cambridge, Faculty of Education.

Butt, G. and Gunter, H. (2005) 'Challenging modernization: remodelling the education workforce', *Educational Review*, 57(2): 131–137.

Butt, G. and Lance, A. (2005) 'Modernizing the roles of support staff in primary schools: changing focus, changing function', *Educational Review*, 57(2): 139–149.

Cajkler, W., Tennant, G., Tiknaz, Y., Sage, R., Taylor, C., Tucker, S., Tansey, R. and Cooper, P. (2007) *A systematic literature review on the perceptions of ways in which teaching assistants work to support pupils' social and academic engagement in secondary classrooms (1988–2005)*, Research Evidence in Education Library, London, IoE EPPI Centre.

Callias, M. (2001) 'Current and proposed special educational legislation', *Child Psychology and Psychiatry Review*, 6(1): 24–30.

Carrington, S. (1999) 'Inclusion needs a different school culture', *International Journal of Inclusive Education*, 3(3): 257–268.

Causton-Theoharis, J., Giangreco, M.F., Doyle, M.B. and Vadasy, P.F. (2007) 'Paraprofessionals: the "sous chefs" of literacy instruction', *Teaching Exceptional Children*, 40(1): 56–62.

Cook, C. (2011) 'Deprived schools lose out in fight for top teachers', *The Financial Times*, 3, 29 January.

Cook-Jones, A. (2006) 'The changing role of the Teaching Assistant in the primary school sector', paper presented at European Conference on Educational Research Geneva, September.

Creemers, B.P.M. (1993) 'Effective instruction as a basis for effective education in schools', paper presented at the Annual Meeting of EARLI, Aix en Provence.

Creemers, B.P.M. (1994) *The effective classroom*, London: Cassell.

Creemers, B.P.M. and Kyriakides, L. (2008) *The dynamics of educational effectiveness: a contribution to policy, practice and theory in contemporary schools*, Abingdon: Routledge.

Cremin, H., Thomas, G. and Vincett, K. (2005) 'Working with teaching assistants: three models evaluated', *Research Papers in Education* 20(4): 413–432.

Davison, J. (2008) 'Why we shouldn't have it all off Pat', *Times Education Supplement*, 14 March.

Department for Children, Schools and Families (2009) *Children with special educational needs 2009: an analysis*, London: DCSF.

Department for Education (2010a) *School workforce in England (including pupil: teacher ratios and pupil: adult ratios) January 2010 (provisional). SFR11/2010*, London: Department for Education.

Department for Education (2010b) *Statistical first release. Special educational needs in England, January 2010 (SFR 19/2010)*, London: Department for Education.

Department for Education (2011) *Support and aspiration: a new approach to special educational needs and disability – a consultation*, London: Department for Education.

Department for Education and Employment (1994) *Code of practice on the identification and assessment of special educational needs*, London: COI.

Department for Education and Employment (1997) *Excellence for all children: meeting special educational needs*, London: HMSO.

Department for Education and Skills (2001) *Schools: achieving success. White Paper*, London: The Stationery Office Limited.

Department for Education and Skills (2002) *Time for Standards. Reforming the school workforce*, London: Department for Education and Skills.

Department for Education and Skills (2003a) *Raising standards and tackling workload: a national agreement*, London: Department for Education and Skills.

Department for Education and Skills (2003b) *Time for Standards: guidance accompanying the Section 133 Regulations issued under The Education Act 2002*. London: Department for Education and Skills.

Department for Education and Skills (2005) *Statistical first release. Special educational needs in England, January 2005 (SFR 24/2005)*, London; Department for Education and Skills.

Downer, A. (2007) 'The National Literacy Strategy Sight Recognition Programme implemented by teaching assistants: a precision teaching approach', *Educational Psychology in Practice*, 23(2): 29–143.

Doyle, W. (1986) 'Classroom organisation and management', in M.C. Wittrock (ed.) *Handbook of research on teaching* (4th edn), New York: MacMillan Publishing.

Dunkin, M.J. and Biddle, B.J. (1974) *The study of teaching*, New York: Holt, Rinehart and Winston.

Dunne, L., Goddard, G. and Woodhouse, C. (2008) 'Teaching assistants' perceptions of their professional role and their experiences of doing a foundation degree', *Improving Schools*, 11 (3): 239–249.

Dyson, A., Farrell, P., Polat, F., Hutcheson, G. and Gallannaugh, F. (2004) *Inclusion and pupil achievement, [DfES Research Report 578]*, London: DfES.

Egilson, S. T. and Traustadottir, R. (2009) 'Assistance to pupils with physical disabilities in regular schools: promoting inclusion or creating dependency?', *European Journal of Special Needs Education*, 24(1): 21–36.

Evans, J. and Lunt, I. (2002) 'Inclusive education: are there limits?', *European Journal of Special Needs Education*, 17(1): 1–14.

Farrell, P., Balshaw, M. and Polat, F. (1999) *The management, role and training of learning support assistants*, London: Department of Education and Employment.

Farrell, P., Alborz, A., Howes, A. and Pearson, D. (2010) 'The impact of teaching assistants on improving pupils' academic achievement in mainstream schools: a review of the literature', *Educational Review*, 62(4): 435–448.

Feinstein, L., Budge, D., Vorhaus, J. and Duckworth, K. (2008) *The social and personal benefits of learning: a summary of key research findings*, London: The Centre for Research on the Wider Benefits of Learning.

Finn, J. D., Gerber, S. B., Farber, S. L. and Achilles, C. M. (2000) 'Teacher aides: an alternative to small classes?', in M.C. Wang and J.D. Finn (eds) *How small classes help teachers do their best*, pp.131–174. Philadelphia, PA: Temple University Center for Research in Human Development.

Fletcher-Campbell, F. (2010) 'Double standards and first principles: framing teaching assistant support for pupils with special educational needs: a response', *European Journal of Special Needs Education*, 25(4): 339–340.

Fraser, C. and Meadows, S. (2008) 'Children's views of teaching assistants in primary schools', *Education 3–13*, 36 (4): 351–363.

Gage, N.L. (1985) *Hard gains in the soft sciences: the case of pedagogy*, Bloomington, Ind.: Phi Delta Kappa.

Galton, M., Simon, B. and Croll, P. (1980) *Inside the primary classroom*, London: Routledge and Kegan Paul.

Gerber, S.B., Finn, J.D., Achilles, C.M. and Boyd-Zacharias, J. (2001) 'Teacher aides and students' academic achievement', *Educational Evaluation and Policy Analysis* 23(2): 123–143.

Giangreco, M.F. (2003) 'Working with paraprofessionals', *Educational Leadership* 61(2): 50–53.

Giangreco, M. F. (2009) *Critical issues brief: concerns about the proliferation of one-to-one paraprofessionals*, Arlington, VA: Council for Exceptional Children, Division on Autism and Developmental Disabilities.

Giangreco, M. F. (2010) 'One-to-one paraprofessionals for students with disabilities in inclusive classrooms: is conventional wisdom wrong?', *Intellectual and Developmental Disabilities* 48 (1): 1–13.

Giangreco, M.F. and Broer, S.M. (2005) 'Questionable utilization of paraprofessionals in inclusive schools: are we addressing symptoms or causes?', *Focus on Autism and Other Developmental Disabilities* 20: 10–26.

Giangreco, M.F. and Doyle, M.B. (2007) 'Teacher assistants in inclusive schools', in L. Florian (ed.) *The SAGE handbook of special education*, pp. 429–439, London: Sage.

Giangreco, M.F., Edelman, S., Luiselli, T.E. and MacFarland, S.Z.C. (1997) 'Helping or hovering? Effects of instructional assistant proximity on students with disabilities', *Exceptional Children* 64: 7–18.

Giangreco, M.F., Yuan, S., McKenzie, B., Cameron, P. and Fialka, J. (2005) '"Be careful what you wish for ...": five reasons to be concerned about the assignment of individual paraprofessionals', *Teaching Exceptional Children*, 37(5): 28–34.

Gibson, S. (2004) 'Managing special educational needs (SEN) in the mainstream school: the role of the SEN team', paper presented at BERA Conference, Manchester, September.

Goldstein, H. and Blatchford, P. (1998) 'Class size and educational achievement: a review of methodology with particular reference to study design', *British Educational Research Journal*, 24(3): 255–268.

Gray, C., McCLoy. S., Dunbar. C., Dunn, J., Mitchell, D. and Ferguson, J. (2007) 'Added value or a familiar face?: the impact of learning support assistants on young readers', *Journal of Early Childhood Research*, 5(3): 285–300.

Gunter, H. and Rayner, S. (2007) 'Modernising the school workforce in England: challenging transformation and leadership', *Leadership*, 47 (3): 47–64.

Hammersley-Fletcher, L. (2006) 'Workforce remodelling – an opportunity for thinking about education?', paper presented at BERA Conference, Warwick, September.

Hammersley-Fletcher, L. (2008) 'The impact of workforce remodelling on change management and working practices in English primary schools', *School Leadership and Management*, 28 (5): 489–503.

Hancock, R. and Eyres, I. (2004) 'Implementing a required curriculum reform: teachers at the core, teaching assistants on the periphery?', *Westminster Studies in Education*, 27(2): 223–235.

Hartas, D. (2008) 'Practices of parental participation: a case study', *Educational Psychology in Practice*, 24(2): 139–153.

HMI (2001) *The National Numeracy Strategy: The Second Year. An Evaluation, HMI (HMI Report 333)*, London: Ofsted.

House of Commons Education and Skills Committee (2006) *Special Educational Needs Third Report of Session 2005–06 Volume I (HC 478–I)*, London: The Stationery Office Limited.

Howes, A., Farrell, P., Kaplan, I. and Moss, S. (2003) *The impact of paid adult support on the participation and learning of pupils in mainstream schools*, London: Institute of Education, Evidence for Policy and Practice Information and Coordinating Centre.

Hughes, M.T. and Valle-Riestra, D.M. (2008) 'Responsibilities, preparedness, and job satisfaction of paraprofessionals: working with young children with disabilities', *International Journal of Early Years Education*, 16(2):163–173.

Hutchings, M., Seeds, K., Coleman, N., Harding, C., Mansaray, A., Maylor, U., Minty, S. and Pickering, E. (2009) *Aspects of school workforce remodelling strategies used and impact on workload and standards, Research Report DCSF-RR153*, London: DCSF.

Jenkins, J.R., Vadasy, P.E., Firebaugh, M. and Profilet, C. (2000) 'Tutoring first-grade struggling readers in phonological reading skills', *Learning Disabilities Research and Practice*, 15: 75–84.

Jones, D. (2007) 'Speaking, listening, planning and assessing: the teacher's role in developing metacognitive awareness', *Early Child Development and Care*, 177(6–7): 569–579.

Jones, P. and Swain, J. (2001) 'Parents reviewing annual reviews', *British Journal of Special Education*, 28(2): 60–64.

Kellett, M. (2004) 'Intensive interaction in the inclusive classroom: using interactive pedagogy to connect with students who are hardest to reach', *Westminster Studies in Education*, 27(2): 175–188.

Kerry, T. (2005) 'Towards a typology for conceptualizing the roles of teaching assistants', *Educational Review*, 57 (3): 374–384.

Kessler, I., Bach, S. and Heron, P. (2005) 'Assistant roles and changing job boundaries in the public services', final report to the ESRC.

Klassen, R. (2001). 'After the statement: reading progress made by secondary students with specific literacy difficulty provision', *Educational Psychology in Practice*, 17(2): 121–133.

Koshik, I. (2002) 'Designedly incomplete utterances: a pedagogical practice for eliciting knowledge displays in error correction sequences', *Research on Language and Social Interaction*, 35: 277–309.

Kounin, J. (1970) *Discipline and group management in classrooms*, New York: Holt, Rinehart and Winston.

Kyriacou, C. and Issitt, J. (2008) *What characterises effective teacher-initiated teacher-pupil dialogue to promote conceptual understanding in mathematics lessons in England in Key Stages 2 and 3: a systematic review. Report: In Research Evidence in Education Library*, London: EPPI-Centre, Social Science Research Unit, Institute of Education, University of London.

Lamb, B. (2009) *The Lamb Inquiry: special educational needs and parental confidence*, London: DCSF.

Lee, B. (2002) *Teaching assistants in schools: the current state of play. (NFER Research summary)*, Slough: NFER.

Lindsay, G. (1997) 'Values, rights and dilemmas', *British Journal of Special Education*, 24(2): 55–59.

Logan, A. (2006) 'The role of the special needs assistant supporting pupils with special educational needs in Irish mainstream primary schools', *Support for Learning*, 17(2): 161–173.

Macbeth, D. (2006) 'The relevance of repair for classroom correction', *Language in Society*, 33: 703–736.

McAvoy, D. (2003) *A price too high*, London: NUT.

McHoul, A. (1990) 'The organisation of repair in classroom talk', *Language in Society*, 19: 349–377.

Maddern, K. (2009) '£5bn spent on SEN fails to boost results, says top official', *Times Educational Supplement*, 16th October.

Mistry, M., Burton, N. and Brundrett, M. (2004) 'Managing LSAs: an evaluation of the use of learning support assistants in an urban primary school', *School Leadership and Management* 24(2): 125–137.

Moor, H., Jones, M., Johnson, F., Martin, K., Cowell, E. and Bojke, C. (2006) *Mathematics and science in secondary schools. The deployment of teachers and support staff to deliver the curriculum. Research Brief – RB708*, London: DfES.

Moran, A. and Abbott, L. (2002) 'Developing inclusive schools: the pivotal role of teaching assistants in promoting inclusion in special and mainstream schools in Northern Ireland', *European Journal of Special Needs Education*, 17(2): 161–173.

Morris, E. (2001) *Professionalism and trust: the future of teachers and teaching*, London: Department for Education and Skills/Social Market Foundation.

Mortimore, P. and Mortimore, J., with Thomas, H., Cairns, R. and Taggart, B. (1992) *The innovative uses of non-teaching staff in primary and secondary schools project: final report*, London: Institute of Education.

Mortimore, P., Sammons, P., Stoll, L. and Ecob, R. (1988) *School matters: the junior years*, Wells: Open Books.

Moyles, J. and Suschitzky, W. (1997) 'The employment and deployment of classroom support staff: head teachers' perspectives', *Research in Education* 58(Nov.): 21–34.

Muijs, R.D. and Reynolds, D. (2001) *Effective teaching. Evidence and practice*, London: Paul Chapman.

Myhill, D. (2006) 'Talk talk talk: teaching and learning in whole class discourse', *Research Papers in Education*, 21:19–41.

National Joint Council for Local Government Services (NJC) (2003) *School support staff: the way forward*, London: The Employers' Organisation.

Nixon, J., Martin, J., Mckeown, P. and Ranson, S. (1997) 'Towards a learning profession: changing codes of occupational practice within the "new" management of education', *British Journal of Sociology of Education*, 18(1): 5–28.

Norwich, B. and Lewis, A. (2001) 'Mapping a pedagogy for special educational needs', *British Educational Research Journal*, 27(3): 313–329.

Nystrand, M. (2006) 'Research on the role of classroom discourse as it affects reading comprehension', *Research in the Teaching of English*, 40(4): 392–412.

O'Connor, U. (2008) 'Meeting in the middle? A study of parent-professional partnerships', *European Journal of Special Needs Education*, 23(3): 253–268.

Ofsted (2002) *Teaching assistants in primary schools: an evaluation of the quality and impact of their work*, London: Her Majesty's Inspectorate of Education.

Ofsted (2004a) *Reading for purpose and pleasure – an evaluation of reading in primary schools*, London: Ofsted.

Ofsted (2004b) *Remodelling the school workforce: Phase 1*, London: Ofsted.

Ofsted (2005) *Managing challenging behaviour*, London: Ofsted.

Ofsted (2006) *Inclusion: does it matter where pupils are taught? HMI Report 2535*, London: Ofsted.

Ofsted (2008) *The deployment, training and development of the wider school workforce*, London: Ofsted.

Ofsted (2010) *The special educational needs and disability review. A statement is not enough*, London: Ofsted.

Ofsted (2011) *Special educational needs and/or disabilities in mainstream schools. A briefing paper for section 5 inspectors*, London: Ofsted.

Ozga, J. (2002) 'Education governance in the United Kingdom: the modernization project', *European Educational Research Journal*, 1(2): 331–341.

Pelligrini, A. and Blatchford, P. (2000) *The child at school: interactions with peers and teachers*, London: Edward Arnold.

Penfold, C., Cleghorn, N., Tennant, R., Palmer, I. and Read, J. (2009) *Parental confidence in the special educational needs assessment, statementing and tribunal system: a qualitative study [DCSF-Research Brief 117]*, London: DCSF.

PricewaterhouseCooper (2001) *Teacher workload study. A report of a review commissioned by the DfES*, London: PricewaterhouseCooper.

Radford, J. (2010a) 'Practices of other-initiated repair and correction in SSLD classroom discourse', *Applied Linguistics*, 31: 25–44.

Radford, J. (2010b) 'Adult participation in children's word searches: on the use of prompting, hinting and candidate offers', *Clinical Linguistics and Phonetics*, 24: 83–100.

Radford, J., Blatchford, P. and Webster, R. (2011) 'Opening up and closing down: comparing teacher and TA talk in mathematics lessons', *Learning and Instruction*, 21(5): 625–635.

Radford, J., Ireson, J. and Mahon, M. (2006) 'Triadic dialogue in oral communication tasks: what are the implications for language learning?', *Language and Education*, 20: 191–210.

Reynolds, D. and Muijs, D. (2003) 'The effectiveness of the use of learning support assistants in improving the mathematics achievement of low achieving pupils in primary school', *Educational Research*, 45(3): 219–230.

Rosenshine, B. and Stevens, R. (1986) 'Teaching functions', in M.C. Wittrock (ed.) *Handbook of research on teaching* (3rd edn), New York: MacMillan.

Rubie-Davies, C., Blatchford, P., Webster, R., Koutsoubou, M. and Bassett, P. (2010). 'Enhancing student learning? A comparison of teacher and teaching assistant interaction with pupils', *School Effectiveness and School Improvement*, 21(4): 429–449.

Rutter, M., Maughan, B., Mortimore, P., Ouston, J. and Smith, A. (1979) *Fifteen thousand hours*, London: Open Books.

Savage, R. and Carless, S. (2005) 'Learning support assistants can deliver effective reading interventions for 'at-risk' children', *Educational Research*, 47(1): 45–61.

Savage, R. and Carless, S. (2008) 'The impact of early reading interventions delivered by classroom assistants on attainment at the end of Year 2', *British Educational Research Journal*, 34(3): 363–385.

Schegloff, E. (2007) *Sequence organisation in interaction: a primer in conversation analysis*, Cambridge: Cambridge University Press.

Schegloff, E., Jefferson, G. and Sacks, H. (1977) 'The preference for self-correction in the organization of repair in conversation', *Language*, 53: 361–382.

Schlapp, U., Davidson, J. and Wilson, V. (2003) 'An 'extra pair of hands'?: managing classroom assistants in Scottish primary schools', *Educational Management and Administration*, 31(2): 189–205.

School Teachers' Review Body (2001) *Tenth report 2001*, London: The Stationery Office Limited.

The Scottish Government (2010) *Teacher census, supplementary data 2010*. Online. Available at: http://www.scotland.gov.uk/Resource/Doc/91982/0109728.xls (accessed 22.02.11).

Sherr, A. (2007) *Professional work, professional careers and legal education: educating the lawyer for 2010*, London: IALS.

Shulman, L.S. (1986) 'Paradigms and research programs – the study of teaching: a contemporary perspective', in M.C. Wittrock (ed.) *Handbook of research on teaching* (3rd edn), New York: MacMillan Publishing.

Slavin, R.E., Lake, C., Davis, S. and Madden, N. (2009) *Effective programs for struggling readers: a best evidence synthesis*, Baltimore, MD: Johns Hopkins University, Center for Research and Reform in Education.

Smith, F., Hardman, F., Wall, K. and Mroz, M. (2004) 'Interactive whole class teaching in the national literacy and numeracy strategies', *British Educational Research Journal*, 30: 395–411.

Smith, H. and Higgins, S. (2006) 'Opening classroom interaction: the importance of feedback', *Cambridge Journal of Education*, 36: 485–502.

Smith, P., Whitby, K. and Sharp, C. (2004) *The employment and deployment of teaching assistants*, Slough: NFER.

Statistics for Wales (2009) *First release (SDR 99/2009): Schools census 2009: Provisional results*. Online. Available at: http://wales.gov.uk/docs/statistics/2009/090701sdr992009en.pdf. (accessed 22.02.11).

Statistics for Wales (2010) *First release (SDR 98/2010): Schools' census 2010: Final results*. Online. Available at: http://wales.gov.uk/docs/statistics/2010/100629supportency.xls (accessed 22.02.11).

Stevenson, H. (2007) 'Restructuring teachers' work and trade union responses in England: bargaining for change?', *American Educational Research Journal*, 44 (2): 224–251.

Svennevig, J. (1999) *Getting acquainted in conversation: a study of initial interactions*, Amsterdam and Philadelphia, PA: J. Benjamins Pub. Co.

Takala, M. (2007) 'The work of classroom assistants in special and mainstream education in Finland', *British Journal of Special Education*, 34(1): 50–57.

Teeman, D., Walker, M., Sharp, C., Smith, P., Scott, E., Johnson, F., Easton, C., Varnai, A. and Barnes, M. (2008) *Exploring school support staff experiences of training and development: first year report*, London: Training and Development Agency for Schools.

Thomas, G. (1997) 'What's the use of theory?' *Harvard Educational Review*, 67(1): 75–105.

Thomas, H., Butt, G., Fielding, A., Gunter, H., Lance, A., Rayner, S. and Rutherford, R. (2004) *Transforming the School Workforce Pathfinder Evaluation Project*, London: Department for Education and Skills.

Thompson, M. (2006) 'Re-modelling as de-professionalisation', *FORUM*, 48(2): 189–200.

Thornley, C. (1997) *The invisible workers: an investigation into the pay and employment of health care assistants in the NHS*, London: UNISON.

US Department of Education (2010) *Part B Data & Notes. IDEA 618 Data Tables. Personnel (2003) (2004) (2005) (2006) (2007)* Available from Individuals with Disabilities Act (IDEA) Data Accountability Center website. Online. Available at: https://www.ideadata.org/PartBData.asp (accessed 18.08.10).

Wallace, T. (2003) *Paraprofessionals*, Minnesota, USA: Center on Personnel Studies in Special Education.

Webster, R., Blatchford, P., Bassett, P., Brown, P., Martin, C. and Russell, A. (2010) 'Double standards and first principles: framing teaching assistant support for pupils with special educational needs', *European Journal of Special Educational Needs*, 25(4): 319–336.

Whitehorn, T. (2010) *School support staff topic paper*, London: Department for Education.

Wiliam, D. (2010) 'How should we use what we know about learning to read?', keynote address at 'Changing Lives': 7th International Reading Recovery Institute, at the Institute of Education, London, 8 July.

Wilkinson, E. R. and Silliman, L. C. (2000) 'Classroom language and literacy learning', in M. Kamil, P. D. Pearson and R. Barr (eds.) *Handbook of reading research* (vol. 3, pp. 337–360), Mahwah, NJ: Erlbaum.

Wilkinson, G. (2005) 'Workforce remodelling and formal knowledge: the erosion of teachers' professional jurisdiction in English schools', *School Leadership & Management* 25(5): 421–439.

Wilson, E. and Bedford, D. (2008) '"New partnerships for learning": teachers and teaching assistants working together in schools – the way forward', *Journal for Education for Teaching*, 34 (2): 137–150.

Workforce Agreement Monitoring Group (2004) *Raising Standards and Tackling Workload Implementing the National Agreement, WAMG Note 10*, London: Workforce Agreement Monitoring Group.

Workforce Agreement Monitoring Group (2008) *The appropriate deployment of support staff in schools, WAMG Note 22*, London: Workforce Agreement Monitoring Group.

Index